Multiplicity and Becoming

Studies in European Thought

E. Allen McCormick
General Editor

Vol. 15

PETER LANG
New York • Washington, D.C./Baltimore • Boston
Bern • Frankfurt am Main • Berlin • Vienna • Paris

Patrick Hayden

Multiplicity and Becoming

The Pluralist Empiricism of Gilles Deleuze

PETER LANG
New York • Washington, D.C./Baltimore • Boston
Bern • Frankfurt am Main • Berlin • Vienna • Paris

Library of Congress Cataloging-in-Publication Data
Hayden, Patrick.
Multiplicity and becoming: the pluralist empiricism
of Gilles Deleuze / Patrick Hayden.
p. cm. — (Studies in European thought; vol. 15)
Includes bibliographical references.
1. Deleuze, Gilles. 2. Empiricism—History—20th century.
3. Pluralism—History—20th century. I. Title. II. Series.
B2430.D454H39   194—dc21   97-12506
ISBN 0-8204-3856-1
ISSN 1043-5786

Die Deutsche Bibliothek-CIP-Einheitsaufnahme
Hayden, Patrick:
Multiplicity and becoming: the pluralist empiricism
of Gilles Deleuze / Patrick Hayden. –New York;
Washington, D.C./Baltimore; Boston; Bern;
Frankfurt am Main; Berlin; Vienna; Paris: Lang.
(Studies in European thought; 15)
ISBN 0-8204-3856-1 Gb.

The paper in this book meets the guidelines for permanence and durability
of the Committee on Production Guidelines for Book Longevity
of the Council of Library Resources.

© 1998 Peter Lang Publishing, Inc., New York

All rights reserved.
Reprint or reproduction, even partially, in all forms such as microfilm,
xerography, microfiche, microcard, and offset strictly prohibited.

Printed in the United States of America.

For Katherine, with love and solidarity

". . . like water in water."
Georges Bataille

Contents

	Acknowledgments	ix
	List of Abbreviations	xi
	Introduction	1
1.	**Transcendental Empiricism and the Critique of Representation**	5
	Situating Repetition and Difference	7
	Difference and Representation	12
	Repetition and Representation	17
	Thought Without Image: Transcendental Empiricism	26
2.	**Immanence and Multiplicity**	37
	Bergson	39
	Nietzsche	48
	Spinoza	56
	Philosophy, Constructivism, and Immanence	68
3.	**Relations and the Radicalization of Empiricism**	79
	Relations in William James' Radical Empiricism	81
	Deleuze on Relations	85
	Radical Empiricism and Rhizomatics	94

4. From Naturalism to Ecological Politics 103

Deleuze on Naturalism in the History of Philosophy 105
Deleuze's Geophilosophy: A Radical Naturalism 114
Radical Naturalism and Ecological Politics 119

Concluding Remarks 133

Notes 135

Bibliography 151

Index 157

Acknowledgments

I wish to express my thanks to Owen Lancer, for his beneficial editorial support, to Jacqueline Pavlovic, for her professional assistance with the production process, to the many colleagues working in the areas of environmental and social justice, for their dedication to the causes of planetary becoming and diversity, and especially to my wife Katherine for her understanding and unfailing encouragement.

Some sections of this book have been adapted from previously published essays. Details of the original publications are as follows:

"From Relations to Practice in the Empiricism of Gilles Deleuze," *Man and World* 28, no. 3 (June 1995), with kind permission from Kluwer Academic Publishers. Parts of this essay form sections of Chapter 3.

"Gilles Deleuze and Naturalism: A Convergence with Ecological Theory and Politics," *Environmental Ethics* 19, no. 2 (Summer 1997), with permission of the editor and publisher. A modified and extended version of this essay forms parts of Chapter 4.

Abbreviations

The following lists a key for the more frequently cited works of Gilles Deleuze.

ATP	*A Thousand Plateaus: Capitalism and Schizophrenia.* Vol. 2. Translated by B. Massumi (Minneapolis: University of Minnesota Press, 1987).
B	*Bergsonism.* Translated by H. Tomlinson and B. Habberjam (New York: Zone Books, 1988).
D	*Dialogues.* Translated by H. Tomlinson and B. Habberjam (New York: Columbia University Press, 1987).
DR	*Difference and Repetition.* Translated by Paul Patton (New York: Columbia University Press, 1994).
EP	*Expressionism in Philosophy: Spinoza.* Translated by M. Joughin (New York: Zone Books, 1990).
ES	*Empiricism and Subjectivity: An Essay on Hume's Theory of Human Nature.* Translated by C. Boundas (New York: Columbia University Press, 1991).
K	*Kant's Critical Philosophy: The Doctrine of the Faculties.* Translated by H. Tomlinson and B. Habberjam (Minneapolis: University of Minnesota Press, 1984).
LS	*The Logic of Sense.* Translated by M. Lester with C. Stivale, edited by C. Boundas (New York: Columbia University Press, 1990).
N	*Nietzsche and Philosophy.* Translated by H. Tomlinson (New York: Columbia University Press, 1983).
SP	*Spinoza: Practical Philosophy.* Translated by R. Hurley (San Francisco: City Lights Books, 1988).
WP	*What is Philosophy?.* Translated H. Tomlinson and G. Burchell (New York: Columbia University Press, 1994).

Introduction

> *Abstractions explain nothing, they themselves have to be explained: there are no such things as universals, there's nothing transcendent, no Unity, subject (or object), Reason; there are only processes, sometimes unifying, subjectifying, rationalizing, but just processes all the same. These processes are at work in concrete "multiplicities," multiplicity is the real element in which things happen.*[1]

In this book I explore the philosophy of Gilles Deleuze across a wide range of his writings. In particular, I examine how Deleuze suggests that his work is to be understood as a pluralist version of empiricism. I was directed toward this specific engagement with Deleuze's thought by a remarkable statement he made in 1986: "I have always felt that I am an empiricist, that is, a pluralist" (*D* vii). This statement is made even more remarkable by the fact that Deleuze's claim of allegiance to empiricism, which is made elsewhere as well, has gone virtually unremarked upon and unexamined by commentators and expositors.[2] It is this pervasive oversight that my study aims to rectify.

Deleuze has been a significant presence in contemporary Continental philosophy since the appearance of his groundbreaking *Nietzsche et la philosophie* in 1962. Yet his publications extend back a decade and a half earlier, with innovative and complex books on Hume and Bergson among them. In all of these early writings, and in those appearing after them, Deleuze attempts to instigate a revolution in philosophy for the purpose of inventing a new image of thought, or rather, new possibilities for thinking and feeling that are not constrained by a single image of what thought is. Deleuze's efforts toward this end are centered on problematizing the assumption that there are universal, "proper limits" of thought which do, or at least ought to, circumscribe and govern the legitimate uses of its faculties. The richness of Deleuze's work consists in promoting what he believes to be the dynamic mobility of a "thought without image," whose multiple exercises and changing dimensions are "opposed to the traditional image which philosophy has projected . . . in order to subjugate it and prevent it from functioning" (*D* 16).

In order to invent new possibilities for thought, however, Deleuze insists that it is also necessary to "find the conditions under which something new is produced," to analyze the current states of things so that something which does not yet exist can be created from existing conditions (*D* vii). It can be said, then, that the following question serves as the basic motivation for empiricism, as conceived by Deleuze: How can that which is new be created from what currently exists? As we will see, this question ultimately relies upon an ontology of real and dynamic difference.

This book may be viewed as an attempt to clarify some of the numerous ways Deleuze poses and answers the question framed above. I should state at the outset that it is not my intention to judge Deleuze's philosophy according to a preexisting standard of what empiricism "is," even if such a standard was available. Nor do I have aspirations to an exhaustive and definitive treatment of Deleuze's thought. My more modest aim is to clarify what it might mean when Deleuze says that his philosophy is an empiricism, and to examine a number of what I consider to be key concepts and issues in his work in order to develop a plausible working picture of this pluralist empiricism. In addition, I discuss possible affinities that Deleuze may have to certain other philosophers, some of whom are generally regarded as belonging to the "empiricist tradition" while others are not. And, in the spirit of Deleuze's philosophy, I take the liberty of putting his empiricism to use in the final chapter by generating an alternative conceptual approach to a matter of current social and political concern: ecological degradation.

The detailed discussions in the following chapters proceed according to a thematic framework. Chapter 1 is devoted to situating Deleuze's empiricism with respect to the "image of thought" propagated in the history of philosophy, by way of a discussion of his conception of transcendental empiricism as contained in his *Difference and Repetition*. I try to explain here how transcendental empiricism calls into question the foundationalist assumptions of traditional representationalism. In Chapter 2, I discuss the important roles assigned to the notions of immanence and multiplicity in Deleuze's thought by way of his interpretations of Bergson, Nietzsche, and Spinoza, and show how he puts these concepts to work undermining philosophical appeals to the transcendent.

In Chapter 3, I consider and expand upon Deleuze's thesis that, from the point of view of empiricism, all relations are external to their terms. Here I utilize the work of William James in order to suggest that, on the basis of the central role accorded to relations throughout both James' and Deleuze's writings, Deleuze's empiricism is pluralistic in a manner strikingly similar to James' own radical empiricism. Finally, in Chapter 4 I discuss Deleuze's views on naturalism as a complementary perspective to his empiricism, and propose that this naturalistic sensibility can be usefully applied in the areas of environmental ethics and political ecology. I then demonstrate how this might initially be done in the concluding section of the chapter. Overall, I show that Deleuze's empiricism is to be considered an antifoundationalist ontology of multiplicity and interacting processes of becomings. Repudiating any absolute unitary principle, Deleuze's empiricist aversion to the transcendent ushers in an affirmation of the immanent, continuous proliferation of multiplicities in this world.

By exploring these different yet interconnected and mutually supportive themes in Deleuze's philosophical thought, I hope to provide a selective yet fruitful conception of one of the most significant directions taken in philosophy today. The emphasis throughout is on a sympathetic reading, concentrating more on illuminating neglected and innovative aspects of his work than on criticizing what might seem, in the absence of a thorough familiarity with Deleuze's numerous writings, puzzling or presumptuously bold positions. I have written this book, then, with the belief that by providing an affirmative understanding of a philosophy committed to opening up new perspectives and new possibilities for thinking and living, there is no telling in advance where it might lead or what it might yield.

Chapter 1

Transcendental Empiricism and the Critique of Representation

Among the many issues that Gilles Deleuze has a special interest in, it can be said that he is particularly concerned with the notion of representation. This is indeed a topic that Deleuze repeatedly addresses, in his own work from his first book on Hume published in 1953, to his collaborative efforts with Félix Guattari appearing from 1970 to 1991. Throughout, what is of paramount importance for Deleuze is to think in terms other than those of representation and in fact to liberate thought from its representationalist image.[1] According to this image, experience can be reduced to the interiority of a self-constituting subjectivity. Deleuze's effort to undo this image becomes the cornerstone of the book that most completely expresses the intricacies of his philosophy, *Difference and Repetition*. In this book Deleuze writes that the model of thought promoted by representationalism inhibits thinking difference and thinking differently, insofar as it distorts the dynamic intensity of the experience of difference: "Representation fails to capture the affirmed world of difference. . . . It mediates everything, but mobilises and moves nothing" (*DR* 55).

Deleuze's general concern is how representation comes to be identified with knowledge and how thought is presented as the medium of representation.[2] Consequently, Deleuze is not presenting the only correct version of reality and *a fortiori* the truth about it as the foundation for knowledge, rather he is attempting to create concepts with which to construct multiple perspectives of what we can do and of how the world can be.[3] We might consider the following remark from his book on Hume as a clear expression of Deleuze's general orientation: "Philosophy must constitute itself as a theory of what we are doing, not as a theory of what there is" (*ES* 133). Deleuze's project is ultimately concerned with the effects that philosophy is able to produce. In this respect it is not only a different way of thinking that matters but, as he writes in *Nietzsche and Philosophy*, it is also "a different way of feeling: another sensibility" that ought to be engendered (*N* 94).[4] These concerns, as I hope to clarify, provide an ethical-practical motivation for Deleuze's philosophy in that they encourage the creation of new values and senses in the affirmative constitution of life and human existence.

Difference and Repetition is a demanding book that presumes familiarity with often obscure regions of the history of Western philosophy. Its principal target is what Deleuze refers to as "the traditional image of thought" (*DR* xvi). By this Deleuze means those philosophical traditions that have sought to promote a model for thought according to the four criteria of representation: identity, resemblance, opposition, and analogy. Deleuze questions these criteria on the basis of the two terms which compose the title of his book. According to Deleuze, the classical model of thought subordinates difference to the four criteria of representation, leaving us unable to think difference in itself. In other words, representation allows only for conceptual difference and not for a concept of difference *as such*, that is, for nonconceptual difference. Repetition itself is similarly unthought, for representationalism considers it as a strictly negative conceptual fault. Representation defines repetition as a form of inadequacy in the identity of the concept, for example as the re-presentation of that which is to be recognized as the same, whereas Deleuze argues that repetition is the productive power of difference. Deleuze's critique of representation is therefore centered around these two themes in order to demonstrate that representation presupposes, yet misunderstands, both difference and repetition. Moreover, these two themes contribute to the elaboration of a new image of thought, or rather to a thought without image, which Deleuze calls transcendental empiricism.

It is this move from the analysis of the criteria of representation to the elaboration of the concepts of difference and repetition that first characterizes Deleuze's philosophy as transcendental empiricism. The importance of this conjunction of terms—transcendental and empiricism—is not to be underestimated, and I will here briefly anticipate the topic of this chapter. Deleuze takes some inspiration from the empiricist tradition in that, on the one hand, his concern is with actual experience as empirical multiplicity or diversity, which has as its condition nonconceptual difference. In this respect Deleuze is opposed to the notion of experience found in representationalist theories which seek to identify the real with the conceptual categories of the possible. On the other hand, Deleuze is also concerned with the necessary conditions of the creation of Ideas, that is, with empirical multiplicity as that which allows for the actualization of the conceptual.[5] In other words, the conditions of difference and repetition set up the space in which thought operates. For Deleuze, then, the empirical is the "transcendental" condition of both actual experiences and concepts.

Yet it is precisely because of these conditions that we cannot speak of a negative limit to thought. This conjunction of the transcendental with the empirical refers instead to the historical, multiple, and singular conditions of the actualization of experience, and to the contingency of actual experiences and ideas that do not merely reflect or resemble their conditions; it refers to the interaction of effects on the basis of internal difference, to effects as the dynamic causes of other effects. The transcendental ceases to be transcendent and timeless and instead becomes immanent and historical. Rather than simply reversing the hierarchy that sets the intelligible over against the sensible and conserving a certain order essential to representation, Deleuze seeks to abolish the distinction itself and thereby to unsettle the "given." Ideas, experiences, and their necessary conditions do not belong to the subject-object domain of representation and are united against it in the case of a radical, transcendental empiricism (*DR* 68). For Deleuze, it is never enough to ask what thought "is" since the question is always that of what thought "becomes."

In this chapter, I will examine how Deleuze develops the notion of transcendental empiricism on the basis of a critique of the representationalist image of thought as it has appeared at various moments in the history of philosophy. Such an analysis will thereby clarify that the purpose of Deleuze's critique is to develop a practical ontology from the perspective of transcendental empiricism.[6] By this I mean an ontology that promotes the theoretical and practical union of ethics, politics, and the thought of being as becoming. What distinguishes Deleuze's ontology is not that it is ultimately concerned with determining what "is" as a fixed realm of Being, but that it is oriented toward elaborating how the emergent becomings of existence can be produced and constituted according to immanent and transformable conditions.

Situating Repetition and Difference

The philosophical as well as historical contexts relating to the writing of *Difference and Repetition* and the general intention of the book are succinctly described by Deleuze as follows:

> The primacy of identity, however conceived, defines the world of representation. But modern thought is born of the failure of representa-

tion, of the loss of identities, and of the discovery of all the forces that act under the representation of the identical. The modern world is one of simulacra. . . . All identities are only simulated, produced as an optical "effect" by the more profound game of difference and repetition. We propose to think difference in itself independently of the forms of representation which reduce it to the Same, and the relation of different to different independently of those forms which make them pass through the negative. (*DR* xix)

For Deleuze, representationalism's failure is to be viewed as a positive moment for philosophy: only with the end of representation can the primacy of difference and repetition be fully acknowledged. As Deleuze indicates, identity is a secondary effect produced as simulacra or "simulations" by the relation of difference and repetition.

In the lengthy "Introduction" of *Difference and Repetition* Deleuze presents the basic arguments of the book, setting the stage for the elaborate analyses carried out in the subsequent chapters. He begins by indicating that repetition is to be distinguished from generality. There are three reasons why repetition and generality are "different in kind" and are not to be transposed. First, generality implies an exchange or substitution of particulars based upon resemblance and equivalence. From the view of generality, repetition is simply the re-presentation of a universal in a particular. In the Aristotelian-Scholastic ontological tradition, universal forms are what "inform" the qualities of individual things; the same form is contained in each of the individuals it informs, and the qualities of each ground their resemblance. The generality of the particular thus finds its form in the equality of that which is repeated.[7]

Against this Deleuze insists that repetition excludes substitution, and that in fact repetition concerns what is irreplaceable. Repetition occurs only in relation to that which is singular and without equivalent. Repetition does not refer to the equivalence of successive individuations of an original identity, but to the full difference that each thing possesses in itself as the first immediately carried to the "nth" power. This reveals a certain paradox of repetition, namely, that repetition repeats the "unrepeatable." Repetition is the displacement of difference and not the reappearance of the identical; it is the internal animation of the singular that prevents it from being equivalent to any other. Thus it is because of repetition that we can speak of the "universality of the singular" without confusing it with the generality of the particular (*DR* 1–2).

Second, generality belongs to the order of laws, in that laws are based on the resemblance of those particulars they subordinate and designate according to terms of equivalence. For instance, laws of nature presuppose only a hypothetical repetition in that phenomena are defined according to a rule of generality that seeks to identify their resemblance to an ideal example. Repetition is conceived as the passage from one generality to another, from one apparently similar situation to another, which in the end represents the equality of phenomena as the permanence of similarity between all things. In a like manner, moral law establishes itself on the terrain of both natural laws and laws of duty, grounded in the formation of habits. One becomes "good" only by repeating what has already been determined as the Good itself—the ordinary, the general, the memorizable—while that which is "bad" is in principle unrepeatable, it is not to be repeated or acquired as a habit.

In contrast, Deleuze argues that repetition is "by nature transgression or exception, always revealing a singularity opposed to the particulars subsumed under laws" (*DR* 5). His point is that experimental reproduction or the integration of moral habits do not account for repetition itself, that is, for the real movement of force that underlies or grounds all conceptual repetitions mediated by the abstract categories of representation. In other words such "external repetitions" presuppose another repetition that always exhibits exceptions to laws precisely because it is not hypothetical but real, singular, new, immediate, and direct. In short, repetition is outside representation.

The third point on which repetition is opposed to generality is that of representation. From the view of generality, repetition is the "abstract relation of the particular to the concept in general" (*DR* 10). At the level of representation there are two aspects through which concepts relate to their objects: that of memory or remembrance, and that of self-consciousness or recognition. These two aspects are made possible when the concept is supposedly endowed with a real infinite comprehension. Here Deleuze draws upon the Scholastic distinction of the comprehension and extension of concepts (the relation between the two being of inverse order). The concept of a particular existing thing is said to have infinite comprehension when it expresses all the elements of that thing to which it refers; for example the concept "human" apparently contains animal, rational, living, and so on. Correlatively such a concept has the least extension (=1) because it can extend to that particular thing only. The concept, then, plays a pivotal role in that it is both the representation of an object in the mind (comprehension) and that which attributes predicates to the subject (extension).

Accordingly, difference is deemed a predicable belonging to the concept. Insofar as difference serves as a determination of the concept the concept itself can be "blocked": "human" becomes something different in Peter and Paul, yet remains the same or fixed in the concept. Since each determination remains fixed in the concept, it defines a merely conceptual difference as a resemblance on the basis of the general or universal nature of the concept (infinite comprehension). Concepts are held to refer to particular things on the basis of their greatest possible resemblance *according to the concept*, and thus on account of representation as mediation. In this manner conceptual determination relies upon the constant evaluation of resemblances. Here difference is understood only as conceptual difference, that is, as a predicate attributed to the subject by the concept. Concepts would relate to their objects by means of a proper re-presentation (the role of memory) according to the model of thought as the recognition of resemblances (the place of self-consciousness). Deleuze's concern is that the same universal concept distributes itself over a possibly infinite number of things such that no actually existing thing can correspond to the concept's generality; each determination is only a logical or "artificial blockage."

Deleuze asks whether there might not be another type of blockage of the concept, one that is "natural" as opposed to artificial. Rather than corresponding to simple logic, this natural blockage refers to a dialectic of existence or transcendental logic. Here the concept itself is forced into place in space and time, causing it to pass into existence in the form of a dispersion of definite individuals. This finite comprehension corresponds to the infinite extension of absolutely identical individuals and "forms a true repetition in existence rather than an order of resemblance in thought" (*DR* 13). Epicurean atoms are an example of such a naturally blocked concept; each individual atom, localized in space, nevertheless belongs to an infinite set of identically composed atoms. There are also concepts of Nature that belong to the mind which observes and represents Nature as mind in alienated form. Such concepts are themselves without memory as they are only reflected in the mind which observes; Nature repeats because it is *partes extra partes* for a dualistic-projective consciousness. Finally, there are concepts of freedom that do possess memory, but which lack self-consciousness or remembrance as the working through of memory. Here repetition appears without recognition of its object, as "the unconscious of the free concept" such as Freud attributed to the effects of repression and resistance (*DR* 14). Repetition is viewed only as the result of a lack of consciousness.

In each example of natural blockage, as with artificial blockage, repetition is invariably characterized according to the identity of the concept. In each case the elements of the blockage come to share the same concept and are therefore determined according to the Sameness of representation. Furthermore, repetition acquires a negative definition, since that which repeats does so by means of either a natural inadequacy attributed to it, or by not comprehending, not remembering, or not recognizing. In each case of blockage, whether logical or natural, the result is disappointing—repetition appears only as the insufficiency of objects represented by the same concept, and difference appears only as conceptual difference. Deleuze finds, then, that the question concerning the essence of repetition still remains to be asked.

What prevents repetition from being recognized for what it is? Deleuze responds that it is ultimately an issue of the relation between repetition and "disguises" (*DR* 16). As previously explained, repetition is not the successive re-presentation of an originary term. Consequently, repetition is not to be conceived according to the form of identity under which repetition appears as the re-presentation of the Same. Real repetition cannot be separated from the singular occurrence of its actual formation and from the difference internal to it. Repetition does not belong to representation, because there is no original model or first term to be repeated and represented. Repetition instead belongs to the symbolic, to the order of signs, and to simulacra. In other words, in constituting itself repetition also disguises itself, that is, it forms itself only by being different each and every time. In effect, difference is included as the disguise of repetition and is expressed by the order of signs, in that signs embody repetition as the self-differentiation of difference and not as the simple association of resemblances. Only by including difference within itself can repetition constitute itself "from one distinctive point to another, from one privileged instant to another" (*DR* 17). Any repeated element that appears to represent the "same" thing under the guise of its concept is, in fact, intrinsically different in virtue of the repetition that differentiates it from all others. The displacement enacted by repetition is that which also disguises it, complicating the order of signs and the ideal of representation. Repetition can thus be positively described as the singularity of presentations, rather than negatively described as the generality of re-presentation.

The implication of Deleuze's insistence on the positive nature and symbolic functioning of repetition is that the process of "signalling" (*signalisation*) is able to replace the mode of representation (*DR* 20). In this process the symmetrical relation of cause and effect is dislocated by introducing a dissymmetry into the system of the "signal." The system of the signal comprises a combination of the dissymmetrical elements of repetition and is opposed to the simple re-presentation of resembling instances under the guise of an identical concept. This dissymmetry is expressed by the sign as the effect of a communication between heterogeneous elements of the differential system; the sign is the expression of the system's internal difference.

Thus Deleuze distinguishes between the repetition which corresponds to the abstract effect of representation and the one which belongs to the dynamic process of signalling.[8] The first is a static repetition that "refers back to a single concept, which leaves only an external difference between the ordinary instances of a figure." The second repetition is that of "an internal difference which it incorporates in each of its moments, and carries from one distinctive point to another" (*DR* 20). Signs appear in the system of signalling not as representative concepts, but as the incarnation of Ideas—as the effects of a dynamic repetition and its excessive difference. Difference is internal to the Idea, while it remains external to those concepts of the understanding that are supposed to represent objects (*DR* 26). We are confronted then with two types of repetition, a static "cadence-repetition" and a dynamic "rhythm-repetition": "The first repetition is repetition of the Same, explained by the identity of the concept or representation; the second includes difference, and includes itself in the alterity of the Idea, in the heterogeneity of an 'a-presentation'. One is negative, occurring by default in the concept; the other affirmative, occurring by excess in the Idea" (*DR* 24).

However, in every case the dynamic repetition is disguised within the static repetition, the latter being the outward and abstract appearance of the former. The interior repetition disguises itself in forming itself and, despite the exterior shell of the static repetition, constitutes the profound essence of every repetition: nonmediated difference.

Difference and Representation

For Deleuze, one of the most important distinctions to be drawn with respect to difference is how one construes its "making." It is important, in other words, to distinguish between a difference that "makes itself" and a difference that requires mediation in order to be made. In the first case, determinations of difference are the effects of a difference that distinguishes itself, "and yet that from which it distinguishes itself does not distinguish itself from it," much like lightning that distinguishes itself from black sky even though black sky does not distinguish itself from lightning (*DR* 28). Difference consists in this type of unilateral distinction in that its own immediate determinations do not depend upon external mediations. Difference makes itself outside the coherency of the concept. In the second case, difference is understood only on the basis of the concept that makes it, in that the concept determines *which* difference will be made. Here, difference arises as a result of conceptual mediation according to the four aspects of a harmonious or organic representation: "identity, in the form of the *undetermined* concept; analogy, in the relation between ultimate *determinable* concepts; opposition, in the relation between *determinations* within concepts; resemblance, in the *determined* object of the concept itself" (*DR* 29).

Through mediating representation the presumably "incoherent" difference that makes itself outside the concept is purportedly saved by relating it to the requirements of the concept. It is thought that difference must be reconciled with the concept in order for it to be coherent. At this point, Deleuze examines Aristotle's work in order to provide an example of how philosophy became associated with the project of determining which differences are to be made. This project arises from the Aristotelian identification of specific differences by concepts in general.

In the case of Aristotelian ontology, the greatest and most perfect difference is that of contrariety in the genus, that is, as the differentia or specific differences of the genus. Difference occurs on the basis of oppositions that belong in essence to the subject with respect to its genus. This difference is the most perfect as it consists of those contraries which define the subjects of each genus on the basis of the essential limitations that the genus attributes: for example, an animal may have feet or it may have wings, but it nonetheless remains an animal.[9] Thus the specific differences or contrarieties in the genus are determined according to the identity that the genus possesses as undetermined concept, and specific differences appear only as particular moments grouped within the sameness of the concept in general.[10] Differences between genera are similarly reconciled on the basis of the categories, or ultimate determinable concepts. It is true that for Aristotle Being (or Unity) is not itself a genus. However, the categories are modes of being that, in effect, function together as the general system of genera that are internally related to Being.[11]

Consequently, the unity characteristic of Aristotelian Being is not collective but distributive and hierarchical. From this concept of Being are attributed the limits of the predicates distributed to beings that equally form a hierarchy from Being to the lowest species. What is capable of performing these distributive and hierarchical functions? Only judgment, whose operation concerns the two functions of the distribution or "*partition* of concepts" and the hierarchization or "*measuring* of subjects" (*DR* 33). Corresponding to these two functions are the two faculties of judgment: common sense and good sense. Common sense and good sense ensure the integrity of judgment through the proper partitioning and measuring of concepts and objects by analogy of the concept with its objects: "Analogy is the essence of judgment, but the analogy within judgment is the analogy of the identity of concepts" (*DR* 33). From the Aristotelian position, therefore, difference seems to be a reflexive concept, a resemblance or likeness found between the Large and the Small or the One and the Many. The reflexive concept of difference is achieved through the complete union of abstract and concrete representation that forms organic representation in the fulfillment of its criteria: identity of the concept, opposition of the predicates, analogy of judgment, and resemblance of perception.

However, Deleuze finds that there is another, perhaps more illuminating, approach to the problem of difference. This alternative is expressed, in different ways, in the works of Duns Scotus, Spinoza, and Nietzsche, all three of whom substitute the proposition that being is univocal for Aristotelian analogy. Consequently, the model of judgment found in Aristotle is replaced by that of the proposition. The propositional model indicates that being is relational and that it designates a plurality of senses distinguished either formally, qualitatively, or semiologically. All the individuating modes of univocal being speak to this plurality of senses, in that the modes are not themselves the same or equal. Yet the different modes nonetheless participate equally in being without changing its essence as that which includes unequal individuating differences. Therefore, while "Being is the same for all these modalities" it is also the case that "these modalities are not the same" (*DR* 36).

In a certain sense distribution and hierarchy still remain, although Deleuze correctly notes that the two now assume completely different affirmations. Where previously distribution implied the "best" division of that which is distributed according to the analogical faculties of judgment and the strict limitations of representation, it now becomes "nomadic" (*DR* 36). Nomadic distribution is not a limiting or measuring of that which is distributed, but rather the self-distributing movement of all beings within a univocal being that is itself undistributed. Hierarchy is similarly transformed. Rather than the measured degree of distance from a principle term which sets a being's limit, it now becomes a question of how a being is deployed according to the various ways in which it exercises its power, while still participating equally in being.[12] Univocal being is therefore at the same time both nomadic distribution and anarchical hierarchy. All beings are different or unequal, and yet, "equal being is immediately present in everything, without mediation" or analogy (*DR* 37; *EP* 46–49). The individuating mode or difference in univocity acts in empirical individuals as "a transcendental principle: as a plastic, anarchic and nomadic principle . . . no less capable of dissolving and destroying individuals than of constituting them temporarily" (*DR* 38). In this manner, the universal is said of the most singular independently of the identity of the concept or the analogy of general concepts.

Even here though, Deleuze finds that a particular kind of representation and dependence on identity persists. Organic representation is characterized by the limitation of those determinations that are to appear as specific differences against a background of general identity. It is therefore a "finite" representation in that it is restricted to the judgment of things. In contrast, univocal being displays a tendency toward the infinite in that limitations cease to matter, so long as individuating differences reside within the totality of being. Thus, univocal being "discovers the infinite within itself," a tumultuous, passionate monstrosity of difference that appears as "orgiastic" representation. Deleuze claims that the decisive concept for orgiastic representation is that of the Whole. All determinations are now represented as pure differences, as infinite, which nevertheless are consigned to a ground (*fondement*) in which the extremes coincide. The infinite thus signifies the identity of extremes as the convergence of determinations in the ground, and in this manner the finite is "engendered in the infinite" (*DR* 44).

For infinite representation the choice is no longer between the Large or the Small, but between the infinitely large or the infinitely small. Into this gap step both Leibniz and Hegel, Leibniz in the direction of an analytic philosophy of the infinitely small and Hegel in the direction of a synthetic philosophy of the infinitely large. Hegel defines difference by the concept of contradiction. Unlike Aristotle, however, Hegel suggests that contradiction is itself the ground in which difference is resolved by making opposition itself infinite; each opposition remains interior to the infinite by itself becoming other, and therefore leads to a new opposition, a process without end.[13] Difference is found only at this point of appearance of oppositions, and is either annihilated or reproduced in relation to the ground of infinite contradiction. In contrast, Leibniz begins with the infinitely small, with cases or properties rather than essences. The essential is contained *in each case*, without the need for contradiction. Deleuze introduces the neologism of "vice-diction" in order to contrast Leibniz's procedure of successive specification to that of Hegel's dialectical contradiction. In Leibnizian vice-diction, difference appears between cases in the form of differential relations within a process of reciprocal and complete determination. The limit returns in the form of a maximum continuity between cases as individual essences, a whole corresponding to a foundational and selective reason.[14] For both Hegel and Leibniz, determination is inseparable from the mediation of representation in that each assigns difference a "reason." Hence, infinite representation subsumes difference to a presupposed principal of identity:

> In both cases . . . infinite representation does not suffice to render the thought of difference independent of the simple analogy of essences, or the simple similarity of properties. . . . Infinite representation invokes a foundation. While this foundation is not the identical itself, it is nevertheless a way of taking the principle of identity particularly seriously, giving it an infinite value and rendering it coextensive with the whole, and in this manner allowing it to reign over existence itself. . . . In either case, difference remains subordinated to identity, reduced to the negative, incarcerated within similitude and analogy. (DR 49–50)

The two examples of finite and infinite representation reveal the problem that Deleuze confronts: the concept of *difference in itself* is confused with the inclusion of difference in the identity of the concept in general. Deleuze does not intend to offer a new theory of difference; rather, he aims to offer an account of difference that will demonstrate that difference does not require representation for its being. His critique of representation is designed to reveal how the four criteria of representation presuppose difference in itself as "a pluralism of free, wild or untamed differences" (DR 50). While the apparatus of representation fails to acknowledge difference in itself, Deleuze's transcendental empiricism is specifically constituted on the affirmation of difference.

For representationalist theories affirmation is only the result of negation doubled. This type of pseudoaffirmation always remains indebted to the form of the negative. Alternatively, Deleuze proposes that affirmation actually produces a "creative disorder or inspired chaos" that challenges the "conservative order of representation" (DR 54). While representation must find opposition in order to affirm, difference immediately affirms itself as that which is and as that which must be created. In other words, affirmation must be engendered and mobilized on the basis of the difference that is affirmed. While representation works from, and brings the represented difference back to a single center, difference in itself invokes a plurality of positions and perspectives that distort representation. Transcendental empiricism is an ontology based on the primacy of difference. Can ontology have a true function, however, without a grounding

Identity? Yes, but it is necessary to recast the ways in which being can be articulated into terms other than those of representation and its criteria.

Deleuze proposes that difference is immediate and sub-representative. As such it is the condition which representation presupposes: "difference is behind everything, but behind difference there is nothing" (*DR* 57). Every person, thing or idea is already a difference in relation to other differences and actual differences are to be viewed as the realization of difference as such. Furthermore, difference does not belong to the barren rationality of representationalism but, as Deleuze states in *Dialogues*, to the "concrete richness of the sensible" (*D* 54). Deleuze defines the very being *of* the sensible as nonconceptual difference that can be directly sensed or apprehended in the sensible (*DR* 56–57). By making difference that which can be sensed directly, Deleuze refuses to abstractly separate actual experience from its conditions. Indeed, it is difference as it is experienced, directly apprehended, and created which "is precisely the object of a superior empiricism" (*DR* 57). This is perhaps Deleuze's most significant proposition regarding transcendental empiricism: nonconceptual empirical difference is the necessary condition immanent within actual experience.

Since difference is the transcendental condition for actual experience, it is also the condition for the creation and application of concepts within experience. The abstract cannot presume to account for the genesis of actual experience, because concepts possess their own processes of actualization and are formed under the pressure of certain social, historical, and political circumstances and events. For Deleuze, the intense world of differences excludes the coherence of a self-representing subject and a represented object. The world of difference cannot be determined as representation would have it. Deleuze notes that transcendental empiricism can also be thought of as "a veritable aesthetic" (*DR* 57). Transcendental empiricism affirms the work of creating difference in much the same way as the work of art affirms the nonrepresentational experience of the sensible. Again, it is not a matter of representation because the transcendental is that *which is sensed directly in the sensible*. The dynamic force of difference as such constitutes the affective domain of the empirical or sensible freed from the closure of subjectivity.

For the reason that representation seeks to mediate difference in the identity of the concept in general, thought becomes limited and cut off from its sensible source. Transcendental empiricism, on the contrary, continually strives to discover "a pure concept of difference in itself" and thereby overturn Platonism and restore the life of difference to Ideas (*DR* 59). To accomplish this task transcendental empiricism must remove the Platonic ground from under the feet of representationalism. At this point, Deleuze questions the association of the dialectic with the negative. Is negation really that which supplies the dialectic with its movement, or is it perhaps rather *problematization*, the problematic as such? Problems have nothing to do with negation, but everything to do with affirmative questioning. Traditionally, the alternative confronting the thought of being is that of a fully positive identical being that does not admit nonbeing, or of a being that admits nonbeing only in order to ground negation. In either case nonbeing is simply the negative, in that it is either illusory or a contradictory part of being itself. Deleuze proposes to think "*both* that there is non-being *and* that the negative is illusory" (*DR* 63). Deleuzian (non)being is at the heart of being in the form of the problematic structure of objects, the nexus of problem and question. (Non)being is the difference internal to things, the positivity of what has not yet been created, and is the necessary problematizing element of being that is expressed in questioning rather than negation.

Deleuze suggests that difference in itself can be thought only if one questions identity as the ground of representation. Questioning the ground of identity involves dissolving the distinction between original and copy, model and form, and looking to the sign as that which interiorizes difference as the condition of its repetition. Simulacra are not copies of originals or imitations of "the thing itself," but signs and things traversed by interior differences. Simulacra are the signs of disparity as the conditions of real experience, that is, of the unlimited repetition of differences themselves. The dynamic and incessant repetition of difference is responsible for the "universal *ungrounding*" of the ground of identity (*DR* 67). In contrast to the categories of possible experience, transcendental empiricism affirms this differential movement in order to expose the subrepresentative domain of real experience. In real experience the transcendental and the empirical are united in the direct, sensible apprehension of difference as such. Difference is both the condition and the reality of experience, and this difference of difference—its active self-differing—appears in the diverse forms of the simulacrum. Thus Deleuze's ontology is not one which asserts how the world essentially has been, is, and will be; rather, it demonstrates that such concepts improperly limit the difference of which the world is composed. It is best understood as a practical ontology of what *can be*, of the generative and transformative forces of difference as such. It is a pluralism that allows us to see many more possible worlds than the one dictated by the form of identity in representation. It is an ontology that flows from difference itself.

Repetition and Representation

Having seen in the previous section the role that Deleuze proposes for difference according to transcendental empiricism, I will now turn to his account of repetition as the power that reproduces difference, generates the disparate, and affirms change and becoming. As with difference, Deleuze argues that repetition explicitly defies the mode of representation. However, the argument now is shifted to related terrain. In the case of difference, Deleuze's concern is with the supposed coherency of objects grounded in the identity of being; in the case of repetition, his concern is with the supposed identity of the transcendental subject as a constitutive representational function. Following his discussion of difference as that which is directly sensed, Deleuze's examination of repetition is formulated around the issue of temporality and the presupposition of a subject whose basic structure corresponds to the intelligible re-presentation of sensible appearances and the subordination of diversity to the subject's continued identity. The representationalist subject is held to be the source of all possible experience, but does actual experience conform to purely rational forms?

Repetition can be considered in relation to three different syntheses of time. The first synthesis of time is that of habit or contraction. As proposed by Hume, the repetition to be found in habit is one that does not change the repeated object "but it does change something in the mind which contemplates it" (*DR* 70).[15] At this point repetition appears as a difference that is introduced into the mind which apprehends each independent presentation of objective sequences: In the case of the sequence AB, what makes one presentation of AB different from another presentation of AB? It is not something different in the elements of AB, but a difference that the mind *"draws from"* their repetition. Elements and cases are contracted in the mind, or more precisely in the imagination, into an internal qualitative impression through a passive synthesis that is prior to memory and reflection. The cases and elements appear as the succession of independent instants that constitute the living present. Although the synthesis is passive it is not a simple receptivity, for it marks a power to contract on the part of the imagination or apprehending mind. Difference is produced in the mind on the basis of the expectation of repeated sequences, in the asymmetrical space of the contraction of particulars in the living present and their projection into the generality of the future (*DR* 71). Sensible contraction or habit thus forms the first synthesis of time, a passive synthesis which is also the foundation of time. Deleuze describes the passive synthesis as that which:

> constitutes our habit of living, our expectation that "it" will continue, that one of the two elements will appear after the other, thereby assuring the perpetuation of our *case*. When we say that habit is a contraction we are speaking not of an instantaneous action which combines with another to form an element of repetition, but rather of the fusion of that repetition in the contemplating mind. (*DR* 74)

In the living present the self is that which is composed of the countless sensible repetitions associated with the habits of a contracting and apprehending imagination. Here the self is not a preestablished identity that undergoes modification, but is a fluid system of repetitions and modifications that dissolves such completeness. Sensible repetitions give rise to habits according to the contractile powers of the body and imagination; the self emerges as an effect through the active contraction of habits (*ES* 64–72).

While the passive synthesis of habit founds time as a living present, it is nonetheless a present which passes; a present that continually moves beyond itself. The first passive synthesis of time brings with it a paradox: "to constitute time while passing in the time constituted" (*DR* 79). Given this situation there must be another time that allows for the synthesis of the living present. The first synthesis of habit is the foundation (*fondation*) of time in that it establishes the present as a certain empirical duration that is lived. Yet what is it that supports this passive synthesis of habit? Deleuze responds that the foundation of time as the passive synthesis of habit must itself be grounded (*fondée*) "by another (transcendental) passive synthesis which is peculiar to memory itself" (*DR* 81). The passive synthesis of memory constitutes the being of the past, that is, the pure past as the ground (*fondement*) of each present. Of course, there is an active synthesis of memory. Yet this synthesis is simply a derivation of habit, and functions as a principle of representation; it is that which reflects the present as present, as well as that which represents former presents.[16]

According to Deleuze there is also a passive and transcendental synthesis of memory that establishes the pure past of time as the presupposition of every representation of the present in the active synthesis. Drawing upon the work of Bergson, Deleuze remarks that the past is not simply that which is constituted after the fact of each present or on the basis of an anticipated future present, but is that which must always coexist with each present whose past it is.[17] This gives rise to three further paradoxes of time. First, the present would not pass, nor would the past be constituted, unless the past and the present were constituted simultaneously: "This is the first paradox: the contemporaneity of the past with the present that it *was*" (*DR* 81). Second, if the present and each past are contemporaneous, "then *all* of the past coexists with the new present in relation to which it is now past" (*DR* 81–82). The present passes into a new present because the past is contemporaneous with it, yet each present has no more claim to the past than any other present. Finally, even though the present passes, the past itself does not pass. It cannot be said that the past was or that it will be; the past *is*, and as such, "it forms a pure, general, *a priori* element of all time" (*DR* 82). Thus a pure and nonrepresentable past in itself preexists each representable passing-present, present-present, and future-present. The repetition of the pure past, irreducible to the re-presentation of the present, forms the condition or ground of time.

With respect to repetition we have seen two cases of passive synthesis: that of habit in which the present is the contraction of separate instants, and that of memory in which the present is the contraction of a coexisting totality of the past. Deleuze further distinguishes the two by describing the former as a material repetition that draws difference from the asymmetrical space of contraction and the latter as a spiritual repetition that includes difference within itself as variations within a Whole (*DR* 84). However, both repetitions are subrepresentative, in that representation can only occur through an active synthesis or reflection which presupposes the already present conditions of the passive material and spiritual syntheses. There is, then, a synthesis of the present and a synthesis of the past: Is there a third synthesis of time that corresponds to the future?

Recall that Deleuze's discussion of repetition is concerned with the supposed identity of the subject. For Deleuze the question of repetition turns upon the introduction of time into thought as such. Effectively utilizing a combination of insights provided by Hume, Nietzsche, and Bergson, Deleuze criticizes Kant's adherence to the idea of a necessary unity of the subject. Kant develops his notion of the transcendental subject by distinguishing between it and the merely empirical self. Kant argues that any possible experience can be so only with the imposition by the subject of necessary and universal criteria, namely, *a priori* intuitions and concepts.[18] The former criteria refer to the passive reception of the appearance of objects in a single temporal sequence and a coherent spatial manifold, the *a priori* or pure forms of time and space (inner and outer sense). The latter criteria refer to the necessity that the forms of intuition be recognized as coherent, according to the *a priori* concepts or categories, in order for experience to be possible (*Critique*, B118–B126).

For Kant, experience is possible only if the subject identifies and recognizes spatio-temporal appearances on the basis of the *a priori* concepts of the understanding that are not themselves dependent on experience (*Critique*, B130).[19] Thus, according to Kant, there must be a pure subject not of real experience but instead of possible experience that possesses an original, "objective" unity independent of the manifold given in intuition (*Critique*, B139–B140). The Kantian transcendental apperception functions to bring the diversity of appearances under a single common representation. The very notion of objective appearances presupposes the unity of the subject, of the "I think" as the condition of possible experience:

> It must be possible for the "I think" to accompany all my representations; for otherwise something would be represented in me which could not be thought at all. . . . All the manifold of intuition has, therefore, a necessary relation to the "I think" in the same subject in which the manifold is found. . . . I call it *pure apperception*, to distinguish it from empirical apperception, or, again, *original apperception*, because it is that self-consciousness which, while generating the representation "*I think*" (a representation which must be capable of accompanying all other representations, and which in all consciousness is one and the same), cannot itself be accompanied by any further representation. (*Critique*, B132)

From these points Deleuze's critique will emerge. Since for Kant it is impossible to experience the transcendental subject in itself, the empirical self of real experience is known only as an object of thought, as it appears to itself as a representation (*Critique*, B156–B158). Kant suggests that the "I think" expressed by the self is the synthetic representative point between that which cannot be known in-itself—the transcendental subject of pure apperception—and the phenomenal world of successive subjective representations (*Critique*, B150–B157). As noted above, Kant concludes that the transcendental unity of apperception is the necessary condition of any possible experience. In other words, possible experience consists in the *knowledge* of the representation of objects as imposed by a single self-conscious subject that is itself a deduction and not an intuition (*Critique*, B157–B159). The transcendental self-consciousness imposes the categorical schema on its diverse intuitions, subjecting this passively intuited diversity to the pure concepts of the understanding. Time is thereby subordinated by Kant to the active synthetic unity of the transcendental subject, which is imposed upon the passive phenomenal subject by something other than itself.

In the Kantian model, repetition is only the subjective re-presentation of appearances under the condition of possible knowledge, the self-same "I think." Hence, the pure form of time that first introduced dissimilarity into the "I" remains relative to the transcendental subject in order to ensure that the unity of subject-identity is maintained. Within the Kantian framework, experience can be understood only as that which conforms to the epistemic conditions supplied by the transcendental subject, "which amounts to a supreme effort to save the world of representation" (*DR* 87). Admittedly, there is a certain positive element to Kant's philosophy, in that the world must be related to some form of human experience. Nevertheless, the strides Kant makes are vitiated by his positing of a unique and transcendent Reason that forever remains external to the contingencies of empirical nature and history. By attempting to save belief in immutable truths it is also necessary for Kant to save representation.

However, Deleuze asks if this pure form of time can indeed be recuperated by a transcendental subject. Is not the pure or transcendental form of time that which always points beyond the ground of the "I think"? If time was relative to the self-identical subject, would it not simply appear as a closed circle subordinated to a chain of re-presented "I thinks," as always the "same" time? The point Deleuze makes is that Kant defines experience only in terms of the categories and on the basis of a transcendental subject that is independent of empirical diversity and that cannot be affected by difference: In short, Kant limits experience to an epistemological, representational sphere and to the maintenance of the form of the identical.

Deleuze's priority is to disengage the pure form of time from Kant's transcendental subjectivity by means of a third synthesis of time. On the one side, the pure form of time appears in Kant as the circular movement of time demanded by the transcendental subject, as the infinite representation of successive presents that unfold within a single temporal sequence. On the other side, the pure form of time for Deleuze is that which *undoes* the circle because time "*itself* unfolds . . . instead of things unfolding within it" (*DR* 88). The pure order of time separates beginning and end by freeing them from the circular figure. The past and future truly become conditions of experience when time is freed from the determination of the "I think" as that which must remain the same. Deleuze therefore defines the order of time as the "purely formal distribution of the unequal in the function of a caesura" (*DR* 89). Liberated from the transcendental subject, time relates to the displacement of differences through the unequal distribution of prepersonal events and the differential repetition of the sensible. Corresponding to this formal distribution are the ideas of a totality and a series. The totality is the fracture or caesura of time understood as a "unique and tremendous event" which draws together the unequal parts of either side of the event—the before and the after. The temporal series is constituted by the fact that the distribution or drawing together enacted by the caesura remains unequal. Since the past, present, and future cannot be determined according to the same criteria, time unfolds unpredictably or unequally.

These features of the pure form of time fragment the self and the "I" with each event and each series: "what the self has become equal to is the unequal in itself" (*DR* 90). Within the caesura of the event and the temporal series everything becomes repetition unaccompanied by a transcendental subject. The "I" has itself become repetition, yet repetition is not an appearance of representation; it is the historical condition under which the new is produced. Prior to being a concept of reflection, repetition is the condition of action that permits the production of the new and yet is also found in these acts of production. The third synthesis of time is that of the excessive repetition, the repetition of the future in the form of the eternal return. The eternal return concerns the pure form of time as the future as such. It is with the eternal return that the past and present function as the transformative elements in the service of the production and creation of the new in the pure order of time, that is, the time of active becoming:

> . . . time as pure and empty form, has precisely undone that circle. It has undone it in favour of a less simple and much more secret, much more tortuous, more nebulous circle, an eternal excentric circle, the decentred circle of difference which is re-formed uniquely in the third time of the series. The order of time has broken the circle of the Same and arranged time in a series only in order to re-form a circle of the Other at the end of the series. . . . In this manner, the ground has been superseded by a groundlessness, a universal ungrounding which turns upon itself and causes only the yet-to-come to return. (*DR* 91)

It is now possible to return to our consideration of the transcendental-empirical relation. For Deleuze, the final synthesis of time demonstrates that the

Transcendental Empiricism and the Critique of Representation

past and the present are dimensions of the future, the past as its condition and the present as the intermediary agent of metamorphosis. It is the future, however, that exceeds both the past and present, for it is only by a pure repetition that the past and present continually return. Both the condition (the past) and the agent (the present) of the future are what they are only by not being the same; past and present continually return, yet it is never the "same" past nor the "same" present. Consequently, the future itself is that which is repeated, but it is always different, as well. The future as eternal return guarantees the independence and originality of the product or the work of historical action. Historical action is, in this sense, the creation of the new under the condition of repetition. Repetition is the transcendental "category of the future," but the future is inseparable from the empirically real historical actions of the past and present (*DR* 94). What becomes autonomous are the actual products and events of historical repetition; they are the differences of history. Repetition is never itself reducible to a particular historical fact since it is the transcendental condition of the production of the new, although it is impossible to consider repetition apart from its historical elements. Transcendental repetition is internal to empirical genesis, in contrast to the external condition of possible, representable experience as portrayed by Kant.

Deleuze considers the example of revolution: The actual historical actions of any given revolution cannot be reduced to the unconditioned which will be the product of these actions. The unconditioned product is without preestablished identity or name and will always in some way exceed the past and present; any particular revolutionary crisis will possess its own signification but its actual future cannot be foreseen. In this way, revolution escapes itself in order to be repeated in the future under different conditions, with different agents, and with different results. The impossibility of reconciling the repetitive natures of past and present to the pure repetition of the future itself leads Deleuze to posit the latter as the "superior repetition" of transcendental empiricism, that is, as eternal return (*DR* 93). Along with difference in itself, Deleuze uncovers a repetition for itself that is both the thought *and the production* of that which is absolutely different. From the perspective of transcendental empiricism repetition is the condition both of the belief in, and the creation of, that which is yet to come. The differential elements of repetition, future, and eternal return are responsible for ungrounding representation and challenging the limitations it would place around the production of the new:

> If there is an essential relation between eternal return . . . and the future, it is because the future is the deployment and explication of the multiple, of the different and of the fortuitous, for themselves and "for all times". . . . Repetition in the eternal return excludes both the becoming-equal or the becoming-similar in the concept, and being conditioned by lack of such a becoming. It concerns instead excessive sys-

tems which link the different with the different, the multiple with the multiple, the fortuitous with the fortuitous, in a complex of affirmations always coextensive with the questions posed and the decisions taken. (*DR* 115)

The eternal return, as repetition for itself, constitutes excessive systems of the production of difference by means of its extension of difference. As we have seen, Deleuze argues that difference can be viewed from two perspectives, each expressed by a single proposition. The first states "only that which is alike differs" (*DR* 116). This is undoubtedly the point of view of representation, which posits resemblance as the condition of difference; two things can differ, according to representation, only on the basis of their analogous relation to an identical concept and on their opposition determined by the three moments of resemblance, identity, and analogy. The second proposition states: "only differences are alike" (*DR* 116). This proposition expresses the perspective of transcendental empiricism. Against representation, Deleuze insists that difference is primary and that resemblance, identity, analogy, and opposition are its secondary effects. If this is the case, then difference must somehow immediately relate its differing terms to one another. In other words, difference must possess its own "differenciator," namely, repetition, which immediately articulates, connects, gathers, and relates differences prior to and outside of representation.

The first characteristic of difference is its organization into systems composed of series that are themselves composed of terms defined by the differences between them. The differences between the constituent terms of each series relate to the differences between series, which in turn form differences between differences within the system of difference. Deleuze proposes that there is an impulse or force of some kind that establishes communication between differences, yet this force is itself constituted by differences in relation as an "*internal resonance* within the system" (*DR* 117). The elemental differences constituting this force are determined by Deleuze to be "intensities." Each system possesses its own intensive character that differenciates it from others, nevertheless, each system also possesses a structure defined by terms and series of differences: "for example," writes Deleuze, "words are genuine intensities within certain aesthetic systems; concepts are also intensities from the point of view of philosophical systems," and the same applies to any system whether it be biological, social or physical (*DR* 118). Deleuze also refers to this differenciator of difference as the disparate itself. The disparate is the difference internal to each system by which each system comes to be determined as different from the others. Resemblances may later be drawn between different systems, but no matter how similar these systems appear, their similarity is only an exterior effect that cannot erase their internal difference or that disparity which functions as the differenciator of each system. Hence, rather than difference being derived from things that are alike, it is because things are different that similarities and identities can subsequently be attributed as secondary effects.

Difference in itself lacks its own identity. Identity emerges as a result of the implication or enveloping of differences in the third synthesis of time. The precursor of every system is pure repetition and the undetermined and original work, which function as the condition under which the system will actually appear. Each system as a whole thus assumes a relational form of complication-explication-implication that affirms the series of divergent and displaced elements synthesized by the future, rather than the past. The subject of each system emerges as a unique element that becomes the support of the system's dynamism: "Each series explicates or develops itself, but *in* its difference from the other series which it implicates and which implicate it, which it envelops and which envelop it; *in* this chaos which complicates everything" (*DR* 124). All the series are simultaneous and coexist prior to the representational successions of before and after, first and second, original and copy. What is decisive are the resonances by which series come to communicate "in the intersubjective unconscious" that is properly outside of such succession and exists only for the future.

The importance of difference and repetition is seen outside of the privileges accorded by representationalism to the identity of originary models and the resemblances of derived copies. The primacy of difference and its interiority to every system ensures that each system is unique and different and that they cannot simply be the reproduction of, or the model for, others. Difference in-itself is the only origin, and repetition as the for-itself of difference is that which causes differences to coexist and relate so that further differences are produced. Systems of difference and repetition are what return, yet each time the systems are different. Thus, not only are the products of each system simulacra, that is, resemblances and identities created as the effects of difference, but so are the systems themselves. According to the Platonic theory of Ideas, there are original and essential models (Forms) defined by their self-identity, and there are copies or imitations judged by their degrees of resemblance to the Forms. Difference is found only between the identity of the original and the resemblance of the copy, as the possible lack of accuracy between the two.

Paradoxically, it is this very distinction postulated by Plato that provides Deleuze with the means to overturn it. The purpose of the ideal model is to allow for the selection of good copies or images, as well as for the elimination of differences as the bad images (simulacra). While the Platonic theory of Ideas established the basis for Aristotelian categories and the institution of representationalism proper, it also inadvertently recognized the ubiquity of difference. What is most disturbing to Plato are those things which simulate identities and resemblances—for example, the thought of Heraclitus or the Sophists, and poetry—and undermine the attempt to establish an order of things based on identity and resemblance. Simulation attests to the constant rumblings of difference beneath the fragile ground of identity. Simulacra are not, then, to be understood as degraded copies of original models but as elements of difference itself, difference incarnate. As a result, the very distinction between model and copy postulated by representationalism is overturned.[20] Things are produced within the multiple and varied intersections of difference and repetition, and their autonomy liberates them from the claim that their legitimacy is derived from resemblance to a never changing and self-identical model.

Thought without Image: Transcendental Empiricism

Deleuze's critique of the representationalist models of difference and repetition forces a reconsideration of the application of representation to thought itself. Doing so involves a "radical critique" of the presuppositions implied by the traditional image of thought, which attempts to identify thought with representation (*DR* 132). Deleuze denounces such an image as nonphilosophical and seeks to offer an account of thought that is not dependent upon the postulates of representation. This account is the culmination of Deleuze's discussion of difference and repetition in that it elucidates the most important ontological elements of his transcendental empiricism. To put this another way, Deleuze is now concerned with elaborating an account of what thought can do and become in terms of transcendental empiricism.

What are the presuppositions or postulates of representation? There are eight that Deleuze examines, although only four of these postulates need be discussed in the present context. The first postulate is the implicit presupposition that serves as the prephilosophical basis for philosophy in the representational mode. This presupposition is implicit or subjective because it takes the form of the phrase "Everybody knows. . . ." In this case, the discourse of representation presumes that "everybody knows" what thinking is, namely, that it is "the natural exercise of a faculty . . . endowed with a talent for truth or an affinity with the true" (*DR* 131). According to this postulate everybody possesses an innate good will for truth, since thought is naturally aligned with the true. This upright nature of thought and good will on the part of the thinker are to be found combined in a *Cogitatio natura universalis*; in a natural good or common sense, the second postulate of representation (*DR* 132).

These two postulates form an image of thought in principle, in light of the universality of good will and common sense with which every mind is naturally endowed. They in turn summon a third postulate, that of recognition, which provides the model for the operation of thought. Recognition is defined by Deleuze as "the harmonious exercise of all the faculties upon a supposed same object" (*DR* 133). Each faculty—perception, imagination, memory, and understanding—operates in accord with the others by virtue of an *a priori* subjective feature that allows the faculties to harmonize with one another: a common sense or *concordia facultatum* that is both the presupposition and the result of the harmonious accord between the faculties.[21] Simultaneously, the collaboration of the faculties is related to a form of identity in the object, thereby assuring a harmonious correspondence between the identity of the subject and that of the object. While common sense provides the norm of identity with respect to a pure Self and the unspecified, good sense provides the norm of distribution with respect to empirical selves and qualified objects. In other words, "common sense contributes the form of the Same," while good sense determines "the contribution of the faculties in each case" in order to maintain a harmonious relation between the faculties and the given (*DR* 134). These three postulates form an ideal image of thought as the universal subjective unity of the faculties aligned with the transcendental model of recognition of the Same object.

Deleuze criticizes this image as misleading because it takes an empirical or everyday fact, that of recognition, and elevates it to the status of a purely transcendental model for what thought is and must be. How is it possible, he asks, to reduce thinking to recognition? In essence, the problem is that a model is formed by abstraction from the empirical, which is then used to "explain" the empirical by making it conform to the abstraction. With representationalism, the abstract and generalized image of thought as recognition precedes actual thinking, and its aim is to explain how this abstract model is embodied in a mode of thinking that resembles the same model. This image of thought dictates that thinking is naturally and inevitably predetermined by the limitations of a transcendental model of possible recognition. Yet, this transcendental model is itself composed of features extrapolated from the empirical realm turned back against the empirical in order to assert an image of thought as complacent obedience to the forms of recognition and representation, and to the seemingly innate and eternal values always rediscovered by the common sense and good will of harmoniously united faculties. The representationalist image of thought portrays thinking not as the creation of new values and new senses, but as the proper allocation and distribution of established values and the verification of its own image.[22] Consequently, thought is "filled with no more than an image of itself, one in which it recognizes itself the more it recognizes things" (*DR* 138). Representation proper thereby emerges as the fourth postulate; as that which subordinates the actuality of difference and repetition to the strictures of identity, opposition, analogy, and resemblance. The world of representation is one shaped by the form of the Same.

To this postulate Deleuze opposes the necessity of a thought without image characterized not by recognition, but by a "fundamental *encounter*" with that which can only be sensed, that is, with the being of the sensible (the *sentiendum*) (*DR* 139). For representationalism, thinking is equal to the recognition of sensible objects by the harmonious exercise of the faculties forming a common sense.[23] Here the sensible refers to qualities of given objects that can be sensed only on condition that each faculty jointly recognizes it as the same. One must be able to perceive, imagine, conceive, and remember—in short, recognize—the "same" object in order to "think." Deleuze insists, however, that what is encountered is not experienced in the mode of recognition, nor is it brought under the exercise of a common sense. Instead, each thing encountered (a person, object, emotion, idea) manifests the being of the sensible in such a way that it "gives rise to sensibility with regard to a given sense" (*DR* 139). There is a particular sense for each object encountered and each sense confronts its object within a discordant, rather than harmonious, exercise of the faculties. Furthermore, that which is sensed is more a sign than an intuition, inasmuch as it poses a problem rather than represents the appearance of a thing to be recognized, remembered, and identified (*DR* 140–41). The sign is the object of contingent encounters, as Deleuze reaffirms in his *Proust and Signs*, and it is what forces us to create the very act of thinking as the developing, deciphering and translating of the unknown that we encounter into Ideas.[24]

Whereas representationalism abstracts from the experience of sensible beings in order to posit separate domains of resembling copies and Ideal essences, Deleuze maintains that only that which can be sensed *is* the being *of* the sensible, the *sentiendum* of difference. Consider an example from Plato's *Republic* (523d) mentioned by Deleuze (*DR* 141): At one point Socrates holds up three fingers, their size and shape are different, yet they are all recognizable as fingers, as the same. The Platonic conclusion is that physically different fingers can be known as fingers because stamped into the memory is the form of an ideal Finger which makes all material versions possible. Plato posits a transcendent realm of ideals hierarchically situated in relation to a lesser world of appearances, unified according to a referential theory of representation. For this theory of representation, the particular is subsumed under the general; recognition is achieved when the particular correctly reflects the transcendent absolute. According to this model, difference is external to that which is actually sensed and is only the conceptual difference of the ideal Form and its resembling copy. For Deleuze, on the other hand, difference is the being of the sensible and is that which is sensed. Actual differences are the result of the internal "differen*c*iation" of difference as such, that is, the dynamic and creative actualization of difference (*DR* 207–221). In one sense, fingers are copies, but they do not refer upward to a metaphysical ideal; they refer to themselves as different, they produce and limit themselves, and only then do they refer to each other. There is no original, ideal Finger which transcends every actual finger and allows us to think "finger." According to Deleuze, difference and the object of an encounter—the being of the sensible and the sensed—are inseparable and there is no transcendent dimension involved. Earthly fingers are simulacra formed within the positive difference that is the being of the sensible. As

Deleuze sees it, the mistake of philosophical representationalism is to fall prey to its own abstractions.

Recognition is based on the form of qualitative opposition that requires comparison and the convergence of the faculties under the determination of common sense. Given that difference is that which is experienced by the senses, Deleuze suggests that recognition, representation, and common sense are thereby without ground. In that case, the faculties themselves must be differentiated by difference. They are characterized by divergence rather than convergence in the guise of an *a priori* common sense. Each faculty is therefore transcendental, *not* because it "addresses itself to objects outside the world," but because it surpasses the rule of common sense and "grasps that in the world which concerns it exclusively, and brings it into the world" (*DR* 143). Each faculty is able to experience only that object or sign of encounter which it alone can sense and is able to sense this object in a manner that cannot be duplicated by another faculty:

> Each faculty discovers at this point its own unique passion—in other words, its radical difference and its eternal repetition, its differential and repeating element along with the instantaneous engendering of its action and the eternal replay of its object, its manner of coming into the world already repeating. (*DR* 143)

Deleuze asserts that this doctrine of the faculties is required by a "properly transcendental empiricism" in order to combat the representationalist image of thought. For this image, the harmonious collaboration of the faculties and the necessity of recognition are the requirements for "possible" experience. Yet how is possible experience to be considered? As discussed in the preceding section, it is to be regarded in terms of the necessary conditions of the possibility of our knowledge of things; accordingly, the *a priori* conditions and presuppositions of knowledge and representable experience are apparently discoverable apart from the empirical. For Deleuze, such a process can only have disastrous results for actual experience. From the perspective of possible experience, the exercise of the faculties and thinking itself can only be represented as faint outlines traced from empirical diversity. The possible can only be defined by generalizing and abstracting cases of the real: To apply the possible to the real as if it dictated what real experience can be is to posit a world of representation rather than to encounter the world of actual experiences. It is to judge experience and thought in advance.

In contrast, Deleuze describes the transcendental and disjunctive exercise of the faculties as they operate in actual experience. Again, the exercise of each faculty is transcendental "precisely because it apprehends that which cannot be grasped from the point of view of common sense" (*DR* 143). What common sense cannot apprehend is difference and repetition, the being of the sensible, and the conditions of actual experience. Thus, transcendental empiricism is concerned with the necessary conditions of experience, yet these conditions are themselves real; they are the conditions that are actualized in different experiences. However, because each experience is able to be actualized only on the basis of those concrete differences which exceed it, empiricism must become transcendental in this unique sense. The transcendental conditions of actual experience are, in truth, on the side of empirical, socio-historical formations and practices imposed from without, and not on the side of a transcendental subjectivity.[25]

For Deleuze, the transcendental is timely and differentiated, not eternal and universal, and transcendental empiricism receives its name precisely because it seeks to understand the *actual conditions* under which new things (from ideas to political organizations) are created and produced. Transcendental empiricism examines the multiplicitous interactions of forces and things in order to delineate their variable compositions; not to formalize them into conditions for the validity of judgments, but to create new concepts and practices of an entirely different nature. In each case, the transcendental is itself variable and transformable according to the historical forces at work and the types of effects created, and the empirical can no longer be characterized merely as the realm of appearances and representation. The dynamic field of the conditions of experience is not simply that which makes one type of knowledge possible, it is also that which *is* constituted, experienced, and acted upon.

What Deleuze offers here is the mutual immanence of particular, actual experiences and those conditions endowed with their own reality upon which such experiences may be actualized and constructed. What is absent is the necessity of a representational correspondence, that is, a resemblance, between experience and its conditions. For Deleuze experience is always able to potentially surpass its given conditions, which is why the conditions of experience must always be actively discovered and freed of teleological illusion, but not by escaping into an other-worldly transcendence. It is not sufficient to posit a transcendent realm of ideal, timeless, or fixed causes over experienced effects; causes are always immanent within what is sensed and experienced and are not to be generalized into self-identical forms or categories. The transcendental is not a universal principle which determines the forms of the empirical on the basis of the resemblance it imposes from without, but is a composition of the differential conditions of real empirical geneses that are themselves constituted in that which is given.

A further difference appears between Deleuze and Kant on this point: While the conditions of experience are, for Kant, on the side of the universal subject in the form of the categories of possible experience, for Deleuze they are on the side of social and historical formation in the sense that real experiences are formed in the objective transcendental field of the chance encounters of events and active forces of becoming.[26] And this transcendental field is also the being of the sensible. Unlike Kant, who aims to determine the real according to the *a priori* concepts of the possible and who thereby establishes an insurmountable barrier between the sensible and the conceptual, Deleuze's transcendental empiricism allows for the actual genesis of concepts by means of the movement of difference within actual experience. Experience cannot be expected to conform to universal concepts and eternal categories, for something new is always produced within its contingent empirical conditions. Thus, "historical formation" has to be understood as itself historical, not in the sense of being "in" History, but in the sense of effects generated by the unfolding of time (recall the third synthesis of time in which historical repetition is the condition of historical action and the autonomy of its products). It cannot therefore be considered as a purely subjective or unchanging category that applies as a rule to all possible experience.

For Deleuze the transcendental conditions of actual experience are not transcendent or suprasensible because they are immanent within the sensible, nor do they conform to the presumed representational requirements of human understanding. The transcendental is the complex of *real*, not possible, conditions of actual experience. Because subrepresentative difference constitutes actual experience, there cannot be a representational correspondence between the conditions of experience and the effects produced within experience. One of the important effects of transcendental empiricism, then, is to problematize the nature of the relations that obtain between empirical effects and their conditions, as well as between the effects themselves. While there must be conditions for the production of empirical effects, there is no causal necessity which regulates what exactly will be produced; actual effects cannot be judged according to the fixed criteria of representational norms because each condition as well as each effect has its own history of becoming. In short, the conditions of actual experience are themselves empirically conditioned. Deleuze expands considerably the understanding of "conditions" beyond what Kant seeks. Kant wants an invariable correspondence between an epistemological cause (a "principle") and its necessary effect, between a pure cause of the "given" and a "given" that must resemble it. On the contrary, Deleuze wants to overcome this dualism, which requires a pure transcendent element, and instead seeks an active, material, and sensible genesis through the mutual immanence of variable causes and effects; a true composition beyond mere resemblance.

Deleuze considers pure difference to be the intensity that "awakens" each faculty. It is that which is sensed and gives rise to sensibility in the encounter. Each faculty is different and apprehends its own exclusive zone of the intensive being of the sensible. The faculties are able to communicate with one another, but they are not governed by the necessity of a common sense because difference always inhabits and fractures sensibility. For each disjointed faculty there exists a differential element that awakens and empowers it and contributes to the determination of its limit: Difference in intensity for sensibility, disparity in the phantasm for imagination, dissimilarity in the pure form of time for memory, and the fractured "I" that is always Other for thought (*DR* 144–45). For each faculty there is always something that forces it to confront its limit: imperceptible differences, the unimaginable, the immemorial, and the unthinkable.

We should note Deleuze's remark that transcendental empiricism is not a "doctrine of the faculties" (*DR* 144). This is so because the exercise and limits of the faculties are transformable, and because there are perhaps "faculties yet to be discovered, whose existence is not yet suspected" or that were "repressed by that form of common sense" (*DR* 143–44). The divergence of each faculty and the difference communicated from one faculty to another form a "discordant harmony" according to their limits (*DR* 146). Those instances of communication which pass from sensibility to thought and back to sensibility are what engender thinking, bringing into being that which is not innate but which must be created from particular conditions, namely, Ideas (*DR* 146–47). There is no common sense that transcends sensibility and determines the appearance of Ideas. Ideas are formed from the discordant harmony or communication of the faculties in their problematic encounter with the being of the sensible. Thought is not simply the orientation of preexistent concepts to their proper objects, but the genesis of thinking itself within the differential conditions of experience. Thinking requires the abolition of the dogmatic image of thought as representation. It is the experimentation of the faculties with the intensities of difference, the problem of the encounter that takes each to their limit: Ideas are generated from, and remain embedded within, thinking as sense experience. In Deleuze's transcendental empiricism, the genesis or actual becoming of thought replaces the imposition of a preexisting Reason by a transcendental subject.[27] This is not to say that thought is essentially "irrational," only that it too must be created, and that it is open to transformation and variation.

Therefore, Ideas are problem-question complexes that give themselves over to processes of solution. However, solutions do not resemble their problems for they do not simply involve the clarification of errors and the possession of generalized concepts. Here Deleuze contrasts learning with knowledge: Knowledge designates only the mastery of rules of solution and general concepts, the rigid method of common sense, while learning refers to the process that privileges the problematic as such, the practice which embodies the experimentalism of empiricists by carrying each faculty to the limit of its transcendental exercise when confronted with a problem or Idea. The method of knowledge is to assimilate thought to the Same, while the infinite process of learning embraces and affirms the act of thinking as difference relating to itself (*DR* 167). For transcendental empiricism, empirical differences are the necessary conditions of thinking. Thought does not constitute the empirical in any abstract manner. Rather, it encounters empirical actualities as its own conditions and thinking consists of the creation of relations between the elements of this empirical diversity. However, Ideas are not simply abstractions or generalizations from experience, as a naïve empiricism might suggest. Because they are not representations, Ideas do not "contain" the elements of their actualization, nor do they explain their own genesis by reference to universal laws of knowledge (*DR* 255). It remains, then, to mention the operation of thought and the characteristics of the Idea.

The Kantian determination of Ideas remains external to the Idea itself; each Idea is determinable only in relation to possible objects of experience and is determined only in accordance with the pure concepts of the understanding. In between the two appears the intermediary of the schema of the imagination, which itself conforms to the categories (*Critique*, B152–B154). Kantian Ideas represent the absolutely unconditioned that transcends any possible experience, under which concepts of the understanding may be applied to objects of possible experience. Hence, the object of an Idea must conform to the categories, which leads to the conclusion that the object of knowledge is not the thing in itself but that appearance regulated by reason. The subjective foundationalism of Kant is completely in accord with his theory of Ideas (*DR* 168–173; *K* 18–27).

In opposition to this, Deleuze seeks to eliminate the Kantian duality of intuition and concept by providing a description of the empirical and genetic determination of Ideas according to the internal requirements of differentiation in difference. This is carried out in three ways: First, the generality of the fixed quantities of intuition (the possible) and the particularity of the variable quantities of concepts (the real) are replaced by a pure element of "quantitability" and continuity that corresponds to the undetermined as such, expressed as "the universal and its appearance" (*DR* 171). The pure element of quantitability is the continuum of the indetermination of both particular and general quantity. Second, within the undetermined as such are the qualitative differences of reciprocal determinations. It is not a particular or general quantity that forces determination, but rather the pure element of "qualitability," that is, the process of the reciprocal determination or synthesis of genetic elements through differential relations. Here, all terms are determinable in relation to one another, in a reciprocal differentiation according to which each term "exists absolutely only in its relation to the other" (*DR* 172). An external intermediary is no longer needed, for the differential relation is the qualitative change integrated by the Idea in its universal function. In other words, the Idea itself is variety or multiplicity and not the variability between intuition and concept. Third, the reciprocal determination of genetic elements corresponds to the reciprocal synthesis of differential relations "in the form of a system of ideal connections" (*DR* 173). This system appears as a *concrete* universal or Idea. Complete determination thus coincides with the becoming actual of the Idea and the final pure element of potentiality, namely, the generative potential of differential relations.

Yet the genetic elements and differential relations of reciprocal syntheses are not the constructs of a transcendental subject, rather they are the difference interiorized by the power of a differential unconscious. The elements of difference are thus to be found in the object as a pure element of potentiality and the Idea is determined according to the power which composes, arranges, forms, and distributes singular points in systems of ideal connections. This system of connections expresses the Idea as the problematic encountered and the solution incarnated within difference itself. Ideas are therefore the differential elements of thought which engender different domains and fields of thinking, and they are variety, multiplicity, and singularity produced as instances or cases of thinking difference:

> Ideas are multiplicities: every idea is a multiplicity or a variety. In this Reimannian usage of the word "multiplicity" (taken up by Husserl, and again by Bergson) the utmost importance must be attached to the substantive form: multiplicity must not designate a combination of the many and the one, but rather an organisation belonging to the many as such. . . . Instead of the enormous opposition between the one and the many, there is only the variety of multiplicity—in other words, difference. (*DR* 182)

Ideas in the form of multiplicities are presented under three conditions: First, their elements are not obligated to possess sensible form or conceptual signification but they are inseparable from an empirical virtuality or potentiality; second, their elements must be reciprocally determined and intrinsically defined, which disallows the independence of ideal relational elements; and third, the ideal differential relations must be actualized in diverse spatio-temporal relationships and the virtual elements incarnated in a variety of terms (differen*c*iation). Taken together, these three conditions allow for the Idea to be defined as a structure, complex theme, and internal multiplicity. In actuality, the Idea is "a system of multiple, non-localisable connections between differential elements which is incarnated in real relations and actual terms" (*DR* 183).

The Idea's genesis is not defined, therefore, according to the realization of the possible, but according to the actualization of the virtual. Deleuze derives this distinction from the work of Bergson. As we have seen, the real and the possible are defined in terms of their resemblance: The possible is represented by abstracting cases from real experience, which are then projected back onto the real as if the possible had actually preceded it. In this case, all that there is has already been given; the real is only the resemblance of the possible and the possible is the image in which the real sees itself reflected (*DR* 183 & 211; *B* 96–98). What is essential here is that no combination of merely abstract terms can produce concrete, empirical actuality. In contrast, the virtual is difference as such, the pure potentiality that is empirically incarnated and actualized in real terms and relations.

Actualization describes the local genesis or creation of the actual (the different) within real virtual conditions (difference) that does not depend upon resemblance, identity, or representation (*DR* 210–11; *B* 96). Thus, while the possible "refers to the form of identity in the concept," the virtual "designates a pure multiplicity in the Idea which radically excludes the identical as a prior condition" (*DR* 211–12). Thought does not revolve around the determination of Ideas as essences through dialectical contradiction, but assumes the double task of evaluating problems at the level of ideal events and of engendering solutions at the level of real events. The two levels coexist on a plane of immanence, and Ideas express the complexity of this coexistence without the one level resembling the other. While the form of the question utilized in representation is "What is X?"—What is Reason? What is the Good? What is the Real?—transcendental empiricism transforms the question into "Which one is?"—Which reason is the one created? Which good is being defined? Which reality is being actualized? Difference, therefore, expresses the reality of the virtual and allows for an explanation of the processes of its actualization in terms of positive creation and composition. The negative Hegelian concepts of contradiction, opposition, and alienation formulate only a false movement that artificially represents the real movement of actualization and obscures the actual empirical genesis of the Idea.[28]

Deleuze concludes, then, that thought cannot be subordinated to the static image of representation, for the sensible multiplicities that are the conditions of actual experience force thought to actively exceed that which is given to it. As presented in *Difference and Repetition*, the aim of transcendental empiricism is to develop an ontology which affirms that experience, including thought, is open and continually subject to transformation by means of its own conditions and modes of constitution. However, while *Difference and Repetition* undertakes the task of elaborating the central elements of such an ontology, nevertheless there remain important questions regarding the effectiveness of Deleuze's emphasis on the primacy of difference. What kinds of relationships can be composed between differences, without reference to any form of ordering transcendence? How can Deleuze conceive of the ubiquity of difference without falling prey to the charge of atomism often leveled against empiricism? How can we consider the "making" of difference in terms of the practices and activities of real experience? In order to answer these questions it is necessary to develop a more complex elaboration of difference, one that accounts for its relations and interconnections not from the point of view of transcendence but from the perspective of immanence.

Chapter 2

Immanence and Multiplicity

It is useful, given Deleuze's critique of foundationalist representationalism, to paint a portrait of the history of philosophy according to two primary tendencies or attitudes toward the world.[1] On the one hand are those philosophies which contend that the world is but an imperfect and transient image of a more significant and eternal realm of transcendent essences, causes, and ideas. The tendency here is to devalue the world as it is experienced in favor of the notion of a metaphysical domain "behind" or "beyond" the world we live in; human beliefs, meanings, and values can be given the appearance of certainty only by an appeal to what transcends the contingencies and exigencies of our experiences. There have been a number of philosophies ranging from the idealistic to the rationalistic that follow this basic formulation of transcendentalism, and which have attempted to represent reality in terms of a discontinuity between the world as experienced and what is generally believed to be a preexisting transcendent realm. Plato is most often regarded as the progenitor of philosophical transcendentalism and others such as Descartes, Kant, and Hegel follow in his path in various ways.

On the other hand is a tradition of philosophies which have a tendency to affirm that the empirical world is the only actual source for the beliefs, ideals, meanings, and values made and transmitted in experience. These philosophies of immanence deny all appeals to transcendent causes, essences, and universal and unchanging principles. Instead, they emphasize the ways we are part of the world that we experience, and the ways we construct, interpret, and change it in order to make new and different things, interpretations, and experiences possible; for them, change is inherent to the immanent world. Here too there have been a variety of philosophies falling on the side of immanence, most often under the names of materialism and empiricism. Certainly Epicurus, Lucretius, and the Stoics are early voices in a tradition that also includes Spinoza, Marx, and Nietzsche. It is to this second line of thought that Deleuze allies himself in an effort to overturn the transcendent point of view. Deleuze contends that "every reaction against Platonism is a restoration of immanence to its greatness and its purity, which prohibits the return of a transcendent."[2]

In this chapter I want to show that Deleuze develops a radical philosophy of immanence through his readings and appropriations of the philosophies of Bergson, Nietzsche, and Spinoza. This philosophy of immanence continues Deleuze's critique of conventional metaphysical foundationalism as discussed in the previous chapter, and may be termed radical because of the central role it accords multiplicity within the immanent world. As a philosopher of immanence, Deleuze weaves a rich and positive account of the world we live in, an account which is resolutely committed to forwarding the notions of plurality, temporality, flux, and change, and to demonstrating the diverse ways in which human existence and its experiences are created. In this manner, Deleuze sets himself the task of undermining the conception of a transcendent foundation upon which all existents are predicated. Yet in his account, Deleuze also gives due weight to the role of the empirical particularity of unity as an actual consequence of an immanent reality. Indeed, it will be seen that for Deleuze multiplicity and unity are inseparable, insofar as he holds that "there is, there must be a unity which is the unity *of* this very multiplicity," which is the effect of the movements of multiplicity and not of a metaphysical principle of totalization.[3]

Moreover, the selection of these three philosophers—Bergson, Nietzsche, Spinoza—and their reinterpretation by Deleuze is at once significant and provocative. It is significant because it indicates that Deleuze wishes to maintain a strong connection to the history of philosophy, and it is provocative because his interpretation of each thinker is an attempt on Deleuze's part to create a "monster" that resists assimilation to this very history.[4] Deleuze's interest in these three philosophers also complements his own attempt to distinguish himself as an empiricist, for he sees in each of them quite varied manifestations of empiricism.

This chapter will proceed by examining in independent yet interconnected sections the essentials of the empiricist philosophies of immanence of Bergson, Nietzsche, and Spinoza, as detailed in Deleuze's writings on each. I will then conclude the chapter with a discussion of one of Deleuze's recent books, *What is Philosophy?*, in order to show that in this work he develops a conception of philosophy which both utilizes and transforms the ideas of Bergson, Nietzsche, and Spinoza. On this basis I hope to demonstrate not only the complexity and variety of sources drawn upon by Deleuze in his effort to elaborate an empiricism committed to immanence, but also to suggest that, by way of this commitment to immanence, Deleuze is able to further his notion of difference as that dynamic power which gives experience its unique unity; the continuity of change, transformation, and diversity, in other words, the continuous repetition of difference. In this manner, Deleuze also responds to one of the greatest questions of philosophy, that of the "one and the many," in terms of the immanent variety of multiplicity.

Bergson

The philosophy of Henri Bergson must first be approached by way of the question of method. What is Bergson's method? It is that of intuition, which Deleuze describes as "a method that seeks difference."[5] Moreover, this method is the foundation of the three notions that most characterize Bergson's philosophy: duration, memory, and *élan vital* (*B* 13).[6] But as Bergson himself made clear, intuition is not simply a sort of "relaxing of the mind" that allows the instincts or feelings to take over from conceptual or intellectual consciousness.[7] On the contrary, the movement is the reverse, in that intuition supersedes instinct by means of the intelligence, reaching a profound state of reflection upon life and the living world, not by trying to place itself outside of this living world but by placing itself firmly within it. Intuition is a method of reclaiming immanence and for this reason it is a strictly formulated method, "rigorously founded on experience."[8] Yet there is one experience in particular upon which intuition depends, that of time, or rather of duration (*B* 13).[9] In Deleuze's interpretation, there are three sorts of acts that are required in order for intuition to develop into a philosophical method possessing precise rules: "The first concerns the stating and creating of problems; the second, the discovery of genuine differences in kind; the third, the apprehension of real time" (*B* 14).

The key terms here, whose relationship I will discuss shortly, are difference, and time or duration. As far as the first rule of intuition is concerned, however, Deleuze notes that it is wrong to believe that knowledge consists only in solutions. This is a theme encountered in the previous chapter. What is more important than solving problems (which is important, of course, in its own right) is being able to *find* and *posit* problems, to invent new points of departure from that which already exists. This is, in fact, the definition of true freedom: The capacity and power to constitute new problems that cannot be resolved by "ready-made" solutions (*B* 15). What is at issue is the recognition that humanity makes its own history and that our freedom is only as great as the problems we set for ourselves. But what is it that defines the truth or falsity of a problem if not the criteria of its possible solution? In other words, is a problem to be defined as true only if the possibility of its being solved seems greater than the impossibility of its being solved? For Bergson, the question is misguided, because the truth and falsity of problems do not depend upon their subsequent solutions, but upon how the questions themselves are formulated.

There are two sorts of "false problems": nonexistent problems, and badly stated questions. The former are the famous "pseudo" problems of the history of philosophy, like those of nonbeing, disorder, and the possible. Bergson reveals these problems to be nonexistent by showing that they depended upon a "retrograde movement of the true" according to which being, order, and the existent are projected back onto a nonbeing, disorder, and realm of possibility that are supposedly primordial. The formulation of these problems is misguided because they are confined to "thinking in terms of more and less," that is, to thinking in terms of dialectical opposition: order is opposed to disorder, being to nonbeing, possibility to reality. False problems are based therefore on negation. For example, in the idea of disorder "there is already the idea of order, plus its negation, plus the motive for that negation (when we encounter an order that is not the one we expected)" (*B* 17). Bergson insists, on the contrary, that there is not simply one general order opposed to disorder, but many irreducible orders (or different realities) that are different in kind and can be indefinitely substituted for one another.

The latter sort of false problem, the badly stated question, is in fact the basis for the first. A badly stated question is one which *disregards* the difference in kind between orders, beings, or existents (*B* 20). Here the difficulty is that of "badly analyzed composites" that substitute arbitrary differences in degree (things which are "more or less" different depending on their opposition to something else) for differences in kind (that which is immediately different in itself) (*B* 18). Such questions introduce a systematic confusion into thinking by means of a naïve classification of difference; something is assumed to belong to either order or disorder in general, but the actual composition of a particular order or reality remains indistinguishable. What is the role of intuition, then, with respect to false problems?

> We tend to think in terms of more and less, that is, to see differences in degree where there are differences in kind. We can only react against this intellectual tendency by bringing to life, again *in* the intelligence, another tendency, which is critical. But where, precisely, does this second tendency come from? Only intuition can produce and activate it, because it rediscovers differences in kind beneath the differences in degree, and conveys to the intelligence the criteria that enable it to distinguish between true and false problems. (*B* 21)

This leads directly to the second rule of intuition, the rediscovery of differences in kind as articulations of the real. This rule is concerned with elaborating a notion of differentiation or division which is not determined by negation. In other words, as Deleuze elaborated in *Difference and Repetition*, difference differentiates itself and it has no need for an extraneous cause of this differentiation. One of the fundamental principles of Bergson's philosophy is that experience offers us an immanent and composite reality. However, the difficulty which arises is that of distinguishing the component elements of these composites, when we have seen only differences in degree and not differences in kind as well. This is especially pernicious in the case of "the two component elements which differ in kind, the two pure *presences* of duration and extensity" (*B* 22). For this reason, a composite must be distinguished according to the component elements, presences, or tendencies that are different in kind and which condition it. This search for the real conditions of actual composites, Deleuze proposes, is a major step for Bergson in the direction of a unique type of empiricism.[10] Intuition moves "beyond experience, toward the conditions of experience (but these are not, in the Kantian manner, the conditions of all possible experience): They are the conditions of real experience" (*B* 23).

The primary distinction Bergson attempts to illuminate, then, is that between difference in kind and difference in degree. Corresponding to this division is the difference in kind between temporal or durational difference and spatial difference, and the difference in kind between two directions of experience: "that of perception which puts us *at once* into matter and that of memory which puts us *at once* into the mind" (*B* 26). Bergson's empiricism is concerned not with determining whether the two lines of perception-matter and memory-mind come together and form a composite, for this composite is the basic fact of actual experience from which philosophical analysis should begin.[11] It is concerned, rather, with going beyond the experience of this composite toward the *conditions* of real experience in order to "rediscover what differs in kind in the composites that are given to us and on which we live" (*B* 26). The second rule of the method of intuition takes the composites given in experience and dissociates them into their component elements that are different in kind. It does this because it understands these mixtures to be complex rather than simple, composed of unequal distributions that cannot be accurately rendered across of scale of differences in degree, that is, from more to less according to a general category that provides the limit to each end of the scale.

Bergson's method attempts to avoid the confusion caused by the use of general categories by seeking the strict conditions of real and not merely all possible experience, because "these conditions are neither general nor abstract. They are no broader than the conditioned" (*B* 27). This means that the method will take a variety of turns with respect to the experience or reality under consideration, first turning outward from it until the particular lines of articulation of which it is composed diverge and reveal their differences in kind, then turning back until they converge or intersect again, not at the same point from which the analysis first began, but at a "virtual image" or virtual point that conveys the "distinct reason" for the composite itself (*B* 28–29). The second rule begins with the experience of a composite, then pursues the real conditions of the composition by differentiating it into its pure constituent elements, and finally reintegrates the lines of composition into a virtual image or point of the given experience. In this way it reveals the differences internal to a composite and the reasons (conditions) for its being what it is, thereby indicating that a properly posed problem tends to lead to its own solution:

> In their divergence, in the disarticulation of the real that they brought about according to the differences in kind, they already constituted a superior empiricism, capable of stating problems and of going beyond experience toward concrete conditions. In their convergence, in the intersection of the real to which they proceed, they now define a superior probabilism, one capable of solving problems and of bringing the condition back to the conditioned so that no distance remains between them. (*B* 30)

The third and final rule of intuition as method dictates that intuition be seen in terms of time rather than space. The second rule pointed to the necessity of distinguishing between difference in kind and difference in degree if composites are to be analyzed adequately. The third rule extends the second by emphasizing the difference in kind between space and time; one of the problems of "badly analyzed" composites is that space and time are allowed to contaminate one another, confusing the distinctive tendencies of each. But there is more to the issue, because not only is it the case that there is a difference in kind between duration and space, but more importantly duration is itself that which tends to bear differences in kind while space is that which tends to bear differences in degree. What is the essential difference between space and duration? Duration is "endowed with the power of *qualitatively* varying with itself," while space is "*quantitative* homogeneity" (*B* 31; my emphasis).

The articulations of a composition can thus be divided into the aspect of space and the aspect of duration, into quantitative differences in degree (augmentation, diminution) and qualitative differences in kind (alteration), but qualitative differences cannot be quantified as can differences in degree. Deleuze considers the example of a dissolving lump of sugar. As matter, the lump of sugar can differ from other things and from itself according to infinitely divisible points that can be counted and contrasted: here it has so many granules, there it has fewer, yet the granules and the lump are still similar in kind for they both are sugar; they are only quantitatively different or different in degree. Yet the lump of sugar "also has a duration, a rhythm of duration, a way of being in time" that characterizes its own alteration, and its difference from other

Immanence and Multiplicity

things, in a qualitative manner that encompasses quantitative differences within time.[12]

Duration indicates a process of continuous variation, or coexistence, while space indicates only discrete exteriorities, or juxtaposition. In other words, an experience possesses its own unique rhythm of duration that cannot be completely broken down into quantifiable and interchangeable degrees of difference. I may be anxious for the sugar to dissolve so that I can drink my cup of tea, so that I experience the duration of its dissolving as an "eternity," while you who have no interest in my cup of tea might barely notice that it took any time at all for the sugar to dissolve. And as the lump of sugar dissolves it becomes not only quantitatively different but also qualitatively different *from itself*, it is *virtually* other than what it was before it dissolved.

Consequently, there is no end to the differences that can be effected between durations, because duration is "always the location and the environment of differences in kind," while space is the location and environment of differences in degree (*B* 32). And it is intuition as a method which allows us to recognize that there are durations other than our own that exist, that is to say, which allows us to affirm and recognize the existence of real differences in kind and avoid subsuming them under general categories (of all possible experience). We should not forget, however, that the second rule of intuition maintains that actual experience gives us *composites*, not discrete elements, formed of the two basic sides of things; that of duration and differences in kind, and that of space (or matter) and differences in degree. Intuition points, then, not only to a specific methodology but also to a "complex ontology" of difference. This ontology is complex because the two facets of difference compose what we will later see Deleuze call the plane of immanence. Differences in degree and differences in kind are like two sides of the same coin, different yet forming a single continuous surface: a unity of differences.

Bergson's "superior empiricism" thus gives us a description not only of the spatial-durational composites of actual or lived experience, but also goes beyond experience in such a way as to give us an account of its real conditions. In so doing it shows that it is not simply opposing difference to identity, or the multiple to the one, because each real condition of experience, whether spatial or durational, is a type of multiplicity. Reality consists of two types of multiplicity which compose a profound surface or plane of difference:

> One is represented by space. . . . It is a multiplicity of exteriority, of simultaneity, of juxtaposition, of order, of quantitative differentiation, of *difference in degree*; it is a numerical multiplicity, *discontinuous and actual*. The other type of multiplicity appears in pure duration: It is an internal multiplicity of succession, of fusion, of organization, of heterogeneity, of qualitative discrimination, or of *difference in kind*; it

is a *virtual and continuous* multiplicity that cannot be reduced to numbers. (*B* 38)

Deleuze notes that Bergson's understanding of multiplicities is influenced by the physicist and mathematician G. B. R. Riemann, who defined multiplicities as "those things that could be determined in terms of their dimensions or their independent variables" (*B* 39). On one side there are "discrete multiplicities" of discontinuous material objects, because space or matter is essentially divisible and extensive, yet it does not change in kind. Take a pound of sugar, a lump of sugar, or a crystal of sugar. The difference here is only one of degree, it is a numerical or quantitative division. On the other side are "continuous multiplicities" of complex states of consciousness, which are not related together in the same way that material objects are because duration does not consist of simple juxtaposed instants, but is the experience of the unity of qualitative variation. These multiplicities do indeed divide or differentiate themselves constantly, yet they change "in kind in the process of dividing up" (*B* 42).

Consider the experience of hearing a particular melody. The melody itself consists of many different elements, its notes, rhythms, speeds, and volumes, but the melody as a whole has a quality that cannot be captured by any single element alone: a single note played is not the same as the melody played in its entirety, and therefore does not represent a difference in degree but a difference in kind between its component elements. Moreover, the melody played at one speed will be qualitatively different if played at another speed, and it will be qualitatively different in each case if I listen to it while I am happy, or sad, or impatient, or exuberant. Yet in any of these cases the experience must involve a unity of heterogeneous elements, that is, a duration that is nevertheless different from another duration *and from itself*, because it is *a unity of change*. The melody cannot be what it is without existing as a whole, but that existence is one of different temporal parts held together in consciousness (both perception and memory). And just as there are many different rhythms of duration, so too are there many different states of consciousness. It is for this reason that duration is the virtual, for insofar as it is *actualized in consciousness* it "creates so many differences in kind by virtue of its own movement" (*B* 43). Whereas in a quantitative multiplicity all of its elements are actual and all of its differences are those in degree, a qualitative multiplicity is defined only by its very actualization, and each actualization is always different in kind. The melody is not a melody until it is played and heard, each experience of its being played and heard is qualitatively different from any other, and the state of consciousness accompanying each experience constantly shifts in a qualitative way. In short, a qualitative multiplicity is one that always makes itself in duration, and in being effectuated a difference in kind is actualized. For Deleuze, this shows that "Bergsonism is a philosophy of difference and its actualization."[13] I will return in a moment to the issue of the virtual and the actual with respect to memory, but first another important aspect of the theory of multiplicity should be mentioned.

This aspect is that the notion of multiplicity avoids the (false) problem of the One and the Many that has been so persistent in the history of philosophy and which found its supreme conception in Hegel's dialectical conception of totality. As traditionally conceived, the "problem" is basically this: If the real is conceived as the One, then the Many is sacrificed; or if the real is conceived as the Many, then the One is sacrificed. Transcendentalism attempts to solve this supposed problem by insisting that non-experiential principles or causes must be brought in to unify an otherwise particularized and differentiated world of experience. Hegel's answer is that if reality is to be seen as a unified whole, dialectical logic must be employed. This places contradiction in the driver's seat, so to speak, forming a single system that is at once One and Many, Universal and Particular, Being and Becoming. In the dialectical process all the opposites are considered as mediating each other in a single system. The One (universal) is such only by way of its self-particularization and reconstitution. The Many (particular) both evolve from the One and reconstitute its unity. For Hegel, then, a dialectical conception of the totality of reality requires understanding the Absolute as involving negation in its inner constitution, first as that which particularizes itself and then as that which regains its unity. The Many and the One are each opposite moments of the same self-enclosed system, the dialectical Absolute driven by contradiction.[14]

From our discussion of intuition as a method, it should come as no surprise that Deleuze's point of attack is against the terms of the dialectical logic on the basis of their extreme generality: "To Bergson, it seems that in this type of *dialectical* method, one begins with concepts that, like baggy clothes, are much too big. The One in general, the multiple in general, nonbeing in general" (*B* 44). The dialectic attempts to recompose the totality of the real on the basis of abstract and general concepts, with the consequence that whenever one general term proves to be inadequately broad or loose, its general opposite is invoked as a corrective.[15] Yet this method can only swing back and forth between opposites as it searches for universality. The difficulty here is that the "singular will never be attained by combining the inadequacy of one concept with the inadequacy of its opposite. The singular will never be attained by correcting a generality with another generality" (*B* 44). As Deleuze sees it, Bergson calls for an understanding of reality not in terms of the One and the Many, because vast general concepts cannot produce the specificity of reality, but in terms of types of multiplicities. There is not simply "the One" or "the Many," but different kinds of multiplicity which coexist without the need for a dialectical resolution of their particularity. Bergson seeks to bring precision to the analysis of composites by asking *what type* of multiplicity, unity, or reality animates a particular problematic. This requires a recognition of two types of multiplicity that are different in kind independently of the negative or negation (*B* 76). It requires, in short, the recognition of actual plurality, for which immanent or nontranscendent difference comes to be the very condition of being as movement and alteration.

We have seen that duration is the realm of both heterogeneity and continuity. This brings us to a fascinating aspect of Bergson's thought which has important implications for Deleuze's own philosophy of immanence, namely, that Bergson reformulates monism in terms of the *virtual unity* of nontranscendent difference. What is Bergsonian monism and how are we to understand it in terms of difference? We can first approach this question by again considering the nature of duration. As mentioned above, duration and matter are different in kind, because matter is quantitatively divisible while duration is not. Space or matter can be divided (even infinitely) and reconstituted without ever changing in kind but only in degree; recall our example of the sugar which remains sugar whether one has a ton, a pound, a cup, a teaspoon, or a single granule.

Duration is much different, however, because it is the qualitative time of movements that cannot be divided into parts which remain the same as their composite unity (multiplicity).[16] For instance, if I am engaged in a certain activity, such as playing basketball, the movements of this activity cannot be reduced to simple positions in space or instants in time, even if we try to reconstitute them by means of succession or juxtaposition. My movements of running, jumping, shooting, defending, and rebounding each occur in a concrete duration that possesses its own quality different from the others. Shooting the basketball cannot be equated with rebounding the ball, but neither can the entire movements of shooting or rebounding be broken down into positions or instants that still remain "shooting the ball" or "rebounding the ball"; they are movements only in the durational unity of their different elements within a specific type of composition. This does not mean that I cannot "freeze" the various aspects of the movement for the purpose, say, of cinematographic analysis, but these aspects thereby become abstract and general and when pasted back together give us only a false movement devoid of concrete duration. Duration is not merely the identical succession of quantifiable and discontinuous instants, for movement is what happens in the interval between such instants on the basis of duration's internal unity. In other words, concrete duration is not infinitely divisible but occurs only as a single unitary process possessing its own quality. From this perspective duration retains an irreducible continuity and heterogeneity. But how are we to understand the unity or coexistence of *different durations*?

Here we must briefly address the role of memory, because duration "is primarily memory" (*B* 51). There are, in fact, two linked aspects of memory that belong to the province of subjectivity, which itself belongs to time: a recollection-memory "oriented and dilated toward the past" and a contraction-memory "contracting toward the future" (*B* 52). The problem thus concerns the relation of past to present, as discussed in the previous chapter with respect to the paradoxes of time outlined by Deleuze in *Difference and Repetition*. Typically, we consider the past to be that which "was" and the present to be that which "is." However, the question arises as to how we are to pinpoint the present which supposedly "is" without, at the very moment we attempt to grasp it as present, passing into a future for which that present is now the past.

Bergson's account of duration and memory reverses the standard determination of time as simple succession by pointing out that "of the present, we must say at every instant that it 'was,' and of the past, that it 'is,' that it is eternally, for all time" (*B* 55). Rather than viewing the past as (formerly) present moments that are no longer present, Bergson argues that the present and the past must be seen as coexisting; each moment splits itself into present and past, a present which passes and a past which is preserved in itself. This coexistence is necessary because the past would never have been constituted if there was not at the same time a present which passed. Yet because each present moment coexists with a past moment, that past moment (which itself was a present) must also coexist with *its* past moment, thereby forming the past in general, the ontological past as a whole which coexists with the present that is passing at each moment (*B* 59).

This is the essential point of Bergson's position: The past preserves itself *as a whole that coexists with each present*. Thus, the past is not a particular past but the past in general which constitutes a pure imperishable recollection that allows for the passage of each particular present. The past therefore serves as the real, ontological condition for the passage of every experienced present. However, while the past in general is real, it remains virtual rather than actual because it serves as the coexistent condition of each particular present rather than as each present itself in the form of an individual consciousness (*B* 55–57). Consequently, this virtual yet real past is the ontological condition of psychological memory and recollection, when the virtual is actualized in every particular present. Time is not simply inside of us (recall Deleuze's criticism of Kant on this point), but is that within which "we move, live and change."[17]

Bergson's superior empiricism is able to bring together both unity (the virtual past in general) and difference (the actualization of particular presents) on the basis of time itself as a real condition of experience. Deleuze summarizes the three aspects of Bergson's position as follows: "There is only one time (monism), although there is an infinity of actual fluxes [i.e., qualitatively different durational rhythms] (generalized pluralism) that necessarily participate in the same virtual whole (limited pluralism)" (*B* 82). There is, then, a single ontological time within which different durations coexist and participate, much like different perspectives upon a shared context. In that case, ontological time is not itself "multiple," it is not quantitatively many different times, but more correctly is to be understood as a multiplicity, as a single time that is nevertheless qualitatively different (*B* 85).

In this way Deleuze draws from Bergson's work an interesting and novel approach to the philosophy of immanence. The diversity of durational experiences within a single ontological time leads to the association of pluralism with monism.[18] Yet the terms of the debate have been rendered unique by Deleuze. The temporal monism of Bergson is not a traditional type of monism. Time is neither transcendent to existence, nor is it a pregiven and enclosed unity; time is real and open, for its actualizations in experience are not predetermined, complete, or absolute. Therefore experience, as it involves or participates in time, is continuously becoming qualitatively different. This leads to the recognition that temporal monism is inseparable from a pluralism of different durations and experiences. Such a position avoids dualism, because time and duration—the real ontological conditions of experience and the diverse actualizations of experiences—are qualitative rather than quantitative aspects of the immanent world. For Deleuze, the coexisting unity of time and pluralism of durational fluxes becomes the perspective from which to characterize existence in terms of multiplicity: "Not only do virtual multiplicities imply a single time, but duration as virtual multiplicity is the single and same Time" (*B* 83). Multiplicities can thus be defined as unities of differences. However, Deleuze's consideration of the immanent relation between time and difference is not limited to Bergson's formula. It is on this same question that he engages with that thinker who is the other great representative of "superior empiricism" in modern thought: Friedrich Nietzsche

Nietzsche

In the opening pages of his book on Nietzsche, Deleuze makes clear how Nietzsche ought to be read:

> Nietzsche's philosophy cannot be understood without taking his essential pluralism into account. And, in fact, pluralism (otherwise known as empiricism) is almost indistinguishable from philosophy itself. Pluralism is the properly philosophical way of thinking, the one invented by philosophy; the only guarantor of freedom in the concrete spirit, the only principle of violent atheism. (*N* 4)

In this section, I will be concerned with outlining Deleuze s interpretation of Nietzsche as a pluralist and empiricist, and with demonstrating how Nietzsche's pluralism, in a manner similar to Bergson's, is to be conceived in association with immanence.

According to Deleuze, Nietzsche develops a philosophical practice consisting of interpretation and evaluation, which hearkens back to the Pre-Socratics, and perhaps to Spinoza as well. For the metaphysical dualism of essence and appearance and for the deterministic relation of cause and effect, Nietzsche substitutes the notion of sense as it applies to human, biological, and physical phenomena (*N* 3). The notion of sense is, in fact, the heart of Nietzsche's pluralism. As Deleuze explains it, Nietzsche does not take a phenomenon to be the appearance of some deeper essence, but rather as the sign or "symptom" of a particular mode of existence or way of life. Phenomena do not refer to transcendent, noumenal realities: Every phenomenon, thing, organism, or society "finds its meaning in an existing force," that is, acquires and expresses a certain sense depending on the force or forces which appropriate it (*N* 3). In this view, there are a plurality of forces whose coexistence and succession constitute a historically changing network of relationships, within which all phenomena are interpreted and evaluated. Hence, the "same object, the same phenomenon, changes sense" depending on its place within these shifting interrelationships of force; because of this "there is always a plurality of senses" (*N* 3).

It is for this reason that the metaphysical dualism of essence and appearance is overthrown by Nietzsche. Nietzsche asserts that there are no single, eternal, unchanging essences underlying all phenomena, events, people, or things, nor are the latter to be understood as mere images or appearances of the former. All such phenomena are to be regarded as empirical actualities that can remain the same while acquiring different senses over the course of their existence. Collapsing the appearance-essence distinction leads to the picture of a single world of experience consisting of a multiplicity of phenomena, all of which acquire different senses within the continually transforming flux of the interrelationships of forces:

> There is no event, no phenomenon, word or thought which does not have a multiple sense. A thing is sometimes this, sometimes that, sometimes something more complicated—depending on the forces . . . which take possession of it. (*N* 4)

The only possible definition of essence that remains for Nietzsche refers to some particular combination of sense and force, where the sense and force in question have the "most affinity" for one another. Essence belongs to interpretation, and thus to what are considered the most important characteristics of phenomena with respect to specific purposes and environments. Consequently, it must be admitted that not all combinations of sense and force have the same value; some combinations are reactive, restrictive, and negative, while others are active, open, and positive. It is the task of pluralism and empiricism to interpret and evaluate all phenomena by investigating which forces and which senses are actively expressive of the qualitative mode of existence of a particular thing, person, or event. This task is known as genealogy.

The picture of the world presented by Nietzsche is that of a dynamic and immanent continuum of differentially related forces. Not only are there different forces that take hold of objects or phenomena, but phenomena are themselves forces, that is, are constituted within and not outside specific relationships of forces. What this means is that phenomena cannot be considered independently of their actual relationships, thus there is no ultimate "in-itself" of things that can be apprehended, but only the different senses of things. This will, of course, be integral to what is known as Nietzsche's perspectivism. However, it is also important to his notion of will to power.

For Nietzsche, force is never singular but always plural; one force is always related to another force. It is this differential relation of force to force that is amplified by Nietzsche's notion of "will to power." Deleuze cites the following passage from Nietzsche in order to relate the notion of force to that of will to power: "The *victorious* concept 'force,' by means of which our physicists have created God and the world, still needs to be *completed*: an *inner* will must be *ascribed* to it, which I designate as 'will to power' " (*N* 49). Will to power does not indicate some autonomous, conscious subject that guides and determines the actions of an individual. Rather, will to power refers to the real differential and genetic conditions that belong to and determine actual relationships of forces. It designates the dynamic differentiation of all the unconscious, bodily forces of life at work in the world: "Nietzsche's concept of force is . . . that of a force which is related to another force: in this form force is called will" (*N* 7). All actual force relations are conditioned and determined by some real element, namely a differential quantity of reality, although this element is neither reducible to the relations themselves nor separable from them.[19] As Deleuze explains, this is because "relations of forces remain indeterminate unless an element which is capable of determining them" is admitted as a complementary condition to force (*N* 51).

The will to power thus functions as that element of reality which contributes to the genesis of the quantitative differentiation of related forces, and to the expression of the qualitatively unique difference of each force that is related. It is for this reason that will to power designates the immanent, generative element of the production of force, which is always plural and relational; it is difference as such. This immanent character of the will to power should not be overlooked, for it is here that Nietzsche is truly an empiricist. As I clarified previously, Deleuze's transcendental empiricism proposes that the conditions of actual experience are themselves conditioned by previous experiences. In other words, contrary to the *a priorism* of Plato or Kant, there can be no *unconditioned* conditions of experience. There are no underlying unconditioned conditions of experience that escape or transcend the immanent world of experience, there are only actually created conditions that belong to this world. The will to power therefore serves as a uniquely empiricist principle, similar to the difference and repetition of Deleuze and to the durational matter-memory composites of Berg-

Immanence and Multiplicity

son. And like these two examples, the will to power constitutes a "superior empiricism" because it refers not to a general, unchanging and transcendent principle of all possible experience but instead to "an essentially *plastic* principle" which is inseparable from, and is transformed along with, that which is conditioned in each real particular actualization of force relations:

> If . . . the will to power is a good principle, if it reconciles empiricism with principles . . . this is because it is an essentially *plastic* principle that is no wider than what it conditions, that changes itself with the conditioned and determines itself in each case along with what it determines. The will to power is, indeed, never separable from particular determined forces, from their quantities, qualities, and directions. It is never superior to the ways that it determines a relation between forces, it is always plastic and changing. (*N* 50)

The notion of will to power can perhaps be further clarified by taking note of Nietzsche's alteration of the philosophical form of questioning. The traditional mode of philosophical inquiry is based on the form of questioning inherited from Platonism: "What is. . . ?" This form of questioning seeks to identify that which "is," namely, essence in the traditional metaphysical sense. It poses its question as if there were only one answer available, the one form or essence which transcends its many particular appearances (inferior copies): "What is Beauty?" or "What is Justice?" and so forth (*N* 76). In contrast, the Nietzschean, or empirical and pluralist, form of questioning asks "Which one. . . ?" or "Which one is. . . ?" For example, the question "What is Beauty?" is transformed into the question "Which one is beautiful?" The former question has only one possible answer that is itself invariable, universal, and beyond experience: "Beauty 'is' Beauty," a self-identical essence underlying appearance. The latter question has many different and particular answers, all ushered in by the rich diversity of existence: "This painting is beautiful," "This sunset is beautiful," "This face is beautiful."

Therefore, the question "Which one is. . . ?" can be answered only by recourse to specific situations, interests, values, durations, and purposes. In other words, this empirical and pluralist form of questioning always refers to "the forces in their various relationships in a proposition or phenomenon, and the genetic relationship that determines these forces (power)" (*N* xi). Again, we see that will to power does not indicate the intentions of an autonomous subject or consciousness, but rather the specific relationship or composition of forces which, in their interrelationship, express the one that is beautiful (or just) at some particular time and place. As Deleuze recounts, the form of inquiry prompted by the will to power refers "to the continuity of concrete objects taken in their becoming, to the becoming-beautiful of all the objects citable or cited as examples" (*N* 76).

A further consequence of Nietzsche's mode of philosophical inquiry is the substitution of immanent perspectivism for transcendent foundationalism. Perspectivism is expressed by the form of the question "Which one is. . . ?" and is composed of interpretation and evaluation. As was noted above, this form of questioning can be answered only by appealing to the real conditions of specific circumstances, actions, passions, and interests, and it seeks not to identify self-identical metaphysical essences behind phenomena but rather to determine what relationship or composition of forces is interpreting and giving sense to the flux of the world of differential forces to which it belongs. It is in this sense that perspectivism incorporates both interpretation and evaluation. Interpretation is that activity which determines the partial and changeable sense of some phenomenon, while evaluation is that activity which distinguishes the values of different senses without, however, eliminating the plurality of these senses. Interpretation sees phenomena as multiple signs or "symptoms" of ways of being or modes of existence within particular contexts, while evaluation distinguishes some modes of existence as being better or more valuable than others (*e.g.*, active rather than reactive). In this way, evaluation ascribes certain values on the basis of particular interpretations and ways of being. Nietzsche offers this description of perspectivism:

> Against positivism, which halts at phenomena—"There are only *facts*"—I would say: No, facts is precisely what there is not, only interpretations. We cannot establish any fact "in itself": perhaps it is folly to want to do such a thing. "Everything is subjective," you say; but even this is an interpretation. The "subject" is not something given, it is something added and invented and projected behind what there is.—Finally, is it necessary to posit an interpreter behind the interpretation? Even this is invention, hypothesis. Insofar as the word "knowledge" has any meaning, the world is knowable; but it is *interpretable* otherwise, it has no meaning behind it, but countless meanings.—"Perspectivism."[20]

There are several points on which to follow up here in order to avoid misunderstanding Nietzsche's perspectivism simply as a version of subjective relativism. First, Nietzsche claims, there are no "facts in themselves" that we can hope to have access to independently of our world-situatedness. He is not asserting that we have no knowledge of the world, or that there is no larger world within which we organize our experiences, only that whatever knowledge we do have is itself a particular interpretation formulated within a specific socio-historical context and informed by previous beliefs, traditions, and values, in short, by other existing interpretations. Second, Nietzsche insists that interpretation does not proceed from a pure, immaterial, and given subject that reflects upon a world of independent objects. That which is called the subject is itself an interpretive construct of certain phenomena, such as thinking, imagining, willing, and so forth, which tend to divide subject and object, cause and effect, doer and deed, without acknowledging that this division itself rests on an interpretation. For Nietzsche, the subject has no existence independent of interpretation and evaluation, and is to be regarded as constituted by various other interpretations and evaluations. Third, Nietzsche denies that there is a passive interpreter behind and separable from the creative activity of interpretation. The interests, passions, and modes of existence of interpreters cannot be divorced from their interpretations. The one who interprets exists in specific ways, takes hold of phenomena and gives them different senses, and evaluates all aspects of life in some manner. An interpretation is the very embodiment of an interpreter.

These three aspects of Nietzsche's perspectivism emphasize the immanent nature of existence: Life is both the product of interpretations and evaluations, and the material for interpretations and evaluations. Life is constituted within networks or webs of existential interpretations with diverse and complex histories, endowed with different senses that are capable of being transformed. Yet because of the historical and cultural contextuality of interpretations and evaluations, it is not the case that simply any interpretation, evaluation, or mode of existence is possible. Due to different historical conditions, some constraints or limitations will hold at any particular time. However, these conditions are not independent of or transcendent to existence in its various modes; such a position would assume that we could have some noninterpretive access to a domain of pure or unconditioned conditions behind or beyond the immanent world as it is experienced. For Nietzsche, not only is God dead, but so too are those *a priori* principles and universal laws that aim to function as the philosophical "shadows" of a transcendent God.[21]

So although Nietzsche's perspectivism does result in a relativism, it is not one which denies knowledge because all claims are supposedly equal. Nietzsche's is an empirical relativism, which holds that the interpretations, evaluations, and senses made of things are relative to the particular circumstances and situations within which different interpreters exist; knowledge cannot be separated from its conditions and situatedness. Nietzsche's perspectivism is also pragmatic, in a certain sense. For Nietzsche, it is not ahistorical truth, as the correspondence of correct beliefs to an independent reality, which is decisive for knowledge. Because Nietzsche regards knowledge as a form of active interpretation, questions of "truth" are not to be divorced from evaluation and thus from the ascription of sense and value within specific experiential contexts or conditions. And in this case, not just any interpretation can be considered adequate or appropriate to the situation at hand. Yet, for the same reasons, neither can any single interpretation claim the status of universal and eternal truth. In short, interpretation, evaluation, and making sense—the ingredients of Nietzsche's perspectivism—cannot operate independently of the historical and cultural contexts of experiences and cannot transcend these contexts in order to attain a complete overview of the world as it might be independent of interpretation. Perspectivism thereby affirms immanence and denies both the duality of noumena and phenomena and the anchoring of a transcendental subject. As Deleuze relates in *The Fold*, "perspectivism amounts to a relativism, but not the relativism we take for granted. It is not a variation of truth according to the subject, but the condition in which the truth of a variation appears to the subject."[22] This returns us to the form of questioning appropriate to Nietzsche's empiricism and pluralism. While the question "What is. . . ?" seeks a disinterested truth or essence that exists independently of experience, the question "Which one is. . . ?" refers itself to the specific circumstances, interests, and ways of being characteristic of the one who interprets. There is another dimension to Nietzsche's method of interpretation and evaluation, which can be understood as an ethical response to a view of the world and existence as dynamic and immanent flux: the eternal return.

In Deleuze's reading there are two aspects to the eternal return, as a cosmological and physical doctrine, and as an ethical and selective thought (*N* 47, 68). The cosmological aspect of the eternal return was discussed in the previous chapter in the context of *Difference and Repetition*, and the explanation is similar in *Nietzsche and Philosophy*. Previously, it was noted that the will to power referred to the differential relations of force to force that constitute diverse phenomena. The cosmological aspect of the eternal return supplies another element to Nietzsche's ontology, concerned with the role of becoming in a world composed of a multiplicity of forces. The eternal return contributes to the production of difference by means of repetition or returning. The problem here is, in fact, greatly similar to that described by Bergson in terms of the pure or ontological past. As Nietzsche recognizes, the passage of time requires that each present moment be something more than a moment "in itself"; it must simultaneously coexist with the past and future and is thus a moment *only in passing*. It is only in relation to the past and future, to other moments, that the present can come to be and pass away. Deleuze notes that the "eternal return is thus an answer to the problem of *passage*" (*N* 48). The eternal return does not mean that the same thing or event recurs again and again; it is not a "cyclical" historical hypothesis. Rather, it indicates that it is difference which returns, in terms of the continuous becoming of diversity: "It is not some one thing which returns but rather returning itself is the one thing which is affirmed of diversity or multiplicity" (*N* 48). In other words, returning, defined as the repetitious reproduction of difference, "is the being of that which becomes" (*N* 48). The continuity of becoming, the necessary return of difference, is seen as the "unity of multiplicity" (*N* 29). Multiplicity is the manifestation of the dynamic unity of becoming as such, that is, the being of becoming.

The eternal return also offers an ethical and selective principle with which to distinguish active and reactive forces, and thereby different modes of existence based on these types of forces. The eternal return elicits a selective thought by first providing a practical rule: *"whatever you will, will it in such a way that you will also will its eternal return"* (*N* 68). The emphasis here should be placed on the act of willing. A thought based on the eternal return as a selective principle must ask itself if it is able to will whatever it wills an infinite number of times. This selective principle requires a complete willing which attempts to eliminate the reactive type of willing done from laziness, complacency, fear, stupidity, cowardice, and so forth. Motivated by the thought of the eternal return, willing becomes creation, the reproduction of becoming in all its different moments (*N* 69). It also becomes the affirmation of chance, because becoming is the production and reproduction of diversity and multiplicity. At this point, the selective principle aims to separate the passive acceptance of the Same from the active creation of the diverse.

Yet the problem still remains that particularly strong reactive forces are themselves able to will according to the thought of the eternal return, resulting in a reactive form of becoming. What is needed is a second selective element in conjunction with the eternal return. This second element pushes the incomplete nihilism characteristic of reactive forces toward its completion and thus its self-destruction. Whereas reactive forces are conservative, in that they seek to preserve weak and diminished modes of existence, complete nihilism signifies the destruction or negation not of life but of the negative or reactive itself. In this sense, nihilism is the *active* destruction or elimination of all that is reactive within oneself; it is the active refusal to be reactive. By actively seeking to eliminate reactive forces, one no longer attempts to will reactively. In doing so, selective thought *creates* a new mode of willing and thus a new mode of existence, by affirmatively selecting that which it wills according to the doctrine of the eternal return. As a consequence, selective thought produces "selective being," the way of living manifested by becoming active rather than reactive (*N* 71). The two aspects of the eternal return are thus united: "Eternal return, as a physical doctrine, affirms the being of becoming. But, as selective ontology, it affirms this being of becoming as the 'self-affirming' of becoming active" (*N* 72).

These are, of course, the themes of Nietzsche's ethical notion of self-overcoming, of the "overman." However, the self-affirming of becoming active makes no appeal to "divine" moral precepts or transhistorical norms. On the contrary, self-overcoming requires the critique and elimination of such transcendental principles, in favor of the affirmation of the diversity, chance, and multiplicity of the immanent world. Becoming active is based in the creative art of interpretation and evaluation, preferring those interpretations which enhance and support rather than restrict and repress affirmative life forces. And this is done not for the promise of a heavenly reward beyond life itself, but for the enhancement of the power and quality of those active, transformative forces which compose and reproduce the becoming of the dynamic world of experience. Nietzsche's philosophy is seen by Deleuze as ushering in "a new way of feeling, thinking and above all being" by means of the affirmation of multiplicity and becoming, that is, from the perspective of immanence rather than transcendence (*N* 71). Along with Bergson, Nietzsche provides Deleuze with the conceptual means to develop a philosophy of immanence on the ontological as well as the ethical register. But there is yet one other thinker who will join Bergson and Nietzsche in this tradition, a thinker regarded by Deleuze as "the prince of philosophers" for his unwavering commitment to immanence: Baruch Spinoza.[23]

Spinoza

There is perhaps no other philosopher more esteemed by Deleuze than Spinoza. According to Deleuze, Spinoza pursued a philosophy of immanence to its fullest extent, because he refused to compromise with transcendence in his quest for freedom (*WP* 48). In two books, *Expressionism in Philosophy: Spinoza* and *Spinoza: Practical Philosophy*, Deleuze reconstructs Spinoza's philosophy of immanence from the standpoint of ontology and ethics. As presented by Deleuze, the strength of Spinoza's system rests upon the double inclusion of ontology in ethics and ethics in ontology, reflected in the fact that Spinoza's major metaphysical treatise is entitled *Ethics*.[24] In other words, Spinoza's ontology of pure immanence finds its meaning in relation to his positive ethics of life, which is the practical manifestation of his ontology. It is from this perspective that one can best appreciate the revolutionary nature of Spinoza's thought.

Deleuze approaches his discussion of Spinoza's ontology of immanence by way of the idea of expression. Why immanence and expression are linked requires a historical analysis beginning with the Platonic notion of participation. As we saw in the previous section on Nietzsche, the Platonic question "What is X?" asks after the essence of an ideal Form, which "is what it is" completely and in itself. Each particular visible thing, however, "is what it is" only insofar as it "participates" in or "partakes" of its corresponding Form. A painting can be said to be beautiful, for instance, because it participates in or partakes of the Form of Beauty itself, yet the painting is not beautiful as such. The cause of its beauty is contingent rather than necessary, since the painting is beautiful only because it happens to participate in what the Beautiful is *per se*. It is for this reason that change occurs in the visible world while the Forms themselves are invariable. Particular things are considered by Plato merely to be the contingently caused copies or imitations of Forms that transcend perceivable reality and remain one and the same in themselves. Consequently, reality is separated by Plato into the realm of independent Forms and the world of the particular things which participate in them. While particular things participate in the Forms, and are copies or imitations of them in the sense that the presence of the

Forms is re-presented in them, the Forms participate only in themselves, that is, they are self-identical.

The difficulty with the Platonic notion of participation is that it "was always sought by Plato on the side of what participates. It usually appears as an accident supervening on what is participated from outside, as a violence suffered by what is participated" (*EP* 169). If a particular thing is a "part" of a Form, then the unity of the Form is threatened because the Form must somehow also participate in the thing. Similarly, if participation consists of imitation there must be some external "artist or demon" who, taking the Form as his model, forces "the sensible to reproduce the intelligible, while also forcing the Idea [Form] to allow itself to be participated by something foreign to its nature" (*EP* 169–70). In short, the problem facing Plato is that of matching the contingent being of multiple particular things to the necessary being of the invariable and unitary Forms. The result of this predicament, as Deleuze notes, is that the sensible is somehow forced to reproduce the intelligible.

Beginning with Plotinus, however, the Neoplatonist tradition sought to invert the problem of participation found in Plato, by seeking a principle for participation not from the side of that which participates, but instead "from the side of the participated itself" (*EP* 170). Contrary to Plato, Plotinus argues that particular things do not participate in the participated itself, if participation is meant to indicate that particular things are parts or copies that must be brought into existence and correspondence by some external or intermediary source. Rather, the participated as such produces, "gives," or emanates from itself that which participates in it. Emanative participation produces particular things as the given effects of its "productive donation" (*EP* 170). Participation takes place, therefore, only through the given, which is produced by a supreme emanative cause or "giver." In this case, productive activity remains on the side of the unitary and emanative cause, while that which participates in it does not do so directly but only indirectly through the given that the cause produces. Thus, the internal principle of participation is a pure transcendental for Plotinus since it is "'above' or 'beyond' participation" (*EP* 170). Even though all things emanate from it, it is not itself participated in, "for participation occurs only through what it gives, and in what it gives" (*EP* 171). Plotinus manages in this way to postulate a cause for all things that retains its absolute unity independently of the many things it produces.

This first principle regards the transcendent One as necessarily superior to its "gifts." However, by insisting that all things flow from the emanative cause, participation is now understood to mean that every being "is" only by being the One. Plotinus eliminates the strict separation found in Plato between the participated and that which participates with the notion that particular things or beings are not mere imitations of the One but instead are its products. Furthermore, for Plotinus the One emanates Intelligence and Being. The Intelligence is that which reflects on itself, and in doing so it thinks its cause, the One. By thinking itself, the Intelligence simultaneously thinks the One, which means that it thinks the entirety of Being. In this manner there arises a mutual immanence of Intelligence and Being combined with the emanative cause. Because Intelligence contains all particular "intelligences and intelligibles" and Being contains all particular "beings and genera of beings," the emanative cause is "a One in which the multiple is present, and which is itself present in the Multiple" (*EP* 174).

This leads to the development of the notions "*complicare*" (to fold) and "*explicare*" (to unfold) in the Medieval and Renaissance philosophies. According to these philosophies, God includes and "complicates," that is folds or combines together all things, while all the things which are present to God involve or implicate and evolve, unfold, or "explicate" him: "Things remain inherent in God who complicates them, and God remains implicated in things which explicate him. It is a complicative God who is explicated through all things" (*EP* 175). Here it is not only important that God is the cause of all things, but also that his effects inhere in him. The cause and its effects are considered inseparable and are defined by the coexistence of the double movements of complication and explication, of folding and unfolding. Even though the cause remains in itself, it is not separable from its effects. This signals another shift away from Plotinus, however, because for him the mutually immanent causes of Intelligence and Being remain subordinate to the emanative cause, the transcendent One from which all things flow (*EP* 177). As Deleuze observes:

> Participation no longer has its principle in an emanation whose source lies in a more or less distant One, but rather in the immediate and adequate expression of an absolute Being that comprises in it all beings, and is explicated in the essence of each. Expression comprehends all these aspects: complication, explication, inherence, implication. And these aspects of expression are also the categories of immanence. Immanence is revealed as expression, and expression as immanent, in a system of logical relations within which the two notions are correlative. (*EP* 175)

With the Medieval and Renaissance philosophies, immanent causality, that is, a causality in which its effect remains immanent, begins to replace and take on greater importance than emanative causality, in which the effect does not remain. Concomitantly, the idea of expression begins to supplant that of imitation. Rather than defining particular things and beings as imitations or copies of transcendent Forms, or as the effects of a superior emanative transcendence, they are seen as the essential "expressions" of the God in whom they inhere. The idea of expression becomes the new principle of participation, insofar as all things are the expression or unfolding manifestation of God's essence. Deleuze recounts that for these philosophers "God expresses *himself* in the world; the world is the expression, the explication, of a God-Being or a One who is" (*EP* 176).

Yet even at this point, the notion of an expressive immanence is seriously compromised by the need for Christian philosophy to maintain the transcendence of God. This is done in two ways. First, the theory of Creation continues on the same path as that of emanation. God is the cause of the creation of the world, but the world is considered only an imperfect likeness of all that God perfectly is. Just as the emanative cause remained above Being, so too does God, as an immutable and immaterial Absolute, remain above the material world. Second, the transcendence of a creator God is supported by an analogical conception of Being which holds that God is, in himself, undefinable and inexpressible. In this case, the expression of God in the material world occurs only indirectly by analogy. The manifestations of God are taken to be a speech through which God makes himself known by divine names (or signs), but God himself is never directly revealed (*EP* 53–54, 177–78). Thus, even though a certain immanence is implied by the idea that all things are in God, this is mitigated by an analogical conception of Being according to which things are in God only because of their imitative likenesses, while God himself remains concealed and transcendent in the end (*EP* 178–79). The eminence of the divine is once again placed above and beyond Being itself.

This hesitancy with respect to immanence and expression comes to an end with Spinoza's philosophy. Deleuze confesses that the "significance of Spinozism seems to me this: it asserts immanence as a principle and frees expression from any subordination to emanative or exemplary causality" (*EP* 180). There are several novel moves made by Spinoza that must be examined if Deleuze's claim is to be understood. In the first Part of the *Ethics*, the idea of expression appears in association with the triad of substance, attributes, and essence: Substance is that which expresses itself, attributes are expressions, and essence is what is expressed (*EP* 27).

About substance, Spinoza's first important move is to challenge two of Descartes' conclusions: First, that there are two substances able to exist by themselves that are the bearers of primary attributes through which they are known and, second, that the real distinction between these substances, namely, that neither substance depends upon the other for its reality, brings with it a numerical distinction, which is that there can be several substances sharing the same attribute.[25] With respect to the first conclusion, Descartes maintains that the substances created by God are extended substance, so called because its primary attribute (or essence) is extension in length, and thinking substance, whose primary attribute (or essence) is nonextended thought. The real distinction between the two substances rests on their different attributes, taking us to the second conclusion. Descartes proposes that all material or physical bodies are modes, that is, inessential or accidental modifications, of a single extended substance. On the other hand, each individual mind must be a distinct thinking substance that shares the attribute of thought with every other mind. Yet the distinction cannot be real, because each individual mind has the same attribute, but rather is numerical; there are many individual minds, each of which are self-contained and distinct substances sharing the same attribute, thought.[26]

Spinoza's criticism of these conclusions is, of course, the basis for his claim that there is only one infinite substance rather than a number of distinct substances.[27] Briefly, his criticism of Descartes takes two forms. First, he notes that if there were many different substances sharing the same attribute, the only way they could be distinguished would be by their modes. However, substance precedes the existence of modes such that modes are themselves dependent upon substance. This returns us to the shared attribute, which, again, cannot be used to distinguish different substances. Second, Spinoza explains that numerical distinction cannot apply to substance, because "substances could only be numerically distinct through the operation of some external causality that could produce them" (*EP* 33). This would be identical to treating substance as if it were an accidental modification that cannot exist by itself. While external causality and numerical distinction are, indeed, applicable to modes, they are not applicable to substance itself since substance is infinite and cannot be converted into measurable parts. The conclusion of Spinoza's argument is that even though attributes are conceived as really distinct they are not numerically distinct. If this is the case, then it cannot be held that there are numerically distinct substances. Rather, "there is only one substance for all attributes," a single substance which is both in itself and conceived through itself (*EP* 34). For Spinoza, on the side of finite understanding there can be only qualitatively or "formally" real distinctions of the attributes of a single, infinite substance, which Spinoza also refers to as God.[28] This leads to the notion of attributes as expressions of a substance which expresses itself.

Deleuze explains that Spinoza conceives of attributes as the expressions of the essence of substance, not as expressions of themselves, following Spinoza's point that attributes do not correspond to numerically distinct substances. For Spinoza, thought and extension (the only two of the infinitely many attributes of which we can be aware) are not attributes of two distinct substances dependent on God, but are attributes of God himself, conceived as a single substance:

> From these propositions it is evident that although two attributes may be conceived to be really distinct (i.e., one may be conceived without the aid of the other), we still can not infer from that that they constitute two beings, *or* two different substances. For it is of the nature of a substance that each of its attributes is conceived through itself, since all the attributes it has have always been in it together, and one could not be produced by another, but each expresses the reality, *or* being of substance. (*Ethics* IP10S)

Because the essence of the attributes belongs to the essence of substance, the existence of substance is expressed by the attributes. Attributes must attribute their essence to the single substance which is the same for all of them, yet substance is expressed only by the formally or qualitatively distinct attributes because it cannot be numerically divided:

> All existing essences relate or are attributable to substance, and this inasmuch as substance is the only being whose existence necessarily follows from its essence. Substance is privileged to exist through itself: *it is not the attribute* that exists through itself, but that to which the essence of each attribute relates, in such a way that existence necessarily follows from the essence thus constituted. (*EP* 43)

The concept of expression will allow Spinoza to combine the existence of substance, the existence of essence, and the existence of the attributes, that is, to make inseparable essence and existence.[29] But first, as I noted above, Spinoza transforms the meaning of attributes. For him, they are no longer attributed, instead they are attributive, inasmuch as each attribute actively expresses an essence which is attributed to the single substance in which they all belong. For Spinoza, attributes are no longer attributed to a number of distinct substances having a possible existence only because they are ultimately dependent upon a transcendent creator God. Instead, they attribute their essence to the one infinite substance which is the same for all attributes, thereby dynamically expressing the necessary existence of substance (*EP* 45). It is on this basis that Spinoza provides another original characteristic to the idea of expression, in the form of the univocity of Being or the immanent unity of all reality.

Spinoza proposes that substance be conceived as that which "cannot be produced by anything else; therefore it will be the cause of itself, i.e., its essence necessarily involves existence, *or* it pertains to its nature to exist" (*Ethics* IP7). He defines "cause of itself" as "that whose essence involves existence, *or* that whose nature cannot be conceived except as existing" (*Ethics* IDef1). Spinoza later states that "God must be called the cause of all things in the same sense in which he is called cause of himself" (*Ethics* IP25S). Accordingly, substance is to be understood as that which is at once the cause of itself, the cause of all things, and necessarily existing. The essence of substance is to exist as eternal and infinite. As such, it has no need for a cause other than, or external to, itself. Because its essence and existence are inseparable, substance can be determined only by its own immanent causation: "God is the immanent, not the transitive, cause of all things" (*Ethics* IP18). Substance is not only immanently caused by itself, but also it is itself the immanent cause of everything else: "Everything that is, is in God, and must be conceived through God, and so God is the cause of all things, which are in him" (*Ethics* IP18D). How does Spinoza make the move from the existence of infinite substance to the existence of finite things or modes? This is where his concept of expression comes fully into play.

As we saw, each attribute expresses an infinite essence or unlimited quality of substance. Yet attributes also "contain or comprehend the essence of modes" (*EP* 47). Spinoza defines modes as "the affections of a substance, *or* that which is in another [i.e., substance] through which it is also conceived" (*Ethics* IDef5). Attributes contain the essences of modes, and modes follow from the attributes. We have, then, a single substance that expresses itself through infinite attributes. However, the attributes are not simply "mirrors" of God's essence, because "what is expressed is at the same time involved in its expression" (*EP* 80). In other words, the essence of substance is at the same time the essence of the attributes, insofar as the attributes constitute the essence of substance through their very expression. This is one of the consequences of immanent causality. The self-constitution of substance does not precede the expression of substance through its attributes. Rather, as it creates itself, infinite substance expresses itself through the unlimited attributes, which are the dynamic components of its own constitution. As a result, there "is a unity of the diverse in substance, and an actual diversity of the One in the attributes" (*EP* 81).

There is more. Not only are the attributes the expressions of an expressive substance, they are themselves expressive of the modes whose essences they contain, making the modes expressions of the attributes. Attributes thus serve as forms of being common both to substance and to its modifications. They express the unlimited qualities of substance, and because modes follow from the attributes, these same qualities are involved in finite things: "God expresses himself in his attributes, and attributes express themselves in dependent modes: this is how the order of Nature manifests God" (*EP* 59). What is not to be overlooked is that all the attributes are the expressions of the same God, substance, or Nature: "God is said to be cause of all things *in the very sense (eo sensu)* that he is said to be cause of himself" (*EP* 67). This is the meaning of the univocity of Being, which is strongly associated with immanence and expression in Spinoza's philosophy. The notion of univocity affirms the equality of all the attributes or forms of being. If all attributes are the expressions of an absolutely infinite substance, it is inconceivable that there would be a form of being either inferior or superior to any other (*EP* 60–70).[30] This last point draws upon Spinoza's criticism of numerical distinction, as well. Because the attributes are expressions of an ontologically single substance, they are only qualitatively or formally distinct. The attributes are qualitatively different expressions or forms of being of a substance that is nevertheless common to them all. For Deleuze, Spinoza's refusal of a hierarchy of causes and of forms of being in favor of a univocity of Being that is equally present in all beings is a direct result of his affirmation of immanence and his opposition to transcendence:

Immanence and Multiplicity 63

> Against Descartes, Spinoza posits the equality of all forms of being, and the univocity of reality which follows from this equality. The philosophy of immanence appears from all viewpoints as the theory of unitary Being, equal Being, common and univocal Being. It seeks the conditions of a genuine affirmation, condemning all approaches that take away from Being its full positivity, that is, its formal community. (*EP* 167)

The convergence of the concepts of immanence, expression, and univocity provide Spinoza the means to affirm the mutual immanence of both unity and plurality.[31] The diversity of the formally distinct attributes establishes the "qualitative composition of an ontologically single substance," while the unity of substance comprises itself equally through all the different attributes (*EP* 182). Every mode is always a certain quantity of power of the qualitatively distinct attributes, such that a mode participates directly in the common substance as an effect which remains in its cause: immanent existence. All of this constitutes the continuous and dynamic production of reality, that is, the immanent flux of expression. Spinoza's ontology thus arrives at its most profound moment with its vision of the world as the product of the continuous interplay and coexistence of multiplicity and unity (*EP* 331–32).[32] At this point it is possible to investigate the manner in which Spinoza's philosophy of immanence operates on the terrain of the ethical.

I will approach this issue by way of an initial consideration of modal existence. On the one hand, the essence of a mode is contained in the attribute, as a real intensive part or degree of power of the attribute itself. On the other hand, the existence of a mode is extensive, since every existing finite thing is a composition of a very great number of parts externally related to one another (*EP* 201, 205–07). However, as I mentioned previously, Spinoza defines essence as "that without which the thing can neither be nor be conceived," and as that which "being given, the thing is necessarily posited" (*Ethics* IIDef2). For Spinoza, then, essence can neither be nor be conceived without the corresponding finite thing or mode, further the mode itself can neither be nor be conceived without its corresponding essence, as well. Essence and existence are inseparable and given together: "a mode's essence is a determinate degree of intensity, an irreducible degree of power; a mode exists, if it actually possesses a very great number of extensive parts corresponding to its essence or degree of power" (*EP* 202). How are we to understand this "correspondence" of essence and existence, of intensive and extensive parts?

According to Deleuze, Spinoza's explanation of modal existence should be understood primarily in terms of the composition and decomposition of relations. Each essence or degree of intensity expresses itself in a certain relation of movement and rest that nevertheless remains irreducible to essence. In addition, extensive parts "come in greater or lesser infinities," that is, there is an incalculable multitude of simple bodies that are extrinsically distinguished from one another and externally related to one another (*EP* 207). A given finite mode comes into existence when a great number of simple bodies "enter into" a given relation of movement and rest, as expressed by a modal essence. Depending on the given relation of movement and rest the extensive parts enter into, and the type of collection formed by the external relations of these parts, a particular finite mode comes into existence. If the given relation of movement and rest is different or is altered, then the collection formed and the existing mode will also be different or altered:

> Extensive parts form a greater or lesser infinite whole, insofar as they enter into this or that relation; in any given relation they correspond to some modal essence and compose the existence of the corresponding mode itself; in some other relation they form part of another whole, correspond to another modal essence, and compose the existence of another mode. . . . An existing mode is thus subject to considerable and continual alteration. . . . A given mode will continue to exist as long as the same relation subsists in the infinite whole of its parts. (*EP* 208)

It should not be forgotten that a given relation of movement and rest is irreducible to the essence in which it expresses itself. This allows Spinoza to resist postulating the essence of a finite thing as the transcendent cause of that thing's existence (*EP* 211). Modes are constituted on the basis of externally related bodies entering into particular relations of movement and rest. Therefore, all modes have a compositional existence corresponding to their essences by means of relations of movement and rest which possess their own laws. Modes cease to exist or acquire a different essence whenever they enter into another relation. For this reason, the existence of each mode is compositional and durational; each existing mode is finite and comes into existence and ceases to exist according to a process of generation in relation to a certain time and place (*EP* 210–13; *SP* 40). Modal existence is summed up by Deleuze in terms of an "expressive triad" that "comprises essence as a degree of power; a characteristic relation in which it expresses itself; and the extensive parts subsumed in this relation, which compose the mode's existence" (*EP* 217).

Deleuze points out that this expressive triad finds an equivalent, second formulation in the *Ethics*. The first formulation corresponds to the question "What is the structure, i.e., the relational composition, of a body?" (*EP* 218). The answer, of course, incorporates three elements: 1) the composition of a very great number of extensive parts; 2) a corresponding degree of power or intensity; 3) a specific relationship of movement and rest. The second formulation corresponds to the question "What can a body do?" and is prompted by Spinoza's assertion that extensive parts endlessly and variously "affect one another" (recall that Spinoza defined modes as the "affections of substance") (*EP*

218). Every existing mode has a certain capacity to be affected by other modes, a capacity which differs from mode to mode: "A horse, a fish, a man, or even two men compared with one another, do not have the same capacity to be affected: they are not affected by the same things, or not affected by the same things in the same way" (*EP* 217). Once a mode loses or in some way cannot maintain the specific relationship between its parts and its capacity to be affected by modes external to it, it ceases to exist. Modal existence is thus inseparable from the actual exercise of the capacity to be affected and the maintenance of a certain relationship of parts. The effort to persevere in existence, that is, to maintain a certain overall relationship and capacity to be affected is, in fact, the essence of existence, which Spinoza terms *conatus*:

> The striving by which each thing strives to persevere in its being is nothing but the actual essence of the thing. . . . So the power of each thing, *or* the striving by which it (either alone or with others) does anything, or strives to do anything—i.e., the power, *or* striving, by which it strives to persevere in its being, is nothing but the given, *or* actual, essence of the thing itself. (*Ethics* IIIP7 and D)[33]

Affections are of two kinds, passive affections and active affections. Passive affections or "passions" are those effects on a body caused by other bodies outside or external to it, while active affections or "actions" are those effects produced by a body itself. Every existing mode possesses both affections to greater or lesser degrees. The existence of a mode is determined and affected by modes external to it and constantly undergoes changes caused by external bodies. Here the capacity to be affected appears as a force or power of suffering. A mode also has the ability to exercise its capacity of being affected with respect to its own essence, that is, its own degree of power, and to thereby produce actions or active affections of which it is the cause. The capacity of being affected is in this instance called a force or power of acting. Furthermore, particularly in the case of humans, the present state of a body's constitution is indicated by certain ideas. Passive affections are involved in inadequate ideas or imaginings that indicate the effect of one body on another, while active affections are involved in adequate ideas which can be explained by the essence of the body that is the cause of its own actions. These two aspects of the capacity to be affected are found together in each existing mode in inverse and varying proportions: the greater the presence of one type of affection, the lesser the presence of the other (*EP* 219–22).

Deleuze demonstrates that the ethical question raised by Spinoza is found in conjunction with his physics and metaphysics: How can an existing finite mode become active, that is, increase its power of acting and of producing adequate ideas? How can we positively exercise our capacity to be affected and challenge the force of suffering which cuts us off from our power of acting? In other words, what can a body do? These questions may be answered by utilizing the physical aspects of Spinoza's theory discussed above. This presented us with three "orders of nature": 1) the order of essences or degrees of power; 2) the order of relations and compositions; 3) the order of encounters or of the spatial and temporal meetings of bodies. The various ways in which these three irreducible orders interact, as determined ultimately by the actual encounters that bodies have (not by any transcendent essences), not only provide the necessary conditions for the existence of finite modes but also affect existing modes and their experiences (*EP* 236–39).

There are two fundamental types of encounters. One type of encounter occurs when the relations of two or more bodies "agree" in such a way that the relational compositions of the bodies are preserved and prosper. This encounter produces a "good" or "useful" affection in each body, a feeling of joy which increases or aids each body's power of action (*EP* 239). The second kind of encounter occurs when the relations of two or more bodies do not agree with one another. Here the bodies are in some way contrary or harmful to one another, either inhibiting the preservation of each body's composition or leading to outright decomposition. As is to be expected, such an encounter produces "bad" affections and feelings of sadness that reduce the power of acting (*EP* 241). Concrete existence is characterized primarily by the dynamic interplay of these two basic sorts of encounters and by the various and quite diverse affections they produce:

> The good is when a body directly compounds its relations with ours, and, with all or part of its power, increases ours . . . the bad is when a body decomposes our body's relations, although it still combines with our parts, but in ways that do not correspond to our essence. . . . Hence good and bad have a primary, objective meaning, but one that is relative and partial: that which agrees with our nature or does not agree with it. (*SP* 22)

These considerations can be translated into an ethical perspective. That which is good is what is useful for a particular body, in that it aids or increases its power of action and helps to maintain its composition. That which is bad is what is harmful for a particular body, inasmuch as it reduces its power of action and inhibits its composition and decomposes or destroys it. What is important here is that "there is no Good or Evil in Nature in general, *but there is goodness and badness* . . . for each existing mode," that is, "from the viewpoint of this or that mode" (*EP* 247). Spinoza's ethical question therefore refers not to transcendent categories of Good and Evil, but instead to immanent criteria which distinguish what is useful or good and what is not useful or bad for each particular body. What is good for a body increases its power of acting and aids its composition. What is bad for a body limits its power of acting and contributes to its decomposition, similar to the effects of poison or toxic matter (*EP* 247).³⁴ Depending on the relations and circumstances of different encounters, bodies will either agree or disagree, aid or destroy one another. Good and Evil are not the expressions of universal essences independently of our actions. Similar actions may be good within the circumstances of one encounter and bad within the circumstances of another. Spinoza's ethical position is, from this perspective, very much like Nietzsche's:

> But because there is no Good or Evil, this does not mean that all distinctions vanish. There is no Good or Evil in Nature, but there are good and bad things for each existing mode. The moral opposition of Good and Evil disappears, but this disappearance does not make all things, or all beings, equal. . . . There are increases in our power of action, reductions in our power of action. The distinction between good things and bad provides the basis for a real ethical difference, which we must substitute for a false moral opposition. (*EP* 254)

The ethical difference proposed by Spinoza is expressed on several levels. A human being who *becomes* strong and reasonable, not in the sense of possessing abstract rationality but in the sense of being able to select and organize good encounters and apprehend relational compositions as they are, as well as free (because one is not simply born reasonable and free) does so by first striving to experience a "maximum of joyful passive affections" (*EP* 262). Only then can one begin to increase one's power of action, gradually becoming capable of "producing affections that are themselves active" (*EP* 262). This does not happen by chance, however, but by means of an active developmental and formative process in which one strives to organize one's encounters. A foolish, weak, and ignorant person is one who is content with sad and passive affections, cut off from their power of action. They remain at the mercy of chance encounters, suffering adverse effects as they happen to come along. Those who strive for freedom, on the contrary, seek to organize their encounters in such a way as to maximize what is useful, agreeable, and compatible, and minimize what is harmful, disagreeable, and inadequate (*SP* 23).

The process by which human beings strive to become reasonable and free can be seen as an "art of organizing encounters," an effort of uniting and combining useful and agreeable relations. And what are most useful and agreeable to humans are, naturally, other human beings seeking to agreeably and usefully combine their relations. By striving to become free, each person seeks what is useful not only for themselves, but for all others, as well. This complex process thereby cultivates freedom and produces "a reasonable association between men" (*EP* 261–62).³⁵ This theme that freedom must constantly be created as the actual effect or product of the process of our "becoming active" reveals, Deleuze says, Spinoza's "profoundly empiricist" inspiration (*EP* 288, 149).

Spinoza's ethical vision depends, then, not on transcendent values but rather on "norms of life," that is, on powers and capacities that relate our feelings, conduct, and intentions to qualitatively different immanent modes of existence: what we feel, do, and think are the characteristics either of a weak, impotent, and enslaved mode of existence, or of a strong, active, and free mode of existence (*EP* 268). The critical and practical task of philosophy is to denounce myths, mystifications, superstitions and all other transcendent or supernatural essences, beings, and values. These are the means used to produce sad passions, devalue Nature and human existence, and keep "us cut off from our power of action" as well as constantly diminish this power (*EP* 270).[36] Sad passions in all their various forms—greed, anxiety, hatred, fear, mockery—are expressions of tyranny, depriving those who are subjected to them not only of power and joy, but ultimately of life and freedom; oppression rules in part by inspiring sad passions (*EP* 271).

Spinoza's philosophy is a genuine philosophy of affirmation, from his positive metaphysics of expressive and productive immanence to his practical ethics of joy and the maximization of our power of action. Such an affirmative philosophy is rightly referred to by Deleuze as "a philosophy of 'life'," which consists in "denouncing all that separates us from life, all these transcendent values that are turned against life . . . all the values in the name of which we disparage life" and turn it into a "death worship" (*SP* 26).[37] All forms of transcendence, all philosophies and ethics which presuppose a transcendent viewpoint, are denied by Spinoza. What Spinoza affirms is the immanent yet complex unity of multiplicity and the diversity of this unity, the productive dynamic of the world, the fluid constitution of life, and the continuous experimental process of composing or constructing qualitatively different immanent modes of existence. The Spinozist notion that a way of life "has to be constructed," and that the world is constantly being composed in such a way that "there is no longer any difference between the concept and life," is carried over by Deleuze into his own formulation of the constitutive function of philosophy (*SP* 122–23, 130).

Philosophy, Constructivism, and Immanence

Although Bergson, Nietzsche, and Spinoza are radically different thinkers whose philosophies are often vastly divergent, for Deleuze they are all united on these points at least: The critique of transcendent realms, causes, values, and principles, and the affirmation of a dynamic, fluid, and immanent world within which human beings exist and create diverse ways of living. In this respect, all three thinkers are regarded by Deleuze as belonging to a philosophical tradition that affirms immanence and criticizes supernatural, divine, or mythical versions of transcendence. The profound influence of the work of Bergson, Nietzsche, and Spinoza on Deleuze's own thought is undeniable, to the extent that Deleuze develops a unique vision of philosophy which incorporates many of their ideas. This notion of philosophy is given expression by Deleuze in *What is Philosophy?*, coauthored with his long-time collaborator Félix Guattari.

After more than twenty years of collaboration dedicated to the constitution of a multidisciplinary theory—manifested through a combination of philosophy, psychoanalysis, anthropology, history, and political theory in *Anti-Oedipus* and *A Thousand Plateaus* as well as other writings—Deleuze and Guattari turn to the specific examination of the nature of philosophy itself in *What is Philosophy?*. Not surprisingly, this book, following the experimental style of their earlier works, attempts to undermine the image of philosophy as the authoritative possessor and protector of canonical rules, standards, and norms. Such an image might profess, for example, that philosophy is the search for unchanging truth, that it assigns eternal values, and that it is the determination of a foundational Absolute or invariable transcendent, and so forth. As Deleuze asserts in *Dialogues*, "An image of thought called philosophy has been formed historically and it effectively stops people from thinking" (*D* 13). In this respect, *What is Philosophy?* represents the consistent extension of Deleuze and Guattari's earlier projects. As a result, it necessarily delineates new lines of thought and invents new themes and concepts as it attempts to immerse philosophy within diversity and thereby release philosophical practice from the conventional restrictions of its dominant foundationalist self-image.

What, then, is the distinctive domain and function of philosophy according to Deleuze? Philosophy is to be distinguished from art and science insofar as it is "the art of forming, inventing, and fabricating concepts" (*WP* 2). This first determination of the philosophical task serves as a repudiation of the theoreticism prevalent in the Western metaphysical tradition because it insists on the active creation of concepts. However, the initial definition of philosophy offered above is further refined:

> [P]hilosophy is not a simple art of forming, inventing, or fabricating concepts, because concepts are not necessarily forms, discoveries, or products. More rigorously, philosophy is the discipline that involves *creating* concepts. . . . The object of philosophy is to create concepts that are always new. Because the concept must be created, it refers back to the philosopher as the one who has it potentially, or who has its power and competence. . . . Concepts are not waiting for us ready-made, like heavenly bodies. There is no heaven for concepts. They must be invented, fabricated, or rather created and would be nothing without their creator's signature. (*WP* 5)

For Deleuze and Guattari, philosophy is not the purely rational contemplation of always present facts or perfectly immobile and immutable ideas. On the contrary, philosophy's task is entirely positive, in the sense that it must itself create that which is proper to it. While Deleuze's type of empiricism understands the concept as that which must be made in order to be had, "Platonic reminiscence and Cartesian innateness or the Kantian *a priori* " are content to treat the concept as a given merely "contemplated from afar" (*WP* 103). Thus, philosophy consists, as we will see, in the effective positioning of singular concepts within a plane of immanence, giving rise to a territory that is possessed only by means of its very creation. The emphasis Deleuze and Guattari place on the singularity of concepts, that is, that new concepts are continually to be created by philosophers, also represents a polemic against what they regard as the idealized notion of consensus. They deny that philosophy could resolve (dialectically or otherwise) the diversity of different modes of existence into a universal intersubjective truth or "consensus" by means of some reflexive edification (*WP* 6–7). As argued by Deleuze and Guattari, what the promoters of idealized consensus overlook is that they depend upon a notion circumscribed by others, such as rational communication, universality, objectivity, majority opinion, resolution of dissension, and so forth, which have very little to do with the creation of concepts and a great deal to do with the elimination of rivals and the possible stultification of diversity (*WP* 28–29).[38] Deleuze and Guattari suggest that the notion of consensus could be used to promote a particular conception of reality at the expense of all others, providing possible justification for the coercion of agreements or the recuperation of difference in the effort to reach "compromise."

Philosophy's function, they propose, calls for the unexpected. To do philosophy is to inhabit the borders of the unforeseen, to skirt unexplored territories. Philosophy is animated by a rigorous and dynamic constructivism, which makes the creation or construction of new concepts incommensurable with both the conformist demands of universalism and the image of philosophy as simply "reflecting on" independent and immutable conceptual entities. In actuality, every constructive philosophical initiative delimits its own unique conceptual space, irreducible to a single absolute system. Yet this introduces an unavoidable and extremely important question: "Why, through what necessity, and for what use must concepts, and always new concepts, be created? And in order to do what?" (*WP* 8). The formulation of this question provides another dimension to the picture of philosophy presented here.

In asking after the use and purpose of the philosophical task of creating concepts, Deleuze provides a pragmatic orientation for philosophy itself. Because concepts are not waiting "ready-made," they must be brought about or produced by the creative efforts of philosophers: philosophers, Deleuze writes, are the "potentiality of the concept" (*WP* 5). The reality of the concept derives from its particular mode of construction. This means that philosophy should be

Immanence and Multiplicity 71

concerned not only with *what* it produces, but also with *how* it produces concepts, and with its active involvement within the creative process. This requires that philosophy abandon the notion that concepts are representations corresponding to transcendent entities beyond space and time, in favor of the view that concepts are the real products of "free creative activity" whose immanent conditions of creation are "always singular moments" (*WP* 11–12).

There are three elements that must be further explained in order to develop the picture of philosophy offered here: the concept, the plane of immanence, and conceptual personae. With respect to the first element, Deleuze and Guattari state that each concept is a multiplicity composed of a finite number of components: "There are no simple concepts. Every concept has components and is defined by them. It therefore has a combination. It is a multiplicity" (*WP* 15). This is because every "beginning" draws upon that which exists within a given field of experience. In addition, the concept brings together its components into a "fragmentary whole" as response to a specific problem: "All concepts are connected to problems without which they would have no meaning and which can themselves only be isolated or understood as their solution emerges" (*WP* 16). Deleuze, drawing upon Bergson, notes that the concept is created in response to one or more problems "which are thought to be badly understood or badly posed" (*WP* 16). It is for this reason that every concept also has a history. Each concept is created as a new response to a previously posed problem, in the process of creation the problem itself is changed. From the point of view of the new concept the problem takes on a different character or quality, and for its construction the new concept draws upon the components of other concepts and problems in unique or original ways: a new multiplicity is produced.

Therefore, the construction of a conceptual multiplicity with respect to a specific problem requires the incorporation of the heterogeneous components of other concepts. The becoming of each concept links it to other coexisting concepts, forming a network of differently composed but nevertheless related concept-problem combinations. For example, a specific concept of the Other is created in response to a particular problem within a given field of experience. This concept not only has a history with respect to other concepts-problems of otherness, but it also branches off and connects to different concepts and problems, such as those regarding perception, judgment, or linguistic expression. In this way a concept takes shape and assumes a reality by intersecting, drawing upon, and transforming various pieces of the conditions of its becoming. Consequently, a concept is not created *ex nihilo* because "every concept relates back to other concepts, not only in its history but in its becoming or its present connections" (*WP* 19).

The created concept is also characterized by its consistency or unity. The components of a concept are diverse and distinct, but the concept itself can be defined as such only because it brings together components that overlap in some way and are not separable. Each component has what Deleuze and Guattari call a "zone of neighborhood" or vicinity of contiguity which allows it to relate to other components, forming an area where the related components become "indiscernible" (*WP* 19–20). While the components of a concept are inseparable within the concept, they are themselves heterogeneous and irreducible despite the fact that they become indiscernible along certain limited points of overlap. Furthermore, the concept's components are akin to intensive processual variations, that is, dynamic processes of continual variation, ordered and organized by their zones of overlap within the order of the concept. This ensures that the components can be reorganized, particularized, and generalized depending on the values or functions attributed to them by a particular concept. The components and the concept thus form an immanent and fluid unity (i.e., a "fragmentary whole") in two directions: First, by means of its overlapping components the concept possesses its own internal consistency or endoconsistency, and second, by means of its relation to other concepts, the concept also possesses an external consistency or exoconsistency.

In addition to these characteristics, Deleuze points out that the concept is incorporeal in that it expresses an event—a creative and constructive *act of thought*—rather than represents a transcendent essence or thing-in-itself. The concept does not refer to something independent of itself, which it must correspond to and resemble. On the contrary, the concept "is self-referential; it posits itself and its object at the same time it is created" (*WP* 22). Because the concept and its object are posited at the same moment, what the concept "refers" to is immanent in the concept itself. The concept is, in this sense, its own object rather than a representation, insofar as the concept is taken to be the product of processes of construction. This, of course, opens the "referent" to the vicissitudes of time and the transformations of history and context, and thus to the creation of new concepts.[39] Concepts, then, are not to be confused with general or abstract ideas; Platonic reminiscence, Cartesian innateness, and Kant's *a priori* are not different names for the same timeless idea simply waiting to be registered by the mind, nor are they responding to the very same problem. Concepts have a becoming and a history; they are made, not found as something already there. As a consequence, philosophy's task "when it creates concepts . . . is always to extract an event from things and beings, to set up the new event from things and beings, always to give them a new event" (*WP* 33). The concept is the continuous production of difference in the world.

The constructivism promoted by Deleuze and Guattari pertains not only to the creation of concepts but also to the plane of immanence which those concepts inhabit: "Philosophy is a constructivism, and constructivism has two qualitatively different complementary aspects: the creation of concepts and the laying out of a plane" (*WP* 36). Whereas concepts are fragmentary wholes that bring together heterogeneous components in order to give rise to new events, the plane of immanence is a nonfragmented yet open Whole or "planomenon" which harbors the concepts themselves. However, the plane of immanence is not itself a concept "nor the concept of all concepts" (*WP* 35). The plane of immanence is the unlimited milieu, the consistent and unified horizon, within which concepts are created and held together. Deleuze and Guattari explain that while concepts are to be regarded as events, the plane of immanence "is the horizon of events, the reservoir or reserve of purely conceptual events" (*WP* 36). Furthermore, the plane of immanence is not a relative horizon, in the sense that it is a static enclosure which varies according to the position of an external observer, but an "absolute horizon" which is itself in movement and is inhabited from within by concepts. This plane serves as the mobile environment that the internal components of concepts incessantly travel in and populate.

Why do Deleuze and Guattari insist that the plane of immanence is not itself a concept? Because it is that which the construction of new concepts presupposes, namely, the indefinite movement of thought. The indefinite movement of thought, or what might be called thought without proper limits, is the absolute horizon on which concepts are constructed. It is in this sense that the plane of immanence is the philosophical presupposition or condition for the creation of concepts. What is not to be overlooked, however, is that this presupposition is *philosophical*, in that it does not exist outside philosophy (*WP* 41). In other words, the plane of immanence is the "prephilosophical" ground that philosophy calls on specifically for the purpose of creating concepts upon it. Even though the plane of immanence is "prephilosophical," since it is not itself a concept, it still belongs to philosophy because philosophy lays it out as the horizon for its own experimentation (*WP* 41).

The plane of immanence thus corresponds to what Deleuze refers to in *Difference and Repetition* as the "image of thought," the implicit, preconceptual presupposition of what is supposed to belong to the power of thinking which every philosophy builds itself upon. This implicit presupposition is expressed by such phrases as "everyone knows what thinking means" or "everyone wants the truth" (*WP* 61). For example, Descartes' cogito can be regarded as the concept from which the Cartesian philosophy begins. Yet what does this philosophical concept itself presuppose in order for it and not some other concept (such as Kant's transcendental ego) to be in this position? It is created upon that which Descartes (or Plato, or Kant, and so forth) implicitly took to belong to thought by right or by necessity; for example, the innate forces belonging to each private subject. Even though the concept occupies and travels the plane of immanence, the plane itself is irreducible to the concept and functions as a necessary condition for the concept's production. The consistency of the concept would not be realized without the plane of immanence. It is therefore possible to understood the concept as an actively created event situated within the horizon, field, or milieu of the plane of immanence. While the plane of immanence is always a single yet fluid milieu, it is true that the image of thought and being has consistently changed. Consequently, "there are varied and distinct planes of immanence that, depending upon which infinite movements are retained and selected, succeed and contest each other in history" (*WP* 39).

We return to the distinction from which this chapter began. At the beginning of the chapter I described two different tendencies animating the history of philosophy, the tendency towards transcendence and the tendency towards immanence. Deleuze maintains that even this is too generous a description, because whatever is inspired by or tends toward the transcendent should be classified as religion rather than philosophy: "Whenever there is transcendence, vertical Being, imperial State in the sky or on earth, there is religion; and there is Philosophy whenever there is immanence" (*WP* 43). Nevertheless, what is characteristic of philosophies of transcendence is that they consider immanence to be immanent "to" something transcendent, while philosophies of immanence have no need for the transcendent and regard immanence as immanent only to itself. For Plato, immanence is immanent to the universal One beyond and untouched by immanence, and for Christian philosophy immanence is derived from an emanative transcendence (God). With Descartes, Kant, and Husserl, immanence is treated as being immanent to the cogito or transcendental subjectivity. Here transcendence appears within rather than beyond immanence, but again only as something untouchable and privileged which still does not truly belong to the immanent world. This form of transcendence posits the activity of consciousness to be a "breaking away" from immanence. But from the point of view of immanence, the power of thinking is continuous with the processual movement or flow of immanence itself; concepts are events produced within the plane of immanence. In each of the two examples of philosophies of transcendence, immanence is enclosed or controlled by transcendence. Transcendence operates to "freeze" or control the infinite movement of thought, in order to "redeem" thought from the threatening chaos of immanence (*WP* 47).

If, on the contrary, immanence is no longer viewed as subordinated to or derived from the transcendent, the dynamic movement of the plane of immanence finds its most suitable philosophical perspective in "a radical empiricism" which "presents only events, that is, possible worlds as concepts, and other people as expressions of possible worlds" (*WP* 47–48). The construction of concepts-events is the process of inventing new modes of existence or possibilities of life on a plane of immanence. Because empiricism is committed to the immanence of the world of experience it "is therefore a great creator of concepts" (*WP* 48). For empiricism, immanence is never immanent to something, whether that something be an emanative God, an eternal Form, or a pure consciousness. If it were, immanence would always be held hostage to the transcendent. It is only from within the limitless, continuous plane of immanence and the infinite movement of thought that new concepts and new modes of existence can be created which will not be betrayed by a transcendence supposedly higher than everything else. In fact, Deleuze and Guattari explain that there are many "illusions" that constantly threaten the free movement of the plane of immanence:

> First of all there is the *illusion of transcendence*, which, perhaps, comes before all the others (in its double aspect of making immanence immanent to something and of rediscovering a transcendence within immanence itself); then the *illusion of universals* when concepts are confused with the plane [of immanence]. But this confusion arises as soon as immanence is posited as being immanent to something, since this something is necessarily a concept. We think the universal explains, whereas it is what must be explained. . . . Then there is the *illusion of the eternal* when it is forgotten that concepts must be created, and then the *illusion of discursiveness*, when propositions are confused with concepts. (*WP* 49–50)

It was mentioned previously that there has been a succession of diverse planes of immanence throughout the history of philosophy, with the result that "we can and must presuppose a multiplicity of planes" (*WP* 50). One reason for this we have already seen: the infinite movements and transformations of thought cannot be stopped. Difference is unstoppable. Another reason is that it is impossible for any one plane of immanence to absolutely encompass that which is constantly becoming. A third, and most profound reason is that "each plane has its own way of constructing immanence" which distinguishes it from all the others (*WP* 50). Each plane of immanence can be thought of as a field of variation, populated by different concepts, which constitute a specific power of thought and a specific power of being. Such planes are the indicators of philosophers who have "changed what it means to think" (*WP* 51).

Moreover, the multiplicity of planes of immanence also compose THE plane of immanence. Yet THE plane of immanence must not be regarded as a fixed, self-identical totality whose structures and order is predetermined; it is not a transcendent realm supporting and organizing the multiplicity of planes. Rather, it is itself the changing, fluctuating, and boundless nonteleological processual product of the plurality of different but coexisting planes. Planes of immanence are distributed and connected in such a way that they form an interleaved multiplicity-in-unity that can be neither separated from the planes nor reduced to a privileged plane(s), much like the layers or strata of the earth form a pluralistic geological composite which is constantly shifting, altering, growing, in short, becoming multiple (*WP* 50, 59).[40] The unity of THE plane of immanence means the infinitely continuous process of the formation of multiplicity, a complex unity that can never be complete or fully apprehended; continuity is not to be confused with the totalizing identity of the transcendent. It can only be said, then, that *THE* plane of immanence begins always already within itself. As a result, *THE* plane of immanence "is, at the same time, that which must be thought and that which cannot be thought. It is the nonthought within thought," the constantly moving outside of thought which is not transcendent to thought but resides in the very heart of thought itself (*WP* 59).[41]

Next we come to the third element of philosophical constructivism: "conceptual personae." This rather ambiguous element exists "halfway between concept and preconceptual plane, passing from one to the other" (*WP* 61). Conceptual personae are unique to each plane of immanence and function to carry out the movements of the plane to the point of the creation of specific concepts; they convey the power of the process of constructing concepts within specific planes of immanence. For example, between Descartes' implicit presuppositions and the constructed concept of the cogito, is the conceptual persona of the Idiot. The Idiot is the private, uninitiated, ordinary thinker, whose thought occurs innately, without reference to the concepts of experts or those who are technically trained: the simple "I think." It is on the basis of this persona that the full-blown concept of the cogito is crystallized as the singular creation of Descartes (*WP* 61–63). Other conceptual personae are the Socrates of Plato—which is not merely a character in Plato's dialogues, but the very basis of his conceptual schema—and the Dionysus of Nietzsche.

"The conceptual persona," Deleuze and Guattari tell us, "is the becoming or subject of a philosophy, on a par with the philosopher" (*WP* 64). By this they mean that the conceptual persona is the agent which the movement of thought utilizes to produce new concepts on a plane of immanence. However, conceptual personae should not be misinterpreted as expressing the authority of a proper name nor as representing the personal identity of the philosopher. This is because the becoming of a philosophy envelops both the philosopher and his or her conceptual persona or personae. Not only does the philosopher become his or her persona or personae, but the personae "themselves become something other than what they are historically, mythologically, or commonly" (*WP* 64). The Socrates of Plato is a basic element in the creation of Platonic thought, but only on the condition that Plato "becomes Socrates at the same time that he makes Socrates become philosopher" (*WP* 65). Similarly, Nietzsche's philosophy begins only when Nietzsche becomes Dionysus or Zarathustra, and Dionysus and Zarathustra become indistinguishable from Nietzsche the philosopher. And in each case, it is impossible to consider Socrates, Dionysus, or Zarathustra to be either the allegorical figurations of Plato and Nietzsche or references back to actual persons. Accordingly, conceptual personae are not merely "mythical personifications or historical persons or literary or novelistic heroes," but rather the very powers of the creation of singular concepts (*WP* 65). In every great philosophy one or more conceptual persona(e) emerge that, apart from their various historical, mythological or literary appearances, serve to infuse thought with the affirmative currents of life. Conceptual personae are the "crystals" or "seeds of thought," the precursors of concepts created by experimentation within the immanent movements of thought (*WP* 69).

As with concepts and planes of immanence, there is a multiplicity of conceptual personae. Even though conceptual personae belong to the power of thinking they also appear in specific social and historical milieus, "since they are constantly arising and vary with planes of immanence" (*WP* 70). Furthermore, the personae on a given plane of immanence appear to be combinations of several different features. The first of these are the "pathic features," which convey the painful, distressing affects of the individual, such as the Idiot, the Madman, or the Schizophrenic (*WP* 70). There are also the "relational features" that indicate the proliferating, branching, and splitting off of personae, from the Friend which branches off to the Claimant and the Rival, to the Couple which splits into the Fiancée and Seducer (Kierkegaard) (*WP* 70–71). In addition, Deleuze and Guattari mention that there are "dynamic features." These, of course, are the intensive movements and alterations, the "pure dynamic difference," of relationally interacting personae (*WP* 71). Not to be overlooked are the "juridical features" by means of which "thought constantly lays claim to what belongs to it by right" (*WP* 72). The history of philosophy is replete with such juridical features; for example, the philosopher as Investigator, Lawyer, or Judge, with reason as Tribunal or Law. And finally there are "existential features," those unique and vital dimensions of a philosopher's life that are related to their development and invention of new modes of existence, which in turn lead the philosopher to "become always something else" (*WP* 73).

The three elements of constructivism discussed here presuppose one another, but each is different and irreducible to the others. In order for concepts to be created there must be conceptual personae, but concepts are not simply deduced from personae. Similarly, conceptual personae require planes of immanence, for they are nothing without the infinite movements of thought. But the planes themselves possess consistency only insofar as they are in keeping with the conceptual personae and concepts created and situated within them. Thus, each of the three element must be constructed by means of distinct yet inseparable activities:

> Philosophy presents three elements, each of which fits with the other two but must be considered for itself: *the prephilosophical plane it must lay out (immanence), the persona or personae it must invent and bring to life (insistence), and the philosophical concepts it must create (consistency)*. Laying out, inventing, and creating constitute the philosophical trinity. (*WP* 76–77)

And it should not be forgotten that these three elements of constructivism are meaningful only when coupled with what should be considered the fourth element, namely, the problem or set of problems to which they respond.

The insistence on immanence as the absolute milieu in which becoming and existence occur is meant by Deleuze to overturn the philosophical tendency toward transcendence. Traditional views of immanence have treated it as either the inferior appearance of some eternal, fixed, and superior transcendent reality or as the threatening chaos to be subdued by the *a priori* rationality imposed on it from without by the transcendental subject. Deleuze rejects this denigration of the immanent world, and argues that the experience of immanence calls not for transcendent causes, categories, and notions (either within or without immanence) but instead for the immanent expression of thought-events, that is, constructed concepts and new possibilities of life. In doing so, Deleuze offers a positive philosophy of immanence that affirms the conditions of existence in the immanent world: temporality, flux, complexity, change, creation, and diversity are the sources and characteristics of life. Yet at the same time Deleuze also affirms the continuity of immanence, as the continuous passage or transition from multiplicity to multiplicity. Immanence is the continuous movement of life, which possesses its own internal dynamic. This allows for the creative renewal of experience, as experience occurs within the transformational movements of immanence, without fixed end or final essence. From this perspective, immanence is what singularizes rather than universalizes experience, for there is no one exclusive way for experiences to be actualized nor is there any kind of Kantian transcendental condition of all possible experience. Deleuze suggests that the problem to which his philosophy of immanence responds:

> concerns the one who believes in the world, and not even in the existence of the world but in its possibilities of movements and intensities, so as once again to give birth to new modes of existence, closer to animals and rocks. It may be that believing in this world, in this life, becomes our most difficult task, or the task of a mode of existence still to be discovered on our plane of immanence today. This is the empiricist conversion. (*WP* 74–75)

As mentioned earlier, Deleuze explicitly designates the philosophical perspective most consistent with the real possibilities of immanence and the articulation of new modes of existence to be a radical form of empiricism. This appeal to a radical empiricism is developed in the following chapter, in light of the important role played by relations throughout Deleuze's writings.

Chapter 3

Relations and the Radicalization of Empiricism

It is not accidental that Deleuze's opposition to foundationalist metaphysics leads him to a theory of immanence which he regards as a radical empiricism. According to Deleuze, the "illusion of transcendence," or the postulating of an ultimate nonexperiential ground behind what is experienced, is to be repudiated in favor of an empiricist sensibility immersed in the dynamic movements of the world, and its flow and flux of immanent becomings (*WP* 47–49, 73). Yet we have also come to see that Deleuze is not abandoning ontological concerns altogether. While jettisoning the claim that a systematic investigation of Being will lead to the discovery of absolute or first principles, he nevertheless derides the claim that philosophy as such is "dead" or "overcome" (*WP* 9). Rather, Deleuze shifts the focus of philosophy away from the conventional task of uncovering transcendent principles ostensibly invested with the hidden power of regulating and containing the entire world, toward the practice of creating and transforming concepts and the planes or fields of immanence that those concepts occupy (*WP* 35–36). The criterion for philosophical activity is not representational accuracy of how the world "really is" as a closed system independent of experience but, given a theory of immanence, the success of the construction of concepts designed to respond to specific problems and real, particular conditions of existence (*WP* 79–83).[1] Thus for Deleuze the goal of an empiricist philosophy is practical: to make a positive difference in life, to invent, create, and experiment. However, in order to clarify why he maintains that the immanent point of view corresponds to a radical empiricism, there is another central theme of Deleuze's philosophy that must be addressed. The theme is that of relations, which is vital for the use to which Deleuze puts empiricism.

In the first section of this chapter I will briefly discuss the radical empiricism of William James as a means of providing a context for articulating the sort of relationship Deleuze might have with this embodiment of the American pragmatic tradition of empiricism. The second section will be concerned with elaborating Deleuze's thoughts on empiricism and relations, and with suggesting that they be seen as following the basic orientation of James' radical empiricism. Finally, I will conclude this chapter by discussing how Deleuze's position on relations is central to the development of his later "rhizomatic" philosophy written in collaboration with Félix Guattari, and highlight what Deleuze sees as the ethical and political relevance of the concept of the rhizome.

Throughout these three sections my primary concern will be to emphasize the ontological aspects of Deleuze's antifoundationalist empiricism. Because Deleuze sees philosophy as an immanent constructivism, his ontology is not to be construed as seeking direct access to some transcendent Being in which all things are anchored. Instead, it views philosophy as taking its place alongside other practices, such as science and art, in organizing experience in different ways. In short, Deleuze's ontology seeks both to reveal the constructed character of the world and to provide some "tools" that can assist in the actual constitution of new becomings and experiences. The pragmatic tenor of Deleuze's constructivism is brought out very clearly in the following well-known remark Deleuze makes in a conversation with Michel Foucault:

> A theory is exactly like a box of tools. It has nothing to do with the signifier. It must be useful. It must function. And not for itself. If no one uses it, beginning with the theoretician himself . . . then the theory is worthless or the moment is inappropriate. We don't revise a theory, but construct new ones; we have no choice but to make others.[2]

This chapter proposes, then, to strengthen the interpretation I have advanced throughout the book that Deleuze's empiricism is inherently pluralistic. I do this by demonstrating that his work can be seen as taking up and transforming certain elements of the project of a radical empiricism initiated by James, and by elucidating a distinctive antifoundationalist ontological view that can be incorporated into the ethical and political concerns expressed in Deleuze's later works.

Relations in William James' Radical Empiricism

I do not think it is too much to suggest that Deleuze subscribes to what can easily be considered the basic postulate of the empiricist philosophical tradition: Philosophy must be practically concerned and engaged with the immanent world and with the diversity of human experiences, whether political, aesthetic, ethical, or scientific. Recall that Deleuze regards Nietzsche as an empiricist because his philosophy "expresses thought as experience and movement" (*N* xiii). However, experience never plays a constitutive role in Deleuze's work, that is, it never refers to some anonymous, transcendental subject or consciousness that underlies and undergoes pure experience in general. Rather, both experience and subject are thought of as being continuously constituted within specific cultural fields of discursive and nondiscursive practices, rules, valuations, and interpretations. Experience and subject are not taken to be universal categories, instead they are regarded by Deleuze as real practical effects or constructs open to change and transformation. This leads Deleuze to a pluralistic empiricism of actual *experiences* instead of a theory of experience in general.[3] His view of empiricism as a unique ontology that appeals to the creative processes whereby experience is continually problematized and transformed is one based not only on immanence, but also on relations. In this respect, Deleuze's brand of empiricism and his engagement with the empiricist tradition can be seen most productively in comparison to William James' radical empiricism and pragmatism.[4]

James' radical empiricism arose, at least partially, as a critical response to the role accorded relations by classical empiricism. According to James the classical empiricists, notably Locke and Hume, translated experience into disconnected, separated terms and thereby failed to take adequate account of relations as also belonging to experience. More specifically, James argues that the earlier empiricists focused only on disjunctive relations, which distinguish things from one another, at the expense of conjunctive relations, which bring things together or constitute degrees of continuity, thereby leaving out a crucial element of actual experience.[5] This emphasis on separation leaves classical empiricism at the level of atomism, unable to describe successfully how the objects of experience can come together in any coherent fashion. When the rationalists and absolute idealists countered by claiming that the unity of experience depended upon transcendental egos or an Absolute that were themselves immune to actual experience, James criticized these positions because their dubious metaphysical presuppositions simply represented a move to the other extreme of a totality beyond or behind experience itself. James points out that the pluralistic rather than atomistic or monistic nature of experience supposes a continuous flux of both difference and unity, and thus that the transformations of experience depend upon conjunctive as well as disjunctive relations (*Essays*

44–52). This recognition is, in fact, what leads to the radicalization of empiricism. For James, relations are as real and necessary to experience as are its parts, and by giving equal weight to the experience of both unity and difference in their various gradations a consistently pluralistic ontology can be maintained. Hence, James writes that one who assumes *prima facie* that pluralism "is the permanent form of the world is what I call a radical empiricist."[6] For James, then, radical empiricism stands on the basis of its treatment of relations as the key feature of experience. There are several further consequences of this position that should be addressed briefly before making our way to Deleuze.

James' argument is supported in the formal presentation of what he intends by radical empiricism in *The Meaning of Truth*. There he writes that radical empiricism "consists first of a postulate, next of a statement of fact, and finally of a generalized conclusion."[7] The postulate, as expected, states that philosophical debate should only be about "things definable in terms drawn from experience" (*Meaning* 6). This postulate proposes that claims regarding the supposed existence of a transcendent realm beyond experience should not serve as material for philosophical debate. We might think of James' postulate in terms of Bergson's critique of those "false problems" which have plagued the history of philosophy. James' point is not to deny difficult, obscure, or abstract questions a role in philosophy. On the contrary, James' view is that the appeal to the transcendent has itself foreclosed the possibility of asking difficult questions and has sought to usher in easy and sure answers on the basis of a domain beyond experience rather than pose further problems that philosophy can constructively address with respect to immanent and experientially derived phenomena.[8]

The statement of fact following the postulate is the central point of his presentation: "The statement of fact is that the relations between things, conjunctive as well as disjunctive, are just as much matters of direct particular experience, neither more nor less so, than the things themselves" (*Meaning* 7). Important here is not only that James affirms the experiential reality of all relations between terms as much as the terms themselves, but also the nature of relations as "between" the terms. More on this will follow, after taking note of the second consequence of James' position useful for our discussion, namely, the generalized conclusion of radical empiricism. This conclusion maintains that because "the parts of experience hold together from next to next by relations that are themselves parts of experience" it is unnecessary to appeal to any "extraneous trans-empirical connective support" in order to account for the structure of experience (*Meaning* 7). Clearly, James rejects any foundationalism that attempts to explain the relationality of experience on the basis of an eternal nonempirical bedrock that underlies and determines it or any *a priori* principles that seek to order the multiplicity of the world into a complete and fixed absolute. On the contrary, radical empiricism is a "mosaic philosophy" influenced by a pluralistic view of the world:

> In actual mosaics the pieces are held together by their bedding, for which bedding the substances, transcendental egos, or absolutes of other philosophies may be taken to stand. In radical empiricism there is no bedding; it is as if the pieces clung together by their edges, the transitions experienced between them forming their cement.... Life is in the transitions as much as in the terms connected. (*Essays* 42)

The centrality of relations, then, is the key to understanding some of James' most important ontological reconceptualizations with respect to empiricism. By means of his treatment of relations, James proposes to support his conception of the flux of the world of experience as pluralistic, that is, composed of multiplicities whose relationships form a kind of "mosaic" rather than absolute holism, and to relate that pluralism to the practical; to different types of creating, acting, doing, and making within a diversity of contexts.

In his essay "The Thing and its Relations" James notes that radical empiricism "must tend to pluralism in its ontology" because of the presence of external relations in experience (*Essays* 54).[9] This does not mean, of course, that the world is without any connections. Instead, the flux of experience, the changing gradations of unity and disunity that characterize actual experience, can be best accounted for by a doctrine of relations that sees them according to their degrees of externality and their immanent function within our experience. As defined by James, an external relation is "*a relation which can change without forcing its terms to change their nature simultaneously*" (*Essays* 55). I will save a full treatment of the notion of external relations for my discussion of Deleuze. It should be noted, however, that James argues in favor of the reality of external and not only internal relations (and thus against absolutism of either the rationalist or idealist variety) because external relations allow for a consistent pluralism, on the grounds that they are "practically workable" and can be altered without thereby necessarily affecting the natures of the terms being related (*Essays* 57). Yet what are the natures of terms?

By "natures" we should not understand nonempirical and atemporal essences but rather the shared interpreted characteristics of an object-for-us as finite beings in particular contexts. For example, the characteristic "nature" of a cup is that it is an object for drinking. But this same cup may be used to hold flowers, or to trap an insect, or to hold down papers on my desk. Although the cup may be placed in different relationships, it still remains a cup. I may drink from it at one moment and use it as a vase at another, but the cup itself does not change in any metaphysically essential manner. What changes instead are the *actual relations* between the cup and other terms, and the various contexts in which the cup is considered. The cup can therefore be both different and the same in a practical sense, and not only one or the other in any absolute sense. The notion of "nature" in this case is that of a temporal, existential, immanent, living and relative nature in contrast with the ideal, eternal, transcendent, and absolute forms that are typically the source of essentialist arguments. The definition of the nature of a term should be seen in this case only in relation to some practical interest or purpose and not as independent of human experience and belief. Certain aspects of a thing may be transformed under different circumstances; its nature may or may not change, depending upon the introduction of a relational context according to our interests, purposes, and activities. These "pragmatic realities" are not metaphysically basic but are value-laden constructions generated on the basis of certain experiences and shared interpretations.[10] James stresses that:

> No philosophy can ever be anything but a summary sketch, a picture of the world in abridgment, a foreshortened bird's-eye view of the perspective of events. And the first thing to notice is this, that the only material we have at our disposal for making a picture of the world is supplied by various portions of that world of which we have already had experience.

He continues, noting that "this radical discrepancy between the absolute and the relative points of view" reveals that "humans are incurably rooted in the temporal point of view."[11]

Internal relations, in contrast to external relations, are those believed to be grounded in the metaphysical essences that inhere in one or more of the terms related, and are to be derived from these essences themselves. The terms and their relations can be only what they are "in essence," as determined by some unchanging foundation. Thus, absolutism is the position that holds reality to be a completely integrated system where *all* relations are internal and dependent upon an underlying, *non*relational totality. In other words, for an absolutist essentialism the relations of some thing can be exhaustively determined by that thing's essence, making relations merely derivative properties. The thing's relations literally could not change for such change would signal the very destruction of the thing itself. On James' view, however, to deny that a formal essence is what determines entirely the actual relations a thing has is to open the possibility for the nature of a term to be defined by context, practical interest, purpose, custom, habit, and history. In that case, the nature of a term is relative rather than absolute, in the sense that the relations a term has contribute to the definition of its nature (or sense) relative to context and purpose.

External relations, then, have a fluidity that sits well with a radical empiricist conception of the fundamentally practical mode of human engagement with the world. In James' account, our experiences are made up of finite things that can enter into many different kinds of relationships without inherent change: "The world we live in exists diffused and distributed, in the form of an indefinitely numerous lot of *eaches*, coherent in all sorts of ways and degrees."[12] Hence the recognition that both difference and unity are practical features of experience. While things are distinguishable they are nevertheless held together (or held apart) by relations that are made (or unmade) between them by means of some activity. External relations are *between* their terms because they are not determined necessarily by the terms and because they possess a distinct reality equal to the terms themselves. Rather than accepting some version of an ideal foundation behind experience serving as its immutable ground, radical empiricism is inclined toward an immanent "mosaic" as the continual creation or composition of relationships of disjunction and conjunction within experience.[13]

Experience can be seen in this light as an interactive process that consists in putting things into and taking things out of relation—for there is as much disconnection in the world as there is connection—and the externality of the relation is what makes it "practical." In an explicit and remarkable affirmation of external relations as central to the project of radical empiricism, James writes:

> Pragmatically interpreted, pluralism or the doctrine that it is many means only that the sundry parts of reality *may be externally related.* Everything you can think of, however vast or inclusive, has on the pluralist view a genuinely "external" environment of some sort. Things are "with" one another in many ways, but nothing includes everything, or dominates over everything. The word "and" trails after every sentence.[14]

Having established James' articulation of radical empiricism as a philosophy which admits the reality of external relations, and which supports a pluralistic view of the world as composed of various relations between things without drawing upon a foundationalist "bedding" or grounding extraneous to this actual composition, I will now consider how Deleuze's own take on empiricism can be seen against this philosophical background. I must stress that the aim of this discussion is not to make Deleuze out to be a "Jamesian," nor to make James into a "Deleuzian," for there are no doubt too many differences between their philosophies when considered in their entirety to do so. My concern is with the broadly interpretive question as to whether Deleuze's thoughts on empiricism and relations can be most interestingly articulated in response to the radicalization of empiricism first carried out by James.

Deleuze on Relations

Unlike James, who bases his radicalization of empiricism upon a critique of what he takes to be Hume's neglect of the importance of relations, Deleuze finds in Hume a profound attention to relations and the resources for a radicalization of empiricism similar to that sought by James. Deleuze's most sustained engagement with the philosophy of Hume appeared in 1953, with the original publication of *Empiricism and Subjectivity*.[15] Like James, Deleuze saw empiricism as providing the tools needed for elaborating an understanding of experience revealing more richness and diversity than that admitted by traditional rationalist metaphysics.[16] However, while concerned with the philosophy of Hume in particular, *Empiricism and Subjectivity* also proves useful for understanding the development and orientation of Deleuze's own philosophy as a pluralist empiricism. What immediately distinguishes Deleuze's reading of Hume from many classical interpretations is that while these interpretations tend to cast Hume in the role of an early positivist attempting to formulate a reductionist epistemology for which experience is primarily cognitive, Deleuze insists that Hume should be seen first and foremost as a political, historical, and moral philosopher (*ES* 27, 33).

Deleuze's point is that Hume sought to make philosophy more practical, in the sense that the philosophic enterprise should understand experience as leading to reflection on our constructive activities. For Deleuze, experience is not merely passively given or received but is dynamically constituted by means of interactions within the immanent world. Experience indicates for Deleuze the processes of mutually differentiated entities interacting with their environments and organizing these interactions in a variety of constantly changing ways. From the perspective of Deleuze's constructivism, our experiences should be seen as the products or effects of the intersection of different historical, cultural, and political conditions. In other words, experience is always actualized in specific *experiences*, in practical modes of activity grounded in some concrete circumstance, environment or situation.[17] It is for this reason that Deleuze claims that "the only possible theory" to be found throughout all of Hume's work "is a theory of practice" (*ES* 32).

One of the most provocative conclusions to emerge from Deleuze's exposition of Hume's practical philosophy concerns the status of relations. According to Deleuze, Hume created "the first great logic of relations" (*ES* x). In his view, Hume's philosophy constitutes the apex of early-modern British empiricism. Yet Deleuze maintains that there is also something more to Hume, "something very strange," he says, "which completely displaces empiricism" (*D* 15). Deleuze notes that it is a sign of Hume's genius to have conceived not only a theory of relations, but more importantly a "practice of relations," which offers empiricism a new and genuinely radical power (*D* 15). In fact, while Kant refers to Hume in the first *Critique* as a "geographer of human reason," Deleuze describes Hume as, on the contrary, a geographer of relations concerned with delineating their constitution and distributions within the world (*D* 56).[18] As mentioned above, because experience is seen as the effect of the convergence (or divergence) of various historical, cultural, and political conditions, Deleuze's concern is with the complex relatedness which constitutes experience as a kind of finite and flexible network of diverse environments. It is for this reason that relations display for Deleuze such potential for an account of the interactive constitution of the world. Yet what does Deleuze mean by the word relation, and how does he utilize Hume in this respect?

There are three characteristics of relations that are important for Deleuze: their exteriority, their nonreducibility to their terms, and their role as effects of human practice. These characteristics arise on the basis of Hume's belief that "association presupposes projects, goals, intentions, occasions, an entire practical life and affectivity" (*ES* 120). With respect to the first characteristic, Deleuze claims that Hume discovered the exteriority of relations by way of his critique of metaphysical essentialism. Generally, the problem here is that of the supposed derivation of internal relations from the fixed essences of things. As discussed in the previous section, internal relations are those believed to be grounded in the nonempirical essences of the related terms. In this view, a term's relations to other terms are grounded in what that term essentially is; the relations follow from its essence. It is in this sense that relations are defined as internal or intrinsic to the being of their terms, that is, grounded in the essence of the things which possess them (*ES* 109).

This suggests, for instance, that given the relation of a cup upon a table, the cup's being related to the table is grounded in the essence of the cup, and the table's being related to the cup is grounded in the essence of the table. The cup's being internally related to the table not only follows from the nature of the cup, but the table's being internally related to the cup in turn follows from the nature of the table. It is assumed that there is something "in" the terms that produces the relation and which each term has *qua* being in that relation. The cup must be related to the table and the table to the cup as required by the essence of each. This certainly implies that a term's relations cannot be altered without also changing the essence of the terms, in other words, the cup cannot be placed under the table or removed from it without somehow changing the essences of the cup and the table. It is difficult to see how the alteration of relations can occur, however, if one accepts the essentialist thesis, for if relations are grounded in the natures of their terms and these natures are unalterable then the relations must remain as determined by their terms. It is only a short step from here to the ontological position that everything is connected to everything else in an inextricable and necessary fashion, and that this absolute monism transcends the plurality and diversity of the world of empirical experience.

One of the most significant points of *Empiricism and Subjectivity* is to show that this notion of internal relations is a betrayal of actual experience and a denigration of the richness and diversity of the life of the world. For Deleuze "the truly fundamental proposition" and the theme common to all forms of radical empiricism is that relations "are external to their terms" (*ES* 98–99).[19] This proposition becomes the basic criterion for empiricism, and Deleuze calls "'nonempiricist' every theory according to which, *in one way or another*, relations are derived from the nature of things" (*ES* 109). Deleuze thus articulates an empiricist conception of relations not only to counter the totalizing tendencies of the essentialist-internalist theory, but also to offer an account of relations that accords them a positive role in the creation of different modes of existence.

In Deleuze's account, empiricists recognize two problems with the theory of internal relations, which are countered by the second characteristic of the nonreducibility of external relations. First, if each internal relation is held to inhere necessarily in its term and is reducible to the term's essence, then there is nothing to distinguish the term from the relation. The relation simply forms an "extension" of the term itself, and its own particularity cannot be discerned. Second, in order for change to occur not only must the relation change, but the terms themselves must change as well, since the relation and the terms are inseparable by nature. The first problem presents a danger in the form of a totalizing image of the world, an organic unity or monistic Absolute that sacrifices relations, individuals, and difference in favor of a closed system that transcends the empirical and pluralist status of all three. The second problem is a consequence of the absolutism implied by the first, namely, that any alteration of a relation must be accompanied by a corresponding alteration in its terms. Deleuze sees this requirement as an attempt to neutralize or limit the fundamental multiplicity of experience, in that the relation must always remain identified with, and therefore reducible to, its term(s): Any alteration on the part of one is met with an equal alteration on the part of the other, such that a thing's essence and its properties maintain a constant identity or generalized equilibrium. In short, the conception of each part, term and relation as having an identity bound up with the Absolute, points to an essential unity that transcends and governs its constitutive parts. Consequently, the purpose of Deleuze's critique is to demonstrate that the theory of internal relations actually prohibits the possibility of conceiving change by positing an Absolute which is homeostatic in nature. Such an Absolute would leave us a world devoid of real difference. To ignore the pluralistic form of the world strikes Deleuze as incomprehensible and is contrary to the point of view of empiricism:

> Empiricism begins from the experience of a collection, or from an animated succession of distinct perceptions. . . . In fact, its principle, that is, the constitutive principle giving a status to experience, is not that "every idea derives from an impression" whose sense is only regulative; but rather that "everything separable is distinguishable and everything distinguishable is different." This is the principle of difference. (*ES* 87)[20]

The principle of difference indicates that the mind cannot perceive an intrinsic connection (in the sense that has been defined here) between distinct perceptions and cannot reveal the supposedly inherent essence of any terms.

Association can realize, then, only external connections or relations that do not belong to the fixed essences of the terms being related. Deleuze's point is that nothing *in the terms themselves* can cause the mind to establish necessary and unalterable relations. Because the terms are not in themselves bearers of essential connections to other objects there is no reason to remove relations from the flux and diversity of experience. The empirical principle of difference does not signal a return to simple atomism on Deleuze's part but instead indicates that the collective aspects of experience, its differential unities or what Deleuze means by multiplicities, represent types of experience whose transitive or relational features constitute an immanent and living continuity of qualitative difference. Experience is not of one simple bit of sense-data followed by another noninteracting bit, but of a teeming multiplicity of things and relations that constantly associate and interact. Experience is of complex unities which are organized in innumerable ways, although never organized absolutely into a single totality, and are held together by means of external relations. This view is also expressed in Deleuze and Guattari's initial work, *Anti-Oedipus*, when they pose the question, "how to think about fragments whose sole relationship is sheer difference—fragments that are related to one another only in that each of them is different—without having recourse either to any sort of original totality (not even one that has been lost), or to a subsequent totality that may not yet have come about?"[21]

As we have consistently seen, difference does not refer to opposition or exclusion but to the perspective that the world of experience is irreducibly multiple in its continuous flux. Our experiences are of distinctive relational complexes and not isolated simples. This position echoes the pluralism of James' radical empiricism: "The world is a pluralism; as we find it, its unity seems to be that of any collection."[22] If we understand unity on the basis of such collections, then unity should be viewed not as an issue of identity, but rather of difference. Constructing a unity presupposes difference (in Deleuze's nonoppositional sense) and external relations, which leaves it open to transformation. A unity based on a fixed essence and necessary relations is no unity at all, but is instead a monolithic edifice which excludes that which does not "properly" belong to it. For the radical empiricist, the world is best understood as a complex network of pluralistic collections or compositions, since some parts of it are related and some are not, or are related only indirectly through a network of intermediary relationships. The view of unity put forth by a radical empiricism is the dissolution of a single absolute Unity into a diffuse network of differential unities or multiplicities that are incomplete, partial, and continuously transforming. Unities of this sort will be the products of dynamic processes of construction which are pluralistic. Multiplicities refer to no other unity than that which they possess and which is open and always in the process of changing.

How, then, are the relations between terms to be established? Deleuze explains that it is the historically contingent "circumstances, actions, and passions" of life which provide for the specific invention and alteration of relations between different terms (*D* 56). Deleuze claims that the relations of experience as well as its parts or terms are endowed with a positive reality because relations are not derivative extensions of the essences of the terms being related, a view James also maintained. Deleuze emphasizes that relations "are not doing the connecting, but rather *they themselves are connected*" (*ES* 26; my emphasis). This is an important point. To the question "How do relations connect things?" essentialism (or foundationalism) has traditionally responded by postulating some type of transcendent ground that both supports the relation and determines its status as a necessary link. For instance, if two terms A and B are joined by relation C, the relation must be thought of as forming some intrinsic part of the terms being related, such that B and C are necessary for the existence of A, A and C for the existence of B, and A and B for the existence of C. The relation C is doing the connecting, then, only because it belongs intrinsically to both A and B; there is, in effect, no other possibility. Neither the terms nor the relation can be considered to be independent or even different in any positive sense, since the relation in question is simply in the terms as something *which is to be found there already*, that is, the relation derives from some sort of essence of these terms. In the end, the complete dependence characteristic of internal relations always presupposes an underlying Absolute that is itself transcendent to the horizon of experience or plane of immanence. But what if the Absolute were unnecessary to explain the connection, or disconnection, of things? Might we not explain relationships as real products of a pluralistic world of thought and action, of becoming rather than Being?

For the radical empiricist, the world is dynamic, partial—that is, it cannot be completely unified all at once—and constantly changing. It is because relations are external to their terms that relations between things may change and things may enter into new relations. The world enters into our experience in this way, indeed constitutes the diversity of the real conditions of experience. We experience the pluralism of the world within ourselves and we continually act upon, invent, and create new versions of existence out of this multiplicity. This brings us to the third characteristic of external relations important for a radical empiricism: External relations are mobile and diverse elements of experience and for this reason they assume a vital role as effects of human practices, habits, and purposes. Relations, Deleuze tells us, are "the means of an activity," they allow us to do and make different things (*ES* 120). Empiricism assigns relations to practice because they make creation possible. Deleuze gives external relations the same status James had given them when he called them "practically workable." Because relations are neither dependent upon nor determined by their terms in an absolute sense, they may be constituted between terms and changed by a variety of actions without affecting the terms themselves. There is no necessary connection or absolute unity to be maintained beyond those relations that are actually established.

In this sense relations fulfill the practical purpose of constructing associations needed for the realization of actions and thoughts, from the functional to the ethical and the aesthetic. Hence Deleuze's assertion that empiricism's theoretical content is devoted to the possibility of practice. I also take this to indicate that all different kinds of experience should not be treated as variations on one supposedly basic and superior type of logical cognitive experience for which "knowing" is opposed to "doing," and that this is why Hume should be read first as a social, historical, and political philosopher rather than as an epistemologist. Deleuze reinforces this position when he writes that "knowledge is not the most important thing for empiricism, but only the means to some practical activity" (*ES* 107).

It is important to note that Deleuze is not denying the interrelatedness of things, although he is challenging the fundamental ontological assumptions of the theory of internal relations. This occurs in several ways. First, as we have seen, Deleuze resists subordinating relations to the essence of things by insisting on the exteriority of relations. This does not mean that relations do not exist between terms, only that they come into existence by actual rather than transempirical means. Furthermore, when the relations between terms are altered there is no requirement that the terms themselves must change, at least "in essence." As mentioned earlier, for the radical empiricist "nature" (or "essence") is context dependent, and is always immanent and situated. It refers to the commonly preferred possibilities, uses, functions, or modes of interaction a thing has with respect to the interests, passions, and actions given in some situation, not to something "more real" and "certain" that is "behind" the immanent world of experience. In other words, reference to the nature of something cannot be made apart from such phenomena as practical activity and evaluation, which are always open or at least susceptible to different possibilities and recontextualizations in relation to the social and physical environments in which they are manifested. This provides a certain freedom to the relational realm which effectively counters any move toward attributing absolute status to an internally-related and closed system.

Second, Deleuze rejects the notion of an all-inclusive totality that transcends the empirical world. Relations lose all practical relevance when they are subordinated to this totality, for in that case the only relations possible are those that inherently tend toward the consolidation of the Absolute. Deleuze explains that real relations are effects of the activities and practices of individuals who are different yet nevertheless interacting. These interactions do not occur within a single comprehensive unity, but take place within diverse social, historical, and political contexts and give rise to qualitatively changing, open systems or unities which may overlap or intersect at certain points.[23] Deleuze thus contrasts a fixed Absolute that transcends its parts to a series of partial or limited wholes that form the immanent and open network of the world.

For Deleuze, our world is composed of open systems produced by social practices, practices which constitute and alter the relations of these unities and thereby the quality of the unities themselves. Deleuze thus promotes a kind of pluralistic contextualism, or in James' terms a mosaic holism, in the sense that relations and their terms combine in any number of ways to form open systems that have a distinct complexion or quality depending upon the particular conditions and contexts of their formation. Such unities are susceptible to change by bringing different elements into relation or by taking other elements out of relation. These elements themselves do not change "in essence" with the alteration of their relations, but are given a qualitatively different context. Because relations do not intrinsically belong to their terms, their composition and alteration does not transform the natures of the terms, instead, the relational unities are qualitatively changed. In other words, as relations are created or altered between terms the unities within which these terms are related change as well, in such a manner that the elements of these kinds of multiplicities are continually becoming something qualitatively new.[24] If we consider our previous example we can see that it would be possible to alter the relation between the cup and the table because the relation is not grounded in any essence and is irreducible to its terms. What is altered is the relationship *between* the two terms. The unity formed by this relationship can be qualitatively changed without affecting the supposed essence of the terms. This way of thinking about relationships allows them to be conceived in such a way as to refuse or resist their subordination to any nonempirical foundation while emphasizing their "practically workable" character, the practical here referring, as it has throughout, to any number of activities including, but not limited to, the aesthetic, moral, scientific, and political. While any particular relational unity is too complex to be simply reduced to its parts, neither can it be elevated to the status of a transcendent Absolute. As James had remarked, there is no "transempirical" foundation or bedding "behind" relations and the open systems that they form.

Accordingly, empiricists are not concerned with determining the essence and intrinsic relation of each thing within a single all-encompassing totality, but with describing how new relations can be actively created between things relative to a specific context in order to produce change in and between the complex unities these relationships form.[25] In this way, relations can be said to be true of things in an external rather than intrinsically necessary way. The processes of creating new relations or altering previously established ones and the effects produced by these transformations assume primacy for radical empiricism. Relations are to be evaluated by their consequences in experience, not by their conformity to an original essence. Radical empiricism's theory and practice of relations therefore supersedes rationalism's and idealism's schemas of fixed and stable essences. For Deleuze the world is thoroughly relational, yet relations are not merely given by a deterministic framework. The world is composed of interconnected yet different open systems whose relational qualities constantly mutate and exceed our attempts to assign them a final order or an absolute configuration.

Deleuze's account stresses the pluralistic manner in which each part of the world is in some way connected and in other ways not; no necessary connection holds throughout all experiences or aspects of the world.[26] It is true that unifying factors are at always at work in that various types of experiences, hitherto unrelated, are conjoined as new philosophical, ethical, scientific, aesthetic, and political perspectives create or actualize new connections. New experiences continually transform earlier experiences. Yet the types of unity engendered will vary with the context, since each context is itself constituted by specific modes of activity, particular interests, temporal sequences, and concrete circumstances. As a consequence, a unity must be considered as always "in process," never absolute, closed, or finished. This brings Deleuze to write that what is most important for such a pluralism "are not the terms or the elements" of experience taken in isolation, "but what there is 'between'," the relations between the terms or elements (*D* viii). In this way he endeavors to show that experience is of neither absolute unity nor indifferent atomism, but always something in between, as long as this "in between" is seen in terms of incessant movement rather than dialectical mediation. Experience consists of particular unities of difference and particular differences of unity in processes of becoming and transformation. And this conviction leads Deleuze to a radical empiricism, a philosophy of relations and compositions inspired by the visions of immanence found in Hume, Bergson, Nietzsche, and Spinoza. Here the *changing relations and conditions* of actual experience are found together in specific combinations. Thus, the types of unities described by Deleuze are best understood as multiplicities that are continuously composed in the fluid transitions characteristic of processes of becoming. Such transitions are dependent upon difference and therefore are not reducible to the containment of any totality.

Deleuze's affirmation of the exteriority of relations, and his argument that they are the selective and interpretive means by which we create and structure different worlds through our practical activity are based in his reading of Hume's empiricism. Although he and James have a somewhat different evaluation of Hume's efforts, they arrive at a remarkably similar conclusion regarding the importance of relations for a *radicalized* empiricism. In order to illustrate and further develop what I have said so far about Deleuze's conception of relations, I wish to explore some of the ways this conception has been put to work in his later writings and in so doing demonstrate how Deleuze is able to augment and advance a version of radical empiricism by means of his "rhizomatic" philosophy.

Radical Empiricism and Rhizomatics

On the one hand, we have seen that essentialist foundationalism and the paradigm of internal relations leads in the direction of absolutism and totalization, the subordination of real and distinct relations and terms to transcendent principles or foundations, and the inability to account for the possibility of real change in the face of the absolute unification of experience. On the other hand, radical empiricism and the theory and practice of external relations has been shown to promote not only a healthy relativism and pluralism but also action, with respect to the practical possibilities of creating new types of association. Perhaps the most innovative use Deleuze finds for his adherence to the exteriority of relations is the concept of the rhizome he develops with Félix Guattari in *A Thousand Plateaus*.[27]

Deleuze and Guattari draw inspiration from the botanical rhizome, the subterranean plant stem that constantly produces new shoots and rootlets. However, they in no way feel constrained to restrict their use of the rhizome to the botanical level, rather, Deleuze and Guattari create a full-blown constructivism of multiplicity: "To attain the multiple, one must have a method that effectively constructs it" (*ATP* 22). Their constructivism can be understood as involving a type of creative associationism that uses the concept of the rhizome as a practical contrast to the hierarchical schema of arborescent structures, and is congenial to a variety of theoretical, social, cultural, and political concerns.[28] Such arboreal or vertical tree-like structures are found within the narrowly rationalist forms of Western epistemology and ontology which organize knowledge according to essentialized, centralized, internalized, polarized, and codified systems of representation that are held to reproduce or mirror a transcendent foundation. The rhizome, on the contrary, is a horizontal and immanent assemblage of external relations open to the productive continuum of the world, and is to be distinguished from the arboreal scheme by six characteristics.

Appropriately, the first two characteristics of the rhizome concern principles "of connection and heterogeneity," according to which "any point of a rhizome can be connected to anything other, and must be" (*ATP* 7). As is evident from the previous section on Deleuze's reading of Hume, the rhizome is placed immediately within Deleuze's position on the exteriority and mobility of relations. The rhizome is defined by its ability to continually establish "connections between semiotic chains, organizations of power, and circumstances relative to the arts, sciences, and social sciences" (*ATP* 7). It is conceived in light of the diverse relations established between variable and multiple terms, both discursive and nondiscursive. Yet rhizomatic relations are not internal, in that they are not derived from self-enclosed essentialist totalities, but external, because they are the effects of practices which associate terms according to specific conditions, contexts, and circumstances. Although always external to their terms, relations are nevertheless enveloped, that is, immanent, within these empirical contexts. On the basis of these particular interactions, rhizomatic relations produce open systems that cannot be self-enclosed. Thus, Deleuze and Guattari argue that there is no such thing as a formal essence or thing in itself, but instead that there are temporary stabilizations of linguistic, perceptive, gestural, environmental, and political components that are assembled in a diverse number of ways (*ATP* 7). These aggregations of functions and qualities are also referred to by Deleuze and Guattari as "vague essences" (*ATP* 367, 407–08). Vague or "fuzzy" essences should be understood in the same sense as the "natures" of things that were discussed in the previous sections, that is, not as fixed, ideal, and formal essences that determine the derivative uses and relations of things but instead as pragmatic and selective interpretations that are themselves the effects of certain circumstances, projects, and activities for which relations are the determinants.

The third characteristic of the rhizome is multiplicity, which Deleuze and Guattari treat as a substantive: It is actual without being a derivation or attribution of some Absolute. A multiplicity is a rhizome in that it is composed of different terms and external relations irreducible to those terms. Multiplicities change their dimensions and magnitudes by altering or expanding their relations, thereby bringing about a qualitative change of the relational rhizome itself. This qualitative transformation of the multiplicity or rhizome is referred to as an assemblage: "An assemblage is precisely this increase in the dimensions of a multiplicity that necessarily changes in nature as it expands its connections" (*ATP* 8).[29] An assemblage is the product of some multiplicities being related to other multiplicities, a collection of multiplicities or rhizomes related on the basis of some particular mode of construction (*ATP* 34). The rhizome, of course, does not possess a formal essence that determines and fixes its relations. Instead, its quality is made up of the interplay of those practically workable relations which compose it, as these connections are altered or new connections are made the multiplicity effectively assumes a new or different quality. The quality of the rhizomatic multiplicity is seen as the effect of the cofunctioning of heterogeneous elements in a fluid unity or arrangement (*D* 69–70). As proposed by Deleuze, external relations are rhizomatic "lines" of becoming that constantly pass or flow between the different complex components (rhizome/multiplicity) of an assemblage, making the assemblage a kind of compositional, open-ended unity (*D* vii–viii).

This lends the rhizome its fourth characteristic, that of the "asignifying rupture" (*ATP* 9). The rhizome, as an open system composed of external relations and heterogeneous elements, is constantly mutating, shifting, and reforming itself on the basis of its multidirectionality. It pursues one line at one moment, a different line at another moment. Deleuze and Guattari also refer to these processes as territorialization, deterritorialization, and reterritorialization, that is, the qualitative transformations of complex assemblages on the basis of proliferating relations between heterogeneous terms. Every assemblage is characterized by the process of constituting a "territory" that holds together distinct or heterogeneous elements, which is simultaneously a movement of deterritorialization or the transformation of the assemblage's previous relational quality, and reterritorialization or the passage from one kind of territorial assemblage to another. It follows that none of these movements can be isolated as the original moment of the process, for they continually pass into one another. The rhizome does not change simply because new terms are brought into play, but because different relations are made to flow between the terms, mutating the relationship as a whole. The rhizome remains although its quality "can no longer be attributed to or subjugated by anything signifying" (*ATP* 10). The rhizomatic assemblage does not resemble, reproduce, or represent any grounding essence that would determine it in terms of correspondence. This is because the quality of the rhizome is engendered in the relational interaction of its elements and forms of expression, which change as the rhizome itself is transformed.

According to Deleuze and Guattari the rhizome is defined also by, fifth, a pragmatic cartography or the active formation of maps of relations and, sixth, a contrast to representational decalcomania, which is the static imitative function of tracing and reproducing images from an originary design. Since the rhizome is foreign to any structural or generative model, it cannot be represented in the form of an infinitely reproducible tracing. Maps, on the other hand, are constructed by means of actual rhizomatic connections, depending on the circumstances and interests at work. Because it is itself rhizomatic, the map "is open and connectable in all of its dimensions; it is detachable, reversible, susceptible to constant modification" (*ATP* 12). In short, "one of the most important characteristics of the rhizome is that it always has multiple entryways," which allows all its other characteristics to flourish (*ATP* 12). What is most important is for the rhizome to be conceived as productively operating within diverse fields of activity and different types of social practices, shaped by and informing those fields and practices. At all points, insist Deleuze and Guattari, rhizomatic multiplicity "*must be made*" (*ATP* 6). It does not simply occur by grace of supernatural or transempirical generation; it is to be created by actual productive processes, whether they be philosophic, scientific, aesthetic, or political.[30]

Because the relations of a rhizomatic multiplicity are immediately interactive, heterogeneous, and variable they are not to be understood as successive derivations of a teleological evolutionary descent that progresses from the least to the most differentiated of terms within an encompassing order of identity. Rhizomes do not evolve from an original essence (model) by means of filiation or correspondence, that is, genetic representation. Instead, rhizomes are anomalous becomings produced by the formation of transversal alliances between different and coexisting terms within an open system (*ATP* 10, 237). Becomings involve relations of a communicable nature, akin to flourishing contagion, that cannot be reduced to relations of strict correspondence. For these reasons, rhizomatic becoming "lacks a subject distinct from itself," a fixed term that marks its point of completion, since the subject is nothing other than the becoming itself, a multiplicity (*ATP* 238). The importance of external relations in this context is vital, for the multiplicity and becoming conceived by Deleuze and Guattari would be rendered completely ineffectual from the point of view of internal relations. Internal relations can only be thought of as secondary derivations from the essential identities of terms, whereas external relations are necessary for the active creation of symbiotic alliances that pass between terms and thus for the composition of open systems (assemblages) that are capable of transformation. Becoming occurs through those in-between spaces that external relations traverse within multiplicities.

This last point may be further considered from Deleuze and Guattari's concepts of the majoritarian and minoritarian, viewing the former from the perspective of internal relations and the latter from that of external relations. In addition to the relational characteristics of these two concepts, Deleuze and Guattari's use of majority and minority are also meant to express the practical and political dimensions of the concomitant notions of molarity and molecularity. The majoritarian functions by confining its subject, defining it as a rigid molar entity formed of privileged oppositional essences or terms intrinsically related to invariable functions, meanings, and identities. The objective of the molar or majoritarian is to remain the same, to remain above or outside becoming, by excluding qualitative transformations in favor of numerical identity, literally, the "majority" which supposedly represents the interests of "all."[31] The molecular, on the contrary, corresponds to processes of becoming-other or qualitative transformations of rhizomatic relationalities. Here, the collective coexistence of heterogeneous elements is made possible by the fluidity of the relations that pass between them.

Deleuze and Guattari explain that all becomings are molecular "because becoming is not to imitate or identify with something or someone," but instead to "enter into composition with *something else*" by means of different relations simultaneously passing between molecular elements; it is to be deterritorialized (*ATP* 272, 274). Molecular becomings thus constitute practices that challenge molar and arboreal systems: "Becoming-minoritarian is a political affair and necessitates a labor of power, an active micropolitics" (*ATP* 292). Micropolitics does not work to institute large, encompassing systems and centralized powers, nor is it based on the notion of an intrinsic identity between the subject and the State. It is instead concerned with a diversity of collective assemblages, with specific relational systems that remain open, and which seek to find new ways of organizing their interactions and drawing connections in virtue of, and not in spite of, their diversity. This is a kind of anarchistic composition of unities, as distinct from the all-encompassing unity of Absolutism: "anarchy and unity are one and the same thing, not the unity of the One, but a much stranger unity that applies only to the multiple" (*ATP* 158). Deleuze's notion of micropolitics, even if not directly influenced by the thought of James, bears a striking resemblance to the anarchist position claimed by James as his own political perspective:

> I am against bigness and greatness in all their forms, and with the invisible molecular moral forces that work from individual to individual, stealing in through the crannies of the world like so many soft rootlets, or like the capillary oozing of water, and yet rending the hardest monuments of man's pride, if you give them time. The bigger the unit you deal with, the hollower, the more brutal, the more mendacious is the life displayed.[32]

The lessons of Deleuze's rhizomatic account of minoritarian practice and becoming that he develops with Guattari are utilized in their analysis of Kafka's writings and what they refer to as minor literature. Again, minor is not a quantitative but a qualitative distinction, and in this case refers to the revolutionary potential of all linguistic practices that challenge the dominance of the binary form of linguistic interpretation by proliferating relations and connections between expression and content. Minor literature comprises a practice of rhizomatic experimentation by mixing asignifying ruptures and intensive utilizations of language in order to create assemblages of acts and statements. Deleuze and Guattari explain that the three characteristics of minor literature "are the deterritorialization of language, the connection of the individual to a political immediacy, and the collective assemblage of enunciation."[33] Minor literature, as an "expression machine" that unexpectedly mixes expression and content in a single intense matter, leaks around the structural or organic correspondence of content and expression that major literature and languages depend upon for their coherence and conformity; it expresses the relational tensions of a language that is in fact infiltrated by multiple languages. At this point, minor literature develops uses of language in such a way that it *"stops being representative in order to move toward its extremities or its limits."*[34] Moving toward these limits is an effect of diverse linguistic practices "which simultaneously combine fluxes of expression and fluxes of content" (*D* 116–17).

The point is not that the minor and the major are two different types of language, but that they are two different *uses* of language: The former invents becomings of language by means of the transformation of relations between linguistic and nonlinguistic (affects, passions, desires, bodily habits, gestures, instruments, rituals) elements within experience; the latter seeks objective constants, universals, and reducible relations according to transcendent principles that determine the supposedly necessary and transempirical conditions of all possible experience while remaining outside it (see *ATP* 101, 106). As Deleuze and Guattari point out, the preference attributed to essentialist or foundationalist principles and standards has often been used for the justification of coercive political authority and majoritarian uses of language.35 Deleuze and Guattari's theory of minor language is thus critically directed at the idea of a universal semiology based on essential dualisms or dichotomies. Their empiricist insistence on the importance of specific social contexts and formations of languages undercuts the attempt to erect an abstract and homogeneous linguistic system that has the purpose of explaining contingent and variable formations on the basis of its universal principles. Central to Deleuze and Guattari's theory is their belief that all languages "are in immanent continuous variation: neither synchrony nor diachrony, but asynchrony, chromaticism [i.e., transformation produced by qualitative differences] as a variable and continuous state of language" (*ATP* 97).

Such variations are the result of placing linguistic elements into different relations, which can be done because the relation between content and expression is not that of an inferred causal infrastructure but instead the effect of a specific productive cause; it is a molecular and rhizomatic becoming, producing assemblages of enunciation, rather than a molar and arboreal evolution. Deleuze suggests that we view the majoritarian/molar in terms of its historical insistence on the verb "to be," and the minoritarian/molecular in terms of the conjunction "and" (*ATP* 25, 98–99). On the one hand, "is" serves as the expression of an absolute foundation, the essential, unchanging ground underlying and transcending the world of experience: A is A, B is B. On the other hand, "and" functions as a conjunctive relation that moves between terms and expresses the continual transformation of actual associations within concrete circumstances; "and" challenges limits and constantly moves elsewhere: A and B and C and D and so forth. As James had remarked, "The word 'and' trails after every sentence." The trailing "and" is thus the primary means for effectuating a minoritarian use of language.36 Essentialism of the majoritarian type utilizes "is" in order to fix rigid boundaries to its form of unity and approves of relationships that are accepted as properly belonging to it only on that basis. Pluralism of the minoritarian kind makes use of "and" in order to form open and flexible compositions that need not be determined by some supposedly intrinsic essence. As Deleuze clarifies, "even if there are only two terms, there is an AND between the two, which is neither the one nor the other, nor the one that becomes the other, but which constitutes the multiplicity" (*D* 34–35).

Furthermore, language does not have the sole function of informing or communicating something that exists independent of one's actions, of representing the world in indicative sentences. On the contrary, language is a type of social practice whose meanings do not lie outside this practice; meaning is immanent in the act. Language consists in the emission, reception, and transmission of "order-words," which are defined by Deleuze and Guattari as "the relation of every word or every statement to implicit presuppositions, in other words, to speech acts . . . accomplished in the statement" (*ATP* 79). It is true that at this point Deleuze and Guattari claim that the relation between the statement and the act is internal, but by this they mean that the relation of one to the other is one of immanence and not one of identity. From the point of view of pragmatics, an action is accomplished "in" a statement, and a statement accomplishes an action, with respect to "the set of order-words, implicit propositions, or speech-acts current in a language at a given moment . . . in a given social field" (*ATP* 79). The immanent relation between the statement and the act constitute "statements-acts" assemblages, yet they do not correspond in any essentially referential manner: "Take as an example the statement 'I swear!' It is a different statement depending on whether it is said by a child to his or her father, by a man in love to his loved one, or by a witness before the court" (*ATP* 94).[37]

Deleuze and Guattari's concern here is to demonstrate that every statement is linked to an act in such a way that neither can be seen as an invariant form in a universal linguistic system. The relation is neither deduced from, nor contained by one of the terms; it is actively established within a given social field, between order-words, immanent actions, and the sense expressed by the statement (*ATP* 79, 83). Deleuze's point is that meaning cannot be confined to a representational model that posits an intrinsic relation from the supposed fixed and stable essence of the subject to its objects. The relations of words and things are not essential in that sense, but are the practical and social associations that are the expressions of diverse modes of existence and different points of view caught up in particular social contexts. Linguistic practices or speech-acts are assemblages that we create and occupy immanently from within which we make claims about the world and other linguistic practices (as well as our own), whether minoritarian or majoritarian. Since the relations of such assemblages are thoroughly practical in character, pragmatics (semiotic and political) becomes the very presupposition of transformational language use. This is because pragmatics defines "the effectuation of the *condition of possibility* of language and the *usage* of linguistic elements" (*ATP* 85).[38] As is to be expected, pragmatics can therefore be associated with neither universal structural organization nor metaphysical grounding, but with the flux of the rhizome and micropolitics.

The pragmatic emphasis on the construction of multiplicities and assemblages points to the novel and contextual nature of experience. As we have seen, Deleuze's pluralism is meant to signify that the world resists all attempts at complete unification, whether by a single principle or an absolutely unified system. For Deleuze, experience means a process of continuous interaction of relations and terms from which emerge a variety of assemblages within any particular context, circumstance, or perspective. The particular perspective, context, or situation discloses or allows for certain relations rather than others, allowing different assemblages to come into play. Different experiences may be sorted and articulated according to the types of interrelationships into which they enter. Thus, relations are both created anew and are given on the basis of previous experiences; although those that are given are themselves products of previous productive activities. This interactive process is at the basis of the making of multiplicities.

It is clear that the theory and practice of relations which Deleuze formulates on the basis of Hume's philosophy is central to his later rhizomatic constructivism. By linking the empirical givenness and transformation of relations with direct involvement and activity, Deleuze seeks to overcome the often presumed static opposition of theory and practice. If the world as we experience it is constantly changing, revealing all the while more dimensions than can be grasped at once, then the abundance of relations given in experience can be admitted without thereby dictating the realization of any specific assemblage that is somehow beyond the reach of transformative practices. The malleability of experience leads Deleuze to contend that the task of philosophy is to diagnose and evaluate the ways that we construct our world in order to postulate and create new types of association and interaction. We can take this to mean that philosophy is the practice of constructing relations when it addresses the issue of inventing modes of thinking and feeling that have yet to be conceptualized.

It would seem that Deleuze also characterizes his philosophy as an empiricism in order to emphasize the experimental nature of our experiences and the hypothetical character of our organizations or compositions of these experiences: "To think is to experiment, but experimentation is always that which is in the process of coming about" (*WP* 111). The compositions of experience are not governed by an intrinsic connectedness but by a differential relationality, which prevents them from being reduced to the terms of which they are constituted or from being identified with transcendent principles or a transcendent foundation. For Deleuze, there is nothing which has only one component, but neither can the unities of this associationism be considered as complete and closed, nor as subsumed under a totalizing Absolute.

From this perspective, what concerns Deleuze is not the project of identifying fixed essences or necessary relations, but rather the ability empiricism has to reveal the social, historical, and political character of relations that have been established and that continue to be established, altered, or abandoned. This radicalized empiricism makes it possible to conceive of a productive practice of relations whose importance consists in qualitatively transforming existent differential unities (assemblages) by remaining open to that which is external to them.

Through his theory and practice of relations, Deleuze provides a means for thinking of alternative ways of inhabiting our world, without having recourse to absolutes that would predetermine our interrelationships and interactions or provide the indubitable standard by which to judge them.[39] In this manner, Deleuze's account of relations moves from the ontological to the ethical and the political by focusing on the inseparability of relations and practices, on the complex interaction of the diverse elements of our experiences, on the types of relations our society either maintains or destroys, and on the actual effects and consequences of these interactions. For Deleuze ours is a world continually "under construction," for which relations have a tremendous relevance.

Deleuze's empiricism, then, is a philosophy of experiences, provided that we understand this to mean not that Deleuze offers an abstract definition of experience *per se*, but rather that his philosophy is an explorational exercise directed toward expanding and enriching the diversity of potential and actual experiences. For Deleuze, empiricism holds a special affinity for life since it strives to be attuned to the becoming of experience. One of the most important ways that this is accomplished is by emphasizing that relations can be viewed as practical and transformative "tools" or means for the improvement and appreciation of the quality of life.[40] Deleuze's constructive philosophy of experiences can therefore be regarded as a kind of experimentalism that seeks to invent "new immanent modes of existence" (*WP* 113). The ontological commitments of Deleuze's empiricism, as we have encountered them in this and in the two previous chapters, include holding to the experiential reality of difference, repetition, immanence, and relations. All of these commitments lead Deleuze to reject essentialism, foundationalism, absolutism, and any supernaturalistic explanation of the world. From this it can be concluded that some sort of naturalism is another ontological commitment of Deleuze's empiricism. Yet the question remains as to how to conceive a naturalism that is consistent with Deleuze's other commitments. It is this topic to which I turn in the next chapter.

Chapter 4

From Naturalism to Ecological Politics

Perhaps the juxtaposition of Deleuze and naturalism seems, at least on the face of it, somewhat enigmatic. The term "naturalism" is rarely, if ever, encountered in the writings of French poststructuralists, and even then most likely appears only as an object of hostile interest. This is the result of naturalism being taken as an equivalent to essentialism, understood as referring to predetermined orders of "natures." Consider, for instance, the following remarks of Michel Foucault in response to the question of whether his later works exhibit a "break" with the naturalism of his earlier works: "What you call naturalism refers, I believe, to two things. A certain theory, the idea that under power with its acts of violence and artifice, we should be able to rediscover the things themselves in their primitive vivacity. . . . And also a certain aesthetic and moral choice: power is bad, ugly, poor, sterile, monotonous and dead; and what power is exercised upon is right, good, and rich."[1]

On this definition naturalism is a theory which holds not only that there is a dualism of absolute essence and incidental appearance, but also that what is essential is intrinsically more valuable morally and aesthetically. However, Deleuze proves to be a significant exception to this general attitude toward naturalism. He not only incorporates discussions of naturalism within the contexts of his many analyses of historical figures, but he also develops a philosophical perspective that, at least implicitly, forwards a version of naturalism compatible with the critiques of essentialism and dualism addressed in the previous chapters. While Deleuze has not offered a systematic account of naturalism, one of the aims of this chapter is to draw together some of the threads of naturalism woven into Deleuze's texts in order to demonstrate how he goes about rethinking this topic.

Another purpose of this chapter, in keeping with one of the central aspects of Deleuze's thought touched upon throughout this book, is practical. I consider environmental ethics and political ecology to be two of the most important arenas in which Deleuze's naturalistic empiricism can be utilized. While poststructuralists such as Foucault and Jean-Francois Lyotard have been concerned with examining social relationships of power or narrative pragmatics, eschewing what they consider to be problematic discourses employing the terms nature or naturalism, Deleuze has taken a different line and actively embraced the question of nature in a variety of ways.[2] For Deleuze, we must not look at either society or nature, as if they were mutually exclusive, but at society *and* nature. As I hope to demonstrate, however, this is not a reintroduction of dualism or essentialism on Deleuze's part. He does not find an unchanging, original nature "behind" society, nor are society and nature opposed and hierarchically divided absolutes. It is my contention that Deleuze promotes a type of naturalism that highlights the immanent, historical interconnections between coextensive social and natural worlds, in such a way that he provides some philosophical resources for integrating ethical and political considerations with ecological concerns, while resisting the reductive temptation to turn nature into a static metaphysical foundation. And as I have mentioned throughout this work, Deleuze insists that philosophy be conceived as a practice whose usefulness derives from the active creation of new and different ways of thinking and feeling. Deleuze is ultimately concerned with the kinds of effects that philosophy is able to produce, insofar as these effects encourage the creation of new values and sensibilities in the affirmative constitution of life.

The overall aim of this chapter, then, is to describe how Deleuze's empiricism can be of assistance in thinking the intersection of the social, political, and philosophical with respect to the elaboration of an ecologically concerned ethical and political theory. This will be achieved in several ways. First, I will detail an alternative history of philosophical naturalism found in a number of Deleuze's works, clarifying the ontological and practical propositions contained in each version. Second, I will discuss Deleuze's notion of "geophilosophy," which he argues is intended to relate philosophical thinking to the earth. I will also explain how Deleuze's appeal to the field of ethology can be used in conjunction with the notion of geophilosophy in order to arrive at a Deleuzian radical naturalism. Finally, the concluding section of the chapter will clarify some of the ways that Deleuze's naturalist sensibilities and political concepts intersect with contemporary ecological politics. I argue here that Deleuze's work can help us to think how the concern with ecological destruction is a legitimate socio-political issue, and therefore that it is possible, indeed necessary, to find a role for nature on the terrain of ethical and political theory and action.

Deleuze on Naturalism in the History of Philosophy

One of the difficulties with discussing naturalism in the context of Deleuze's work is that naturalism has been so variously defined and employed throughout the history of philosophy that it is impossible to offer a single definition of the term. Some have understood naturalism to be a view that excludes any reference to supernatural or transcendent principles, beings, or entities, with possible consequences ranging from the belief that the world is explicable only in scientifically verifiable terms, to the assertion of some form of humanism or secularism. Others contend that naturalism is meant to indicate the continuity or unity of the human and nonhuman, and stress that human behavior and human institutions have their basis in natural phenomena such that there is no exclusive opposition between nature and society.[3] Although there are many possible versions of naturalism with differing points of emphasis ranging from the ontological to the epistemological and the methodological, I believe that Deleuze's take on naturalism can be seen as having the most affinity with contemporary strains of American naturalism, itself born from the dual influences of pragmatism and empiricism. While it is impossible here to offer a discussion of naturalism in twentieth-century American thought, what is relevant for our purpose is to note that American naturalism, influenced by such thinkers as Aristotle, Spinoza, and Darwin, argues that naturalism can be characterized as a perspective that seeks to eliminate the dualism and transcendentalism of traditional metaphysics, in favor of the view that humans and their cultures belong within a larger natural reality that cannot be overridden by any extranatural essence. In other words, this position denies that there is any independent supernatural realm having ontological priority over whatever there might be. This view is clearly in accord with Deleuze's empiricism as portrayed up to this point. It has a particular affinity, as well, with the radical empiricism of William James that was discussed in the previous chapter. What should now be examined are the defining features of naturalism as presented in Deleuze's own accounts.

In this section I will be taking a look at the various ways Deleuze approaches the issue of nature and naturalism in his writings. For the purposes of this section I will present Deleuze's comments in a fashion that corresponds not to the order of his works, but roughly to the history of philosophy. While I will briefly mention the ethical aspects Deleuze believes accompany these versions of naturalism, I will reserve a more extended discussion of ethics and naturalism for the following sections. With that in mind, we can look first, then, to Deleuze's relation to Plato and the Platonic tradition. As we have seen, this relation is quite complex and takes the form of a fundamental encounter within Deleuze's thought as a whole. However, the essays collected together and published as an appendix to *The Logic of Sense*, entitled "The Simulacrum and Ancient Philosophy," are useful as a means of entry to our topic.[4] In the essay "Plato and the Simulacrum," Deleuze's task is that of "reversing Platonism." This reversal is first defined as "the abolition of the world of essences *and* the world of appearances," that is, the elimination of the Platonic dualism that postulates a realm of metaphysical essences separate from and more real than the natural world itself, which is consigned to the status of mere appearance (*LS* 253). These themes have appeared repeatedly throughout our study.

Yet it is also important to point out the motive supporting the Platonic project: The dialectical method of division. As Deleuze sees it, the primary purpose of the Platonic method of division is not to divide a genus into contrary species, but "to distinguish the pure from the impure, the authentic from the inauthentic . . . the true pretender from the false one" (*LS* 254). How does it carry out this purpose? By uniting myth and dialectic into a foundational model "according to which different pretenders can be judged" (*LS* 255). On the Platonic model, only by providing absolute criteria of selection is it possible to determine which particular things, persons, or claims are the most adequate pretenders to the ideal Forms. Emanating from the "Unparticipated" Forms are graded hierarchies along which participants are ranked and judged according to whether they are true or false pretenders, that is, whether they are "true" copies or "false" copies of transcendent essences. "True" copies are well-founded appearances because of their resemblance and internal relation to the Forms or Ideas. "False" copies, on the contrary, are appearances built upon dissimilarity and insinuation, upon external relations and deviation, and are therefore without proper resemblance. These "false" copies or simulacra are the targets of the method of division and are singled out by Plato for repression. This has a paradoxical consequence, however, for in this manner Plato discovers "that the simulacrum is not simply a false copy, but that it places in question the very notations of copy and model" (*LS* 256). In other words, if all appearances are copies of transcendent essences or models, how can a "false" copy be accounted for unless there are also "false" Forms?

Because the simulacrum is built upon and contains difference, it cannot be defined simply as a resembling copy formed by an always self-identical model. For Plato, the simulacrum implies a constant transformation and deformation of points of view, a continuous becoming of difference which engulfs the observer. Platonism initiates the attempt to limit and master this becoming implied by simulacra, erecting a philosophical domain "of representation filled by copies-icons, and defined not by an extrinsic relation to an object, but by an intrinsic relation to the model or foundation" (*LS* 259). In the previous chapters we have encountered many of the consequences Deleuze sees as resulting from the legacy of Platonic representationalism. One of the most troublesome results has been the designation of an unconditioned Absolute, a pure transcendent Being, which circumscribes and rules the natural world of becoming and diversity. But the power of the simulacrum, insofar as it constantly unsettles and ungrounds all attempts to erect an essence-appearance or model-copy dualism, is that of conjoining the diversity of the natural world with its real conditions of immanent difference and disparity, not in a single, fixed center but in a continuous, inclusive process of becoming (*LS* 261–63).

"Reversing" Platonism can thus be regarded as a naturalistic strategy aimed at eliminating the dualism of essence and appearance, and affirming difference, repetition, immanence, external relations, and the continuous becoming of diversity. With this reversal unity ceases to be that of the Same, of an all-encompassing Absolute, and becomes instead the simultaneous coexistence of differences: It is the open system of multiplicities, and is neither completely given nor finalized. This naturalistic reversal begins by insisting that "the conditions of experience in general must become conditions of real experience," of actual, changing *experiences* whose conditions cease to be privileged as transcendent Platonic essences (*LS* 260). Real experiences are then no longer measured according to a model of resemblance, but are regarded as powerful movements of experimentation within an immanent natural world whose differential conditions they express (*LS* 260–61).

In addition to the sources we have already discussed, there is also a naturalistic tradition Deleuze draws upon in developing his empiricism. This tradition has its beginnings in the Epicureanism of Lucretius, who formulated the basic principles of naturalism as an anti-Platonic philosophy: "the positivity of Nature; Naturalism as the philosophy of affirmation; pluralism linked with multiple affirmation; sensualism connected with the joy of the diverse; and the practical critique of all mystifications" (*LS* 279).

In the second essay, "Lucretius and the Simulacrum," Deleuze pursues the line of thought which holds that a naturalism based on the changing conditions of real experience, and not a representationalism which withdraws from the empirical into a realm of formal structures, is the practical and speculative object of philosophy. Naturalism is, in this case, based on the presence of three intertwined aspects of natural or biological diversity: "the diversity of species; the diversity of individuals which are members of the same species; and the diversity of the parts which together compose an individual" (*LS* 266). All the elements of the natural world, the individuals, species, rivers, plants, and places which constitute, inhabit and traverse it, are inseparable from the real conditions of diversity. For Lucretius, nature is understood as a distributive rather than collective power; it is that which produces the diverse, yet it does not totalize the diverse into the transcendent One, Whole, or Being to which Platonic anti-naturalism aspires.

> The Epicurean thesis is entirely different: Nature as the production of the diverse can only be an infinite sum, that is, a sum which does not totalize its own elements. There is no combination capable of encompassing all the elements of Nature at once, there is no unique world or total universe. . . . Nature is not collective, but rather distributive, to the extent that the laws of Nature . . . distribute parts which cannot be totalized. Nature is not attributive, but rather conjunctive: it expresses itself through "and," and not through "is". . . . Being an addition of indivisibles, sometimes similar and sometimes different, Nature is indeed a sum, but not a whole. With Epicurus and Lucretius the real noble acts of philosophical pluralism begin. (*LS* 266–67)

Because nature is conjunctive and disjunctive, that is, differentially interrelated rather than unifying in any absolute sense, it produces itself through new combinations of its heterogeneous elements. Yet no single combination can encompass all the elements of nature at once. Rather, there are particular finite compositions of elements and relations produced in the continuous movements of becoming. In this respect naturalism can be equated with pluralism since Lucretius thinks of nature in terms of multiplicity, as a nontotalizable sum of diverse individuals, species, and environments.

The pluralistic naturalism of Lucretius is further expressed by two complementary points of view, which Deleuze refers to as the "speculative point of view" found in the atomic-physical theory of the *clinamen*, and the "practical" or "ethical" point of view manifested by a concern for pleasurable and joyful existence. The *clinamen* serves as "a highly structured principle of causality," which illustrates the productivity of nature without a totalization of its multiplicity (*LS* 268). The physics of Epicurian-Lucretian naturalism (inherited from Democritus) is worked out through a series of propositions. First, the minimal unit of all compositions is the atom: "The atom is the absolute reality of what is perceived" (*LS* 268). Second, the sum of atoms and the void with which they are interlaced are both infinite. Their correlation forms a third infinity that is their infinite sum. Third, the basic relation of one atom to another is due to the *clinamen*. Each atom moves through the void in a unique direction initially determined by the *clinamen*. It is not a secondary or accidental modification of the atom's direction, but the original differential curvature or "swerve" which sets the atom on a course of collision and interaction with other atoms.

Fourth, since the *clinamen* is both necessary and unique to each atom, it follows that it "manifests neither contingency nor indetermination" but rather "the irreducible plurality of causes or causal series, and the impossibility of bringing causes together into a whole" (*LS* 270). Fifth, although there is an infinity of atoms, they exhibit regularity of size and shape. Sixth, atoms cannot combine with every other atom in order to form a single infinite combination. Their constant movements and collisions lead to composition as well as decomposition. Seventh, combinations cannot be formed by one kind of atom alone; they are constituted only by a diversity of atoms. Each composition is a finite unity of heterogeneous elements, although some compositions possess more of one type of atom and less of others. Eighth, nature is not only the power of the diverse and its production, but also of its reproduction. This is because each composition is produced within determined, complex settings which supply replacement elements as that compositional entity transforms or decomposes. The physical theory at the heart of Lucretius' naturalism thus presents a picture of nature not as a passive, inert object separated from humanity, but as a highly complex, (re)productive, infinite sum of dynamic processes within which humanity is included.

While it is true that this physical theory signifies the emergence of a position strongly opposed to the dualism and transcendentalism of Platonic metaphysics, it nonetheless remains "the speculative point of view" of naturalism (*LS* 272). In the Lucretian philosophy, it is "practice and ethics" which becomes the primary object of naturalism, for the obligation to be assumed by humans is the protection of the diversity produced by the immanent nature within which all things reside and live (*LS* 272). This is in recognition of the fact that if natural diversity is harmed or diminished, the potential for a pleasurable existence is lessened. Lucretius' naturalism also indicates that our actions are to be guided not by adherence to supernatural myths and illusions, but rather by the affirmation of the positive power of an immanent and multiple nature, and by joy resulting from the diversity of its elements. Myths and illusions rest upon the belief in gods and eternal souls, on divine entities and transcendent forms which mysteriously escape natural existence. Such myths are themselves scornful of the material, sensuous, and temporal existence accepted by naturalism, and serve to transpose divine will into a human will (or spirit) set over and against nature. In contrast, the naturalist "speaks about nature, rather than speaking about the gods" (*LS* 278).

The speculative and practical objects of naturalism coincide on this point: the enterprise of demystification through philosophical, scientific, and ethical activity broadly intended to free humans from the illusions of ontotheological transcendence (*LS* 278–79). It is important to notice that this position does not oppose nature to social convention, custom, and invention *tout court*. Instead, it is opposed to those social forces which depend upon myth and illusion in order to consolidate their power by negating the multiplicity and diversity of nature and society, sowing sadness rather than reaping joy:

> One of the most profound constants of Naturalism is to denounce everything that is sadness, everything that is the cause of sadness, and everything that needs sadness to exercise its power. From Lucretius to Nietzsche, the same end is pursued and attained. Naturalism makes of thought and sensibility an affirmation. It directs its attack against the

prestige of the negative; it deprives the negative of all its power; it refuses to the spirit of the negative the right to speak in the name of philosophy.... The multiple as multiple is the object of affirmation, just as the diverse as diverse is the object of joy. (*LS* 279)

The spirit of the negative is what brands the sensible as nothing more than mere secondary appearance and links the intelligible to the absolute realm of timeless essence. What appears with Lucretius' naturalism, then, is a critique of Platonism's antinaturalistic repression of the multiplicity of life and the diversity of nature, along with an affirmation of the flux of natural reality.

A similar naturalistic emphasis in Spinoza's philosophy is embraced by Deleuze. As with Lucretius, nature is characterized by Spinoza as a positive and productive power. Whereas Cartesian metaphysics devalued nature by depriving it of its immanent power, making it the creation of a transcendent God and placed the thinking subject outside of nature, Spinoza's positive naturalism insists that it is from and within infinite nature that all finite things exist as a plurality of modes: "This naturalism provides the true thrust of the Anticartesian reaction ... it is a matter of re-establishing the claims of a Nature endowed with forces or power" (*EP* 227–28). For Spinoza, nature is its own dynamic source of creation and it relies not at all upon a transcendent foundation or "occult entities," but expresses itself through immanent and actual powers that, in acting, are parts of nature (*EP* 228). The notion of an expressive nature thereby "forms the basis of a new naturalism" (*EP* 232). One of the most important factors making Spinoza's naturalism "new" is that while he finds nature to be dynamic (expressive), he denies that it is teleological. Nature is a complex process without any predetermined end, and naturalism need not account for its movement by postulating the existence of some more fundamental realm which explains this process. There is no ultimate foundation outside of nature, but immanent powers, relations, and bodily compositions constitutive of nature itself.

This position, it will be recalled from Chapter 2, follows from Spinoza's theory of immanent causality. Immanent causality "refuses the intervention of a transcendent God" no less than it does the hierarchy of emanative causality (*EP* 109). Instead, the existence of nature as a productive causality is inseparable from its immanent essence, which is constituted by the very effects belonging to it, namely, the attributes and modes. In this way *natura naturans* (naturing nature) and *natura naturata* (natured nature) are interconnected by a mutual immanence. What is essential here is the univocity of nature; the uniquely differentiated modifications of infinite substance are expressions of formally (qualitatively) distinct but ontologically equal attributes. This makes it possible to speak of the equality of differences without resorting to an ordering hierarchy or a reduction to sameness. Instead what are important are the relations between different modes, insofar as finite modes are dynamic compositions within immanent nature. Spinoza's naturalism fully emerges from the connection of immanent causality with univocity:

> Naturalism in this case is what satisfies the three forms of univocity: the univocity of attributes, where the attributes in the same form constitute the essence of God as naturing nature and contain the essences of modes as natured nature; the univocity of the cause, where the cause of all things is affirmed of God as the genesis of natured nature, in the same sense that he is the cause of himself, as the genealogy of naturing nature; the univocity of modality, where necessity qualifies both the order of natured nature and the organization of naturing nature. (*SP* 92–93)

This presents us with a conception, akin to that found in Lucretius, of a nature which is the infinite sum of multiple relational compositions. Nature is multiple, but the multiple forms an open system because it is constituted by ever-changing compositions or multiplicities. These complex relational compositions or multiplicities, which are different yet ontologically equal, correspond to the dynamic physical universe of bodies.

In Spinoza's naturalism the "encounters" between complex bodies will also be evaluated in ethical terms. As Deleuze suggests, those encounters that agree with the natures of each body are "good" and help to form other relations between them, which allow for mutual flourishing and preservation. Other encounters that disagree with the natures of the bodies concerned are "bad" and contribute to the destruction and decomposition of the relations that support their ability to persevere in existence. The order of these encounters, which coincides with the order of compositions and the order of relations, can be defined as "the Common Order of Nature" (*EP* 238). Spinoza's notion of ethical goodness, then, lies in striving to maximize mutually compatible relations and in preventing the decomposition, poisoning, and toxification of what is necessary to maintain these relationships with diverse natural bodies. Thus, it becomes imperative to be positively active in light of such affects as love, generosity, and joyfulness, rather than to be acted upon and negatively reactive on the basis of such affects as hatred, cruelty, contempt, and fear. In the end, the difference is that between freedom and slavery. Deleuze finds in Spinoza a naturalistic ethical principle warning against the erroneous and destructive closure of the powers of diverse, natural bodies since we "do not know what a body can do," and/or what its potentials might be.

From what has been said so far, it should be clear that Deleuze regards naturalism as a critical practice aimed at eliminating the great static dualisms, such as human/nature, reason/nature, mind/body, and culture/nature, so important to the Platonic and Cartesian traditions. Because of the way naturalistic philosophers such as Lucretius and Spinoza conceive of nature, it is impossible in their philosophies to abstract the human realm from its wider natural moorings. The ontological perspective adopted by naturalism thus leads to a social and political philosophy that enhances the propositions we have seen to be basic to its perspective. This is one of the projects Deleuze finds at work in Hume, whose naturalism focuses on the agreement between nature and human nature, insofar as human belief and invention function within and as part of nature itself (*ES* 132–33). For Hume the distinction between nature and culture is indeed a false one, reflected not only in the dualistic philosophy of the rationalists but also in the abstractions of the social contract theorists. Similar to the mutual immanence of *natura naturans* and *natura naturata* in Spinoza, Hume contends that nature and society form a "composite" or "indissoluble complex," although the one cannot be reduced to the other (*ES* 44, 46).

Thus the social realm, the site of human invention, custom, artifice, and convention is not ontologically opposed to nature. Human society and history are modes by which the dynamic, creative, and active power of nature manifests itself. Consequently, every human invention is no less natural for being an invention because "humanity is an *inventive species*" (*ES* 44). This allows Hume to radicalize the notion of society; society is not an artificial limitation of our natures, but rather a positive invention of a cultural world compatible with our active and formative natures. That is why convention replaces contract in Hume's social theory, for contract theory presupposes the conception of a state of nature that precedes society and which leads society to be conceived on the basis of a dualistic "break from nature." Hume contends that this results in an ahistorical definition of society, whereas he emphasizes the gradual, historical, unreflective, and contingent invention and adoption of a variety of conventions found to be socially useful through experience, which draws upon previously established conventions and not an abstract "promise."[5] Hume criticizes such theories because "they define society only in a negative way; they see in it a set of limitations of egoisms and interests." In contrast, Hume understands society as "a positive system of invented endeavors" (*ES* 39).

Far from regarding society as simply the rational limitation of egoistic motives, Hume considers it to be the extension of nature itself by means of an inventive human nature. In one sense society is natural, and in another it is artificial, although these two senses are complementary rather than antithetical. This is because the elements or "ingredients" of society are naturally given in the passions, sympathies, and natural instincts of the members of families.[6] The problem here is that natural sympathy is partial and extends most easily to those whom we love or are close to, such as friends and peers. Families, the basic social units or communities to which everyone always belongs, tend to exclude one another because they are partial, that is, the sympathies of family members exhibit a natural partiality. And yet partiality is not egoism. A theory of egoism maintains that society is a negative limit that places restrictions around each individual's otherwise boundless self-interest. For Hume, on the contrary, partiality is merely the "inequality" of our affections, that is, the fact that our affections are at first naturally limited to our family, friends, and neighbors (*ES* 38). According to Hume, then, society should be understood as the attempt to integrate and then extend this natural partiality by means of the positive invention of social or "moral" institutions:

> The artifice guarantees to sympathy and to natural passions an extension within which they will be capable of being exercised, deployed naturally, and liberated from their natural limits. *Passions are not limited by justice; they are enlarged and extended.* Justice is the extension of the passions and interest, and only the partial movement of the latter is denied and constrained. (*ES* 43)

Hume proposes a combined natural-social historical passage from the fundamental social state of clans and family communities, to the "artificial" state of culture made possible by the creation of political institutions. For naturalism, justice must be extended as far as possible, quite literally made to move across the earth. What is important to note here is that Hume both denies a presocial human condition and affirms the special role of moral and political invention. The immediate, natural human condition is social, yet culture is itself properly political and therefore the result of artifice, invention, and convention (as are rights, in contrast to the proposals of the contract theorists).[7] What Hume never loses sight of, though, is that nature "includes the artifice" while political society includes "the principles of nature in its organization" (*ES* 44, 40). Society as a whole is thus both natural and artificial for Hume, since it is neither simply given nor strictly opposed to nature (*ES* 44–48). In this way Hume bypasses the notion of social contract, because the question to be addressed is not that of passing from a presocietal to societal condition on the basis of a rational, reflective promise, but that of passing from a natural society to an invented political society, from natural social institutions to political institutions. It should not be forgotten, however, that Hume does not simply posit natural society as a harmonious and peaceful organic unity from which differences later emerge to threaten it. Rather, differences, in the form of a partiality of interests and sympathies, compose the threads of a fragile social existence from the very beginning. Political existence is the realm invented in order to protect these differences while striving to strengthen the social bond.

It would be a mistake, I believe, to suggest that Hume's naturalism is simply an essentialism or romanticism which would legitimize any social formation simply on the basis of its "naturalness." This is because every social institution, regardless of its place in nature, is not a mere given but rather a particular invention that presupposes specific rules and goals of organization which determine its unique characteristics. Moreover, Hume's argument shows us that moral goodness or rightness does not necessarily follow from the sheer fact of existence. This, of course, follows in line with the observations of Spinoza and Nietzsche that Good and Evil are not fixed moral categories inhering in a static nature.

As Hume stresses, it is human invention that specifically generates an ethical and political domain irreducible to a pure state of nature because the political is a different mode of a multiple nature. Human societies are seen by Hume as a part of a larger natural reality that cannot be transcended. Humans are conceived then as cultural beings, but this is their role within nature. In effect, Hume both naturalizes humanity and humanizes nature. There are only natural phenomena, but nature is neither the nonhuman alone, nor is it exhausted by the myth of the given; it is in this sense that ethics and politics are in our nature: "it is not our nature which is moral, it is rather our morality which is in our nature" (*ES* 38). This confronts us with the difficult recognition that ethical evaluation cannot appeal to transcendent, supernatural, or external standards beyond nature, but must be justified by reference to real conditions which are themselves part of nature.

We are faced, then, with the question of how to integrate the implications of Deleuze's picture of the history of philosophical naturalism with the matter of ecological destruction as a contemporary social and political issue. If ethical evaluation is to be considered from the perspective of a naturalism that includes human culture within a dynamic nature, what values are we to appeal to in order to develop and assess the ecological effects of our social practices? I want to suggest that Deleuze's writings contain an important and innovative extension of the naturalist sympathies exhibited in his historical analyses, and in this respect can prove useful for contemporary environmental ethics and political ecology. In the following section I examine some of the ways Deleuze carries out this extension.

Deleuze and Geophilosophy: A Radical Naturalism

In his own works and in those written with Guattari, Deleuze articulates a strongly naturalistic account of philosophy, according to which "thinking takes place in the relationship of territory and the earth" (*WP* 85). What is unique about the earth is that it "is not one element among others but rather brings together all the elements within a single embrace while using one or another of them to deterritorialize territory" (*WP* 85). On the one hand, the practice of philosophy occurs only when thought inhabits some territory, a time and place, in relation to the earth. Yet this relation is mobile, for while no territory can by itself encompass the earth neither can the earth be fixed to a single territory. On the other hand, then, even though the earth embraces all territories it is also the force of deterritorialization and reterritorialization, since its continuous movements of development and variation unfold new relations of materials and forces.

Thus, the earth generates difference and is a source of becoming. In this sense, the earth is considered distributively, that is, as an open system of a plurality of elements in constant interaction, rather than as an absolute order of Being transcending that which is constituted in nature. What Deleuze and Guattari call "geophilosophy" is the attempt to formulate a mode of thinking in association with, and as the affirmation of, the diversity and multiplicity of the immanent becomings of "natural reality" (*ATP* 5). In effect, this amounts to the effort to construct a new way of thinking that is naturalistic and ecologically oriented, because it seeks to eliminate the traditional dichotomy separating humanity (as subject) and nature (as object) by "stretching out a plane of immanence that absorbs the earth (or rather, 'adsorbs' it)" (*WP* 88).[8] Bonding with the earth in this manner serves to undercut the antinaturalistic tendencies fostered by the dualistic, transcendentalist, and anthropomorphic presuppositions found in much of Western philosophical and religious thinking.

One way this project is pursued is by emphasizing the interaction of the human and nonhuman in terms of immanence and relationality. The notion of "milieu," one of the meanings of the Greek *oikos* from which the common "eco" derives, plays an important role here.[9] Throughout their work, Deleuze and Guattari formulate a nonteleological, nonfinalistic evolutionism according to which the immanent world is characterized by constant change which grows from within a diversity of milieux connected in various complex ways.[10] There is, however, no progressive, preordained developmental tendency exhibited in these changes.

"Milieu" is the word Deleuze uses to refer to all that is involved in the interactions between elements, compounds, energy sources, and organisms from the molecular to the molar levels. Milieux grow "from the middle" when molecular materials and substantial elements are exchanged and organized around a reversible boundary or membrane, forming a "unity of composition" that is qualitatively unique: "Thus the living thing has an exterior milieu of materials, and interior milieu of composing elements and composed substances, and intermediary milieu of membranes and limits, and an annexed milieu of energy sources and actions-perceptions" (*ATP* 313).

The notion of milieu is thus used to indicate the conditions under which becoming takes place. Taking ecology to refer to the interrelationships of living things and their environments, a milieu is the site, habitat, or medium of ecological interaction and encounter. A complete milieu is made up of the relational interactions of several sub-milieux (climate, geography, populations, soils, microbes, and so forth). Yet the milieu possesses a relative rather than absolute equilibrium, since it is itself open to transformation on the basis of its supple boundaries and alterable relationships, with the consequence that its populations can be affected as well. Organisms and milieux therefore develop, grow, and change together within continuous and intersecting processes of becoming, a view with significant ecological importance.

As argued by Deleuze and Guattari, the full diversity of life is exhibited through natural processes of change and becoming. The effects of these processes cannot be identified on the basis of their descent from a common origin, since the creative and transformational "a-parallel" evolutionism proposed by Deleuze and Guattari regards them as the products of distinct milieux, environmental variations, and transversal interactions (*ATP* 10–11). They contend that we cannot account for the current forms of organisms and habitat by assuming that their features developed according to a progressive hierarchy from the primitive to the more advanced, from the weaker to the stronger, from the less intelligent to the more intelligent, or that survival is simply a matter of developing more advantageous adaptive mechanisms. Instead, Deleuze and Guattari call for a rhizomatic conception of evolution based not on a centralized directionality of species development, but instead on the active, unfinalized flux of constantly circulating relations and encounters, along the lines of horizontal dispersion and shared transformation. "More generally," they write, "evolutionary schemas may be forced to abandon the old model of the tree and descent. . . . Evolutionary schemas would no longer follow models of arborescent descent going from the least to the most differentiated, but instead a rhizome operating immediately in the heterogeneous and jumping from one already differentiated line to another" (*ATP* 10).

If this is the case, what is significant with respect to the movements of natural reality is not whether organisms can be represented according to their progression or regression along a fixed line of descent, but whether the continuous change and diversification of life and the immanent, mobile relationships of the various organisms that inhabit certain ecological or environmental milieux are to be affirmed and recognized as both necessary and desirable. This is nothing less than a recognition of the importance of becoming and of what Deleuze and Guattari call symbiotic "alliances" between and among the diversity of milieux and organisms: "If evolution includes any veritable becomings, it is in the domain of *symbioses* that bring into play beings of totally different scales and kingdoms" (*ATP* 238). Symbiosis is the cofunctioning of two or more different organisms, often in a mutually beneficial, cooperative relationship of reciprocity. Deleuze's treatment of relations showed that they cannot be reduced to the supposedly fixed essences from which they are then derived. Rather, the characteristics and qualities of a specific locus of interaction are attributable to the types of relations taking hold of the terms involved, while the relations are themselves susceptible to change, transformation, or even elimination.

In other words, the relationship becomes a kind of alliance between heterogeneous terms in symbiosis.[11] And this alliance accompanies the kind of becoming that happens in between the related terms, that is to say, it is initiated in the middle of their interactions within different ecological milieux. For example, there is an alliance between the roots of a plant and the microorganisms in the soil in which the roots take hold. Yet this alliance can itself be affected by the introduction of toxic chemicals into the soil, or by an early frost, or a foraging animal. So too are the alliances between humans and their complex natural-social milieux influenced by a variety of biological, geological, cultural, and technological factors. Whatever process of becoming occurs, it is constituted through relations of alliance that are articulated in terms of a particular milieu that overlaps with several other milieux (WP 110). This clearly suggests that the dynamic movements of nature are always coming about within ever-changing zones of immanent interactions between diverse ecological factors.

Another way Deleuze furthers his naturalism is by arguing for the inclusion of ethology in his description of philosophical practice. Ethology refers both to the study of animal behavior, and to the study of the formation and evolution of human *ethos*. While ethology has taken many divergent forms, from vitalism to behaviouralism and sociobiology, Deleuze uses the term in several of his works in order to emphasize the nondualistic continuity of human and nonhuman life forms and their complex environmental interrelationships, as well as to propose an overlap between the physical, biological and chemical, and the social, ethical and political. For instance, Deleuze draws from Spinoza the conception of a "*common plane of immanence* on which all bodies, all minds, and all individuals are situated" (SP 122).[12] This "one Nature" is common to all things because it is there that different ways of living are simultaneously installed and constituted. Life is understood according to its relations of movement and rest, and each body, whether human or nonhuman, by its capacity for affecting and being affected. It is nature "that distributes affects," and each thing living in nature "is defined by the arrangements of motions and affects into which it enters" (SP 124). The dynamic capacities of each living thing to act and be acted upon intersect at various points with those of others, some affects are shared, some are not. Each thing is different or singular, yet all are situated in the affective realm of nature, a common environment constituting an open system "which applies equally to the inanimate and the animate, the artificial and the natural" (ATP 254). This implies an extensive spectrum of encounters between all bodies (taken broadly) together with the consequences or effects of such encounters. Writes Deleuze:

> Ethology is first of all the study of the relations of speed and slowness, of the capacities for affecting and being affected that characterize each thing. For each thing these relations and capacities have amplitude,

thresholds (maximum and minimum), and variations or transformations that are peculiar to them. And they select, in the world or in Nature, that which corresponds to the thing; that is, they select what affects or is affected by the thing, what moves or is moved by it. For example, given an animal, what is this animal unaffected by in the infinite world? What does it react to positively or negatively? What are its nutrients and its poisons? What does it "take" in its world? Every point has its counterpoints: the plant and the rain, the spider and the fly. So an animal, a thing, is never separable from its relations with the world. The interior is only a selected exterior, and the exterior, a projected interior. The speed or slowness of metabolisms, perceptions, actions, and reactions link together to constitute a particular individual in the world. . . . Further, there is also the way in which these relations of speed and slowness are realized according to circumstances, and the way in which these capacities for being affected are filled. For they always are, but in different ways, depending on whether the present affect threatens the thing . . . or strengthen, accelerate, and increase it. (*SP* 125–26)

Nature is thus seen by Deleuze as an immanent plane of life upon which all things enter into both their own unique compositions and a variety of "more or less interconnected relations" with other compositions (*ATP* 254). In fact, the earth can be considered the fundamental yet never fixed plane of immanence on which the constitution of multiplicities takes place. It is important to note, however, that the compositions and relations of all living things are not fixed by an invariable order and that each thing is not *directly* connected to *every other thing*. The idea that nature is that which distributes affects provides not only a basis of continuity between each thing in the world, but also a basis for recognizing the multiplicity of nature since it makes possible a rich differentiation of all things in terms of the kind of variations, interactions, requirements, circumstances, and capacities applicable to each thing and its local habitat. That the world is constituted in this profusion of becomings and appears everywhere as multiplicity can be seen as an endorsement of the concept of biodiversity. As our discussion of Lucretius pointed out, Deleuze argues that naturalism is dedicated to the entire variety of nature's diversity. Biodiversity is comprised of all species of microorganisms, plants, animals, the milieux or ecosystems of which they are a part, and the specific assemblages formed by the relationships and processes flowing between these elements.

This position stresses not an undivided totality transcending particular things and milieux, but rather the complex of continuities *and* differences distinguishing all these things traversing the world, without falling back onto a dualism of the human/nonhuman. In doing so, it affirms the multiplicity of ecological milieux, the diversity of their interactive elements, and the dynamic relations between milieux, elements, and circumstances, because each thing must constantly connect to an immanent exteriority in order to become what it is. Here the mutual folding of inside and outside is a natural corollary to the symbiotic alliance referred to earlier. Just what relationships obtain, however, cannot be accounted for on the basis of an indifferent and closed system, but should instead be explained in terms of the active interactions and transformations of unique bodies and habitats. If different types of relationships, combinations, or symbioses were rendered indistinguishable, it would be impossible to determine whether certain beliefs and actions had either detrimental or beneficial ecological consequences. Deleuze considers this insight to be one of the most important supplied by ethology.

In addition to the above, ethology also "studies the compositions of relations or capacities between different things" (*SP* 126). The ethologist seeks to understand not only what relations are suitable or unsuitable for a particular thing, but also what new, "extensive" relations can be formed between different things in order to compose "assemblages," societies, or communities favorable to all of those individuals belonging to them: "How can a being take another being into its world, but while preserving or respecting the other's own relations and world? And in this regard, what are the different types of sociabilities, for example?" (*SP* 126). This passage suggests several features for a radical naturalism: 1) there are different types of "sociability" in nature; 2) sociability is not reserved only for humans but is characteristic of nonhuman beings, as well; 3) it is possible to create social/communal compositions that respect and protect the diversity of human and nonhuman beings and milieux, and strengthen and promote what is particularly good and useful for them. Here the concerns of the naturalist make an explicit shift from the assessment of existing ecological conditions to the proposal that new ways of thinking, feeling, and acting be created, informed by the knowledge of what is beneficial to the flourishing of all life on earth. Consequently, what must be considered now are the ethical and political implications of Deleuze's naturalism.

Radical Naturalism and Ecological Politics

The strength of Deleuze's affirmation of naturalism is that it possesses significance for the reconsideration of ethical and political issues associated with the degradation of the earth's multiple environments, ranging from the decline of urban centers to the erosion of arable lands, the clear cutting of ancient forests, the mass contamination of air, water, and soil, and the forced extinction of living beings. In other words, Deleuze provides philosophically for the possibility of articulating ethical and political responses appropriate to the destruction of many of the earth's combined natural-social habitats. In fact, Deleuze's version of naturalism is in my estimation ideally suited to environmental ethics because it refuses to refer existence to transcendent values. As Deleuze frequently asserts, to find transcendent values such as Good and Evil in a static nature is to misapprehend nature as the ultimate moral determinant. Ethics, on the contrary, is a companion to what Deleuze refers to as the knowledge of immanent modes of existence. This distinction can assist in clarifying how Deleuze's naturalism is antiessentialist, and help pave the way for an active ecological ethics or *ethos* in contrast to a reactive and negative moralism.

Even though Deleuze strongly criticizes the moral tradition, there is nevertheless a constructive role for ethics in his work. At the heart of Deleuze's critique is the thought that morality "always refers existence to transcendent values" and functions as a "system of judgment" (*SP* 23). Moral theories, such as those articulated by Plato, Aquinas, and Kant, have typically started from a dualism between mind and nature, claiming that it is the rational insight, introspection, and apprehension of transcendent values or principles which make moral conduct possible, while seeking to justify moral values within the framework of universal, absolute, transcendent criteria imposed upon empirical circumstances. The basic features of morality have often been established as the privileging of reason, disinterestedness, and impartiality in order to assign value to something as a representation of its "worth," and to be able to act from an understanding of its principles as universal.

These characteristic features of moral judgment tend to support a dualistic account of an essentially rational human self separated from the bodily, affective, desiring, animal, in short, "natural," elements of human and nonhuman existence. The supposed universality of moral systems of judgment thus include what is "proper" to or identified as rational within the sphere of moral consideration, while excluding or ignoring what is different. Moreover, in such a framework the legitimacy of moral principles is derived from their abstractness, that is, their application across widely different circumstances, periods, and situations, rather than their specificity with respect to any given locale and time. Consequently, what Deleuze calls morality imposes its transcendent criteria from without upon the multiplicity of the real conditions of existence.

Deleuze argues that ethics, in contrast to morality, receives its motivation not from that which transcends natural reality, but instead from within given concrete situations and moments, and from particular modes of existence within a dynamic nature:

> There is not the slightest reason for thinking that modes of existence need transcendent values by which they could be compared, selected, and judged relative to one another. On the contrary, there are only immanent criteria. A possibility of life is evaluated through itself in the movements it lays out and the intensities it creates on a plane of immanence. (*WP* 74)

Deleuze defines ethics as a "typology of immanent modes of existence" which does not measure types of existence against external, fixed standards as does morality, but seeks to create knowledge of the "qualitative differences" marking the multiplicities of nature (*SP* 23). For Deleuze, morality does not provide knowledge, it merely institutes prohibitions, imperatives, and constraints. Ethics is a kind of knowledge, however, whenever it cultivates a fluid understanding of the changing affects, capabilities, needs, and powers of specific human and nonhuman modes of existence. For Deleuze, the difference between morality and ethics is that "morality presents us with a set of constraining rules of a special sort, ones that judge actions and intentions in relation to transcendent values," while "ethics is a set of optional rules that assess what we do, what we say, in relation to the ways of existing involved."[13]

Deleuze's conception of ethics insists that the evaluation of each mode of existence is ongoing and never-ending, because an evaluation is itself a way of being, the "style of life" of the one who actively evaluates (*N* 1). Evaluation is seen as an affair of nature in the sense that it always belongs to a specific mode of existence. Evaluation thereby exhibits the same flow of constant becoming characteristic of natural reality. The continuous change of all phenomena necessitates that the evaluations of things change accordingly, if evaluation is not to become reactive. When evaluation ceases to be creative and open to transformation, values are regarded as fixed, transcendent categories imposed upon a seemingly inert and lifeless nature (*N* 6).

But if all evaluations change as natural reality changes, is not Deleuze haunted by the specter of relativism? Certainly, a naturalistic or pluralistic empiricism does create a relativization of existing values but only because it regards all values as having a historical emergence and genesis. Values are "relative" or related to the conditions of their creation and use. Deleuze emphasizes that evaluations in nature are not justified by reference to transcendent values, conditions, or principles which are not subject to natural change. Whereas a doctrine of ethical relativism might hold that there are no criteria by which to determine that any one value is preferable to any other, Deleuze insists that there *are* criteria, but that they are immanent, historical, and emergent rather than transcendent, essential, and static. How might we understand this with respect to a Deleuzian naturalistic ethics?

As we have seen, Deleuze's version of naturalism contends that the powers of thought belong to nature. Thinking is not the manifestation of the interiority of a knowing subject apart from its various existential environments, but exists as the fluid effect of the interactions that take place *between* the forces of the body and the environmental conditions in which it exists. It is the dynamic, reciprocal, reversible folding of the inside and the outside on a plane of immanence. The reciprocal relationality of bodies and milieux underscores the fact that each has certain effects on the other. The evaluation of modes of existence must therefore proceed from the recognition of this reciprocity or symbiosis.

This requires careful attention not only to the changing natural-existential conditions of the emergence of given phenomena, but also to the effects or consequences of specific modes of existence with respect to these conditions, as much as this is possible. In other words, the evaluation of modes of existence is immanent and ongoing. It takes time to develop and is always provisional, flexible, and nonreductive since it requires the ability to act in ways that are appropriate to qualitatively different human and nonhuman needs and conditions. As a result, our beliefs and evaluations are ultimately justified only by the relationships they have with concrete (ecological) conditions and thus with real, immanent criteria of existence rather than some transempirical values or authority. This is to say that evaluation must emerge from "in the middle" of actual experiences and not simply impose preestablished, absolute values upon different and changing ways of being.

Hence, even though Deleuze concludes that evaluation is a continuous process that goes on within diverse milieux, this does not imply that it is impossible to distinguish some values, beliefs, and modes of existence as more desirable than others. But these distinctions concern what is good or bad *for* a particular thing over the course of its existence, and not whether that thing "is" morally good or evil as measured against some absolute standard. As Deleuze sees it, ethical experience is not the progression toward some ultimate fixed goal that abstract reason can formulate in terms of universal maxims or categorical imperatives. Instead, it is an ongoing process that moves toward new possibilities for thinking and feeling in order to cultivate the positive forces of life. In this process, ethical evaluations should be regarded as hypotheses to be verified by experience in relation to their effects upon human and nonhuman existence.

In Deleuze's case, then, ethics can be seen as the "critical and creative" practice of developing an *ethos* according to which one actively works to promote the continued well-being of the various members of diverse yet interconnected milieux on the basis of their unique needs and capacities (*N* 1). A Deleuzian ecological ethics would thus consider ethical evaluations as emerging constantly from a provisional and revisable understanding of the relations and interactions between the different members of complex milieux and the effects or consequences of these relations and interactions. This would require an openness to active experimentation and difference, and a rejection of the poverty of absolutism and the sterility of reactive moralism.[14] Experimentation is best understood not as an attitude of "anything goes," but as a willingness to find or create what is most advantageous for life on earth while exercising prudence and precaution with respect to that same life (*D* 138–39). The fundamental consideration here is that of which concepts, practices, and values best promote the collective life and interests of the diverse modes of existence inhabiting the planet. It follows that this basic consideration entails the practical evaluation of the social institutions through which humans define, access, and intersect with each other and nonhuman nature.

In this way Deleuze provides a political perspective to his naturalism. Indeed, the naturalism found in Deleuze's work is a form of political philosophy, but a political philosophy articulated in ecological terms. As noted at the conclusion of the previous section of this chapter, when considered ecologically all life is social life, provided that sociability and the composing and organizing of what Deleuze and Guattari term "collective assemblages" is not considered an exclusively human activity. "Social" should be understood to encompass the various reciprocal interconnections of human and nonhuman modes of existence. An assemblage acquires unity or "consistency" only on the basis of the relational cofunctioning or symbiotic alliances it establishes between its "different natures" (D 69–70). If this is the case, then it is through a wide variety of symbiotic assemblages that the life and the becoming of nature takes place. And it is through these different assemblages, which Deleuze describes as "the set of relationships which at a particular moment unites man, animal, tools, and environment," that ethical evaluation is carried out (D 73). The lesson taught by Deleuze is that no evaluation takes place in isolation from the ongoing processes of social composition in nature. Since these include human social institutions, it is vitally important to realize that ethical evaluation requires an examination of the practices of specific human social institutions as they relate to nonhuman social activity. The naturalistic integration of humans in nature as carried out in Deleuze's empiricism therefore correlates with an ecologically oriented conception of ethics and politics.

The conjunction of naturalism and politics at this point is based on the view that awareness of ecologically dangerous relationships can be used to formulate active political interventions aimed at transforming or overcoming those relationships in order to create new values and interactions that are beneficial to the diversity of the earth. Thus, Deleuze's thought presents an important contribution to political ecology. This is not to say that "ecopolitics" would supplant or assimilate all other political struggles and forms of intervention, for as Deleuze insists there are "many politics" addressing a number of problems at specific points on a complex social network (D 135–47). It is to say, however, that certain institutionalized beliefs and practices based on disregard for the earth and contempt for the life-needs and health of its inhabitants, while appearing in different forms and shapes, constitute a serious political issue shared by many across the planet. Yet for ecopolitical activism to compose itself effectively, it must steer clear of universalized abstractions and carefully study the specific needs and alternative possibilities within localized situations.

It is for this reason that Deleuze's notion of "micropolitics" can be especially useful for a political activism engaged with qualitatively different ecological milieux. The singularity of diverse ecological milieux calls for modes of intervention that are plastic and fluidly defined in terms of the problems and conflicts involved, and of the means that are available with respect to each habitat, ecosystem, or biotic community and its unique needs. This does not prevent the combining or the formation of alliances between different ecopolitical movements and milieux, or between ecopolitical struggles and those engaged in other forms of social and political resistance, but in fact presents the optimum condition for doing so.

Neither does the micropolitical approach rule out the "macropolitical." As Deleuze acknowledges, "every politics is simultaneously a *macropolitics* and a *micropolitics*" (*ATP* 213). In other words, larger social structures and forms of organization are typically generated by the intersections of multiple smaller, local practices and conditions, which are in turn themselves effected by the influences and activities of macropolitical institutions. Yet it is inaccurate to consider the micropolitical and macropolitical as corresponding symmetrically, and the one to be reducible to the other. Deleuze's point is that a more nuanced understanding of the specificity and reciprocity of the micropolitical and macropolitical, and greater attention to the diversity of the actual practices and current conditions of local situations are required for a useful political philosophy. Thus, while many existing ecological problems undoubtedly present a danger to the entire planet, a micropolitical focus on the particular needs, conditions, and interests of diverse local habitats and inhabitants will better contribute to the creation of effective ecopolitical interventions than will operating solely from a unitary, large-scale framework.

Nevertheless, from the Deleuzian perspective, ecological problems are always to be considered as simultaneously local and global, since local habitats overlap and combine with others at various points throughout the entire planet and have a global impact. While many environmental problems have global consequences—one need only consider the planetary threats presented by the depletion of the earth's protective ozone layer and by transboundary air pollution—the problems, resources, and needs encountered often require particular actions or measures that can only be appropriately addressed at the local or regional level. This is the case especially given the lack of global consensus on how to define, much less confront, ecological degradation. However, the issue then becomes one of attempting to relate the various regional approaches into an international perspective without sacrificing their integrity, flexibility, and effectiveness. Local, regional, national, and global linkages must therefore be addressed from a decentralized approach that is at once micropolitical and macropolitical but nonreductive, thus allowing for the active engagement of all parties concerned.

It should be noted that none of this amounts to what Deleuze calls the "grotesque" gesture of calling for a return to "a state of nature" (*D* 145). Not only does Deleuze reject a simple reversal of dualism and binary opposition, he also rejects the view that there is or ever was an original, nonproblematic natural condition that can be reclaimed. Deleuze clearly upholds that all of nature, including its human elements, are in constant flux and that there is no essential, foundational, or sacred state to be found or reclaimed. In this respect, Deleuze follows Nietzsche in demanding a "de-deification" of nature that would eliminate interpretations of nature as the site of divine purposiveness, static essences, and transcendent moral ideals.[15] Deleuze's naturalism is not an essentialistic theory nostalgically seeking a return to some pristine nature that is an object apart from human existence, conceptualization, and intervention. Rather, it is a critical perspective that attempts to show that humans and their cultures are, for better or worse, a integral part of the existing natural, biophysical reality which cannot be transcended, but which *can* be destroyed by certain exploitative, ecologically insensitive beliefs, practices, and ways of being. Human history and natural history are therefore caught up together in the same immanent movements of change, and political intervention aimed at ecologically destructive values and practices cannot be based on any reactive appeal to transcendence, but rather on current situations and experiences. This implies the active creation of, and not a return to, modes of existence that exemplify appropriate, sustainable, and beneficial relationships between human and nonhuman beings and their simultaneously local/global environments.

A micropolitical approach to such issues has both similarities and differences with some contemporary ecological or "Green" movements. Social ecology and deep ecology are perhaps the most visible examples today. Social ecology, pioneered by Murray Bookchin, is oriented primarily toward the examination of the relationship he sees between environmental degradation and social structure. More specifically, Bookchin argues that the human domination of nature follows from the domination of human by human as found in certain kinds of hierarchical and oppressive social arrangements. He writes that "ecological degradation is, in great part, a product of the degradation of human beings by hunger, material insecurity, class rule, hierarchical domination, patriarchy, ethnic discrimination, and competition."[16] Social ecology is thus premised on the view that "the basic problems which pit society against nature emerge from *within* social development itself," and that "human domination of human gave rise to the very *idea* of dominating nature."[17] According to Bookchin, this is particularly evident in the technical-economic system of constant and aggressive expansion characteristic of modern capitalism. Referring to himself as an avowed naturalist with an aversion to "spiritualism" and "mystical" approaches to ecological problems, Bookchin argues that radical cultural, political, and economic changes in the current social order, as well as the development of a new "ecological sensibility," constitute the appropriate responses to a precarious ecological situation.

Consequently, Bookchin contends that a society oriented by the "grow-or-die" attitude toward humans and nonhumans alike is destined to confront insurmountable natural limits. Only fundamental changes in capitalistic modes of production and consumption can avert ecological catastrophe. These changes are centered around such notions as the decentralization of communities, a complex evolutionism rooted in mutualism or symbiosis, the necessity of cultural and biophysical diversity, bioregional federalism, and the development of ecologically appropriate alternative technologies.[18] The general outlook of social ecology presented so far would seem to find some strong points of agreement with the naturalistic and micropolitical aspects of Deleuze's thought. Deleuze has, of course, consistently criticized the destructive effects of a "universal capitalism," the totalizing functions of State apparatuses, the oppression of nationalist, racist, and sexist "majoritarianisms," and the dangers presented by the basic tendency to divorce the creative becomings of life from social existence. There are, however, important differences that would lead Deleuze to reject some of the specifics of Bookchin's position.

One of these is Bookchin's excessive reliance on a rationalistic paradigm for social development. He contends that because humans are "nature rendered self-conscious," the perfection of human subjectivity will lead to a "rational" society that is able to serve as a benign steward for the rest of nature.[19] On this basis, Bookchin has taken a hostile stand against recent critiques of the category of reason, regarding them as evidence of mere "irrationalism" and "anti-humanism."[20] He argues that any retreat from the province of reason amounts to "misanthropic" mysticism. Bookchin's unwillingness to question the generic notion of an inherent, universal reason, and his basic assessment of oppression as simply the result of "irrationality"—as if rationality and domination were mutually exclusive—indicates that he retains some problematic, foundationalist assumptions that have been challenged in various ways by critical theorists, poststructuralists, and feminists, among others.[21]

In addition, Bookchin's rationalism has also led him to embrace a Hegelian model of development and progress, which considers the appearance of a truly rational society to be the dialectical manifestation of a latent "potentiality" contained in nature.[22] He frequently offers a picture of "nature rendered more and more aware of itself" as human societies have "organically" unfolded "from their own inner logic," proceeding from the "primitive" to the modern and ultimately to the "rational."[23] For Bookchin, the realization of a rational society would reveal "nature's potentiality to achieve mind and truth."[24] Bookchin's transcendentalist leanings are clearly in evidence with the preceding remarks, in which he indicates that a fragmented nature will gradually (re)unite with itself as it attains increasing self-reflexivity and eliminates social contradiction. These examples are not intended to dismiss Bookchin's work altogether, but to point to specific positions that Deleuze would obviously reject as burdened by deterministic presuppositions of traditional essentialism, foundationalism, and humanism.

What of deep ecology, another significant contemporary ecological theory? Perhaps the most prominent deep ecologist is the Norwegian philosopher Arne Naess, who coined the term "deep ecology," but others who have contributed to its development are Bill Devall, George Sessions, and Warwick Fox. As Naess conceives it, "deep" ecology is so called because of three basic points: 1) it rejects "shallow" environmentalism seeking minor reform of a few basic socio-economic practices; 2) it asks "deeper" questions about how and why these practices are in place; and 3) it embraces a "total world view" based on the intrinsic, spiritual identification of self and nature.[25] Devall and Sessions claim that deep ecology "attempts to articulate a comprehensive religious and philosophical worldview" according to which the "spiritual and material aspects of reality fuse together" into an "organic whole."[26] What is referred to as deep ecological consciousness is the view that the world exists as an "unbroken wholeness" with no discontinuities or boundaries between human and non-human nature.[27] Deep ecology insists that everything is a part of and connected to everything else in an overarching unity founded on internal relations.

In terms of its ethical and political response to ecological problems, deep ecology argues that "reformist" actions such as recycling and the cleaning up of highly polluted sites are only short-term measures which leave intact the dominant paradigms legitimizing human exploitation of nature. Naess contends that self-realization and biocentric equality are two "norms" that can aid in a radical transformation of these paradigms. As presented by Naess, self-realization is a process in which the self is identified with as much of the world as possible, since difference is taken to be a hindrance to the awareness of the "sameness" uniting all things into a "greater Self." A full realization of the individual self can only be accomplished with its integration into the larger Self of the entirety of nature:

> We, as egos, have an extremely limited power and position within the whole, but it is sufficient for the unfolding of our potential, something vastly more comprehensive than the potential of our egos. So we are more than our egos, and are not fragments, hardly small and powerless. By identifying with greater wholes, we partake in the creation and maintenance of this whole. *We thereby share in its greatness.* New dimensions of satisfaction are revealed. The egos develop into selves of greater and greater dimension, proportional to the extent and depth of our processes of identification. . . . The ecophilosophical outlook is developed through an identification so deep that one's *own self* is no longer adequately delimited by the personal ego or the organism. One experiences oneself to be a genuine part of all life. (*Lifestyle* 173–74)

Naess goes on to argue that the wider identification characteristic of the "deep, comprehensive and ecological self" contributes to an understanding of biocentric equality, that all things in nature are equal with respect to their ability to achieve self-realization. This implies that harming other entities is equal to harming one's own self through the elimination of present and future potentials for self/Self-realization.

It appears that there are more differences than similarities between Deleuze's naturalism and deep ecology. While Naess uses language similar to Deleuze when he claims that "diversity, complexity, and symbiosis" are fundamental "potentials," and that realizations of these potentials should be plural and qualitatively different, he assigns them this importance only insofar as they are integrated into the totality of comprehensive Self-identification (*Lifestyle* 200–02). This may be a consequence of Naess' assumption that difference can only inhibit the awareness of biocentric equality and is to be equated with "indifference," in the sense that if a strong identification of sameness is absent only negative indifference will remain (*Lifestyle* 174).

Naess grounds this belief in the idea of "microcosm mirroring macrocosm," of each natural entity mirroring "the supreme whole" (*Lifestyle* 200). This, again, seems to indicate a denial of difference, for the individual self and the supreme Self simply reflect one another in a mirror of sameness. I believe, however, that by grounding concern for others in resemblance or identification, this position presents a greater opportunity for ethical indifference than would an account based on respect for the coexistence of interrelated differences. Furthermore, such an attitude may fail to pay sufficient attention to the unique needs, interests, and capacities of different modes of existence; seeing them as identical could lead to greater ecological harm than if their differences and particular interactions are acknowledged and understood as such. In addition, Naess openly adheres to a "back to nature" attitude and a "Nature mysticism" which Deleuze would also clearly reject as dangerously reactionary, with the possibility for limiting the creation of alternative discourses and practices and for falling back into a kind of moralistic longing for the "golden age" (*Lifestyle* 183, 176). And finally, it is doubtful whether Deleuze would have any sympathy for the constant appeal to an essentialistic and psychologistic "depth" of self in deep ecological theory.

Not surprisingly, the position most compatible with Deleuze's thinking on these matters is Guattari's "three ecologies" argument. As outlined in his small book *Les Trois Ecologies*, Guattari makes the case for a series of critical and creative "ecological praxes" situated within the contexts of three distinct, yet interconnected "ecologies": social ecology, environmental ecology, and mental ecology.[28] These three ecologies correspond to the "ecological registers" of social relations and production, the natural and dynamic environment, and human subjectivity and thought. When taken together, the three registers require an "ethical-political articulation," which Guattari names "ecosophy," capable of addressing the dangers presented to life on earth by the combined effects of environmental disequilibrium, progressive deterioration of social existence, and ossification and standardization of thought and behavior (*Ecologies* 11–12). Critical of the belief that the dominant economic-political systems of what

Guattari names "Integrated World Capitalism" will be either willing or able to cultivate significant transformations in the planetary situation, Guattari calls for a simultaneously micropolitical-macropolitical ecological revolution:

> There will not be a true response to the ecological crisis except on a planetary scale and on the condition that it brings about an authentic political, social, and cultural revolution, reorienting the objectives of the production of material and immaterial goods. This revolution must not be concerned solely with the visible relations of forces on a grand scale but equally with the molecular domains of sensibility, of intelligence, and desire. (*Ecologies* 13–15)

Guattari regards the three ecological registers to be "existential territories" characterized by unique problems and conditions requiring the construction of new fields of possibility for both human and nonhuman nature. This is to be undertaken in terms of the individual and collective "resingularization" of the world, inspired by aesthetic as well as ethical creation (*Ecologies* 21). Working from the perspective that culture and nature are inseparable, Guattari argues that there are three complementary points of transversal interaction relevant to ecopolitical praxis: the socius, the psyche, and the environment. Responding ethically and politically to the "simultaneous degradation of these three areas" must be done in terms of the "*contemporary conditions* of the objectives and methods of each and every form of movement of the social" (*Ecologies* 32–33). Hence the need for three ecologies.

Of these ecologies, social ecology is the theory and practice concerned with the degradation of social conditions, and with the reconstruction of human relations and liberty at all levels of the socius, or social field. Such phenomena as urban decay, capitalistic expansion and exploitation of territory and labor, subjugation of women, the unemployed, immigrants, the homeless, and children, the rise of religious fundamentalisms and cultural intolerance, are to be considered as effects of the decline and pollution of the social environment. These phenomena are indicators of the disappearance of "the words, expressions, and gestures of human solidarity" (*Ecologies* 35). Social ecology is concerned with the ways in which humans interact and with how their social practices have an impact on the natural environment.

In comparison, environmental or natural ecology is the theory and practice concerned with the degradation of the diverse natural conditions upon which all life inhabiting the planet depends, as well as the protection and enrichment of these conditions. The widespread ravages of the earth's complex ecosystems and the increasingly rapid loss of natural species and habitat enacted by the various exploitative technologies of an international market economy, or Integrated World Capitalism, have lead to a steady deterioration of worldwide living conditions. The link between environmental ecology and social ecology is clear.

Finally, mental ecology is the theory and practice concerned with the degradation of the conditions for creative subjectification and singularization. In Guattari's analysis, the spread of Integrated World Capitalism has been accompanied by the infiltration of homogenizing norms into the production of subjectivity at all levels of daily life, whether "individual, domestic, conjugal, neighborly, creative, or personal-ethical" (*Ecologies* 44). Such norms desingularize different modes of subjectivity and experience, and propagate images of thought as somehow "outside nature," centered on concepts, discourses, and regimes of control, instrumentalization, and representationalist identity. Mental ecology aims to enable the singularization of human existence in terms of an immanent subjectivity that both affects and is affected by the natural reality in which it is immersed. Here the central concern for Guattari is with the fluid processes characteristic of the becoming of thought, especially with the capacity to create new modes of ecologically aware existence that are no longer dependent upon transcendent values and the narrow confines of a culture defined by corporate profit and authority.

Each ecology, then, confronts a specific problem area, yet these areas are not separate from one another because they are transversally interconnected and are degrading simultaneously. This allows Guattari to propose a generalized ecology viewed through the lenses of each of the three ecologies, united by their common principle:

> The principle common to the three ecologies consists of the following: each of the existential territories with which they confront us exists, not in and of itself, closed upon itself, but as a precarious, finite, finitized, singular, singularized for-itself, capable of bifurcating into stratified and mortified reiterations, or opening up, as a process, into praxes that enable it to be rendered "habitable" by human projects. It is this praxic-openness that constitutes the essence of the art of the "eco," subsuming all the ways of domesticating existential territories, concerning intimate modes of being, the body, the environment, the great contextual ensembles relative to ethnic groups, the nation, or even the general rights of humanity. (*Ecologies* 49)

While the struggles and aims of each ecology are different, their common aim is to "organize new micropolitical and microsocial practices, new solidarities, a new gentleness or kindness, conjoined with new aesthetic practices and new analytic practices of formations of the unconscious" (*Ecologies* 45–46).

In this way, Guattari articulates an ecological vision aimed at developing different forms of social action "which cannot be achieved by top-down reforms" on the part of professional politicians, but by the creative proliferation of new value-systems, alternative modes of subjectivity, innovative human and nonhuman relationships and forms of alliance, across the social network of everyday practices intersecting with the natural movements of global becomings (*Ecologies* 57).

All that has been elucidated here makes it clear that Deleuze would agree with most, but perhaps not all, of the elements of Guattari's account. What is most important is their agreement that in order to resist ecologically destructive beliefs and practices, it is necessary to engage in the creation of specific alternatives at the level of local yet overlapping habitats, which allows for the formation of mutually beneficial alliances and relationships of ecological solidarity on a planetary scale. On this basis, it may be possible to formulate a more extensive dialogue between Deleuze, Guattari, and other current theorists concerning ecology, and begin to develop micropolitical analyses of various ecological conditions, problems, and modes of intervention.

What is particularly important about Deleuze's rejection of antinaturalism is the suggestion that we eliminate moral judgments that are dependent upon faith in a transcendent order which is held to be the source of eternal values. Deleuze's naturalism does not entail essentialism because it does not seek to pronounce moral valuations based on narrowly defined models of what human and nonhuman nature "is." Instead, he urges us to create new values and sensibilities that *do* enable life on the planet to thrive.

Deleuze sees our values, beliefs, relations, and institutions as susceptible to reevaluation and reconstruction. Yet this requires a willingness to experiment, to develop ethics as the practice of exploration and discovery, to carefully create and determine which modes of living enhance or destroy life, and to cultivate respect both for unforeseen possibilities as well as for those ecological limits that cannot yet be determined or overcome. For such a practice it is vitally necessary that we learn from what the earth can teach us, and perhaps, in the process, we can then strive to elaborate a new *ethos* of ecological becoming. Such an *ethos*, as suggested by Deleuze's writings, would seek to assert the imaginative capabilities of individuals, organizations, nations, and the international community for the purpose of creating new forms of solidarity embracing all of the planet's diverse inhabitants.

Concluding Remarks

Philosophy has traditionally set itself the task of uncovering transcendent essences and absolute foundations while subsuming difference under the ideal of the identical. Deleuze argues for overturning such traditional ventures in all of their idealist and rationalist guises, and actively promotes a philosophical project that embraces the constantly changing sensible world of becoming and multiplicity. This positive philosophy of difference, vigorously attuned as it is to the perpetual flux of actions, thoughts, and desires in this immanent world, constitutes a pluralistic variety of empiricism. Attentive to the transformative conditions, contexts, processes, and relations of existence, it never ceases to look to the singularity of our experiences and to strive for new configurations of thinking and feeling, especially those that would reestablish contact with the world.

    Such an effort is the vital core of Deleuze's thought. It seeks to bring us back into contact with the complexity and richness of the world by means of an uncompromising affirmation of difference. Through Deleuze's writings I have tried to explore how this affirmation is variously manifested in his radically pluralist empiricism. One of the most important suggestions this book makes, I hope, is that we must actively work to create a habitable world, while recognizing our place in a natural, living reality that is complex, interrelational, symbiotic, and, ultimately, whose changing limits or dimensions are inseparable from our own continued existence. If that is the case, Deleuze's empiricism amounts to the practical affirmation of the common destiny shared by all modes of life on earth, not in spite of, but because of their multiple, flowing, yet always intersecting and fragile lines of difference.

By necessity, however, and out of respect for the principles expressed in Deleuze's work, this exploration leaves many territories undiscovered and numerous answers unfound. Similarly, I trust that it is also more than a beginning, but much less than an end. As I noted at the outset, I did not intend this book to be a final, definitive statement about all of Deleuze's philosophy. There is too much to Deleuze to even begin to entertain such a grand and probably misguided notion. What I have tried to do is sympathetically examine some aspects of his work that either have not been noticed before or have not always received the attention they deserve. Above all I have sought to show how the remarkable power of problems and questions, of problematization, rather than the presumed certainties of preexisting answers animate his thought. Problems, and thus their solutions, are not "givens" Deleuze tells us, but rather "are the differential elements in thought" (*DR* 162). They are provoked by our encounters with the unknown and provide the conditions for creative and continuous processes of becoming.

How can we create something new? How can we think differently? How can we literally make, and respect, difference without succumbing to the illusions of closure, of finality, or of essentialist absolutes? In taking up and cultivating such questions, Deleuze proposes a compelling and elusive vision of the work of philosophy. The promises as well as the risks of such a position are, as Deleuze so often maintains, the necessary conditions for the practice of a pluralist empiricism which seeks to open up new possibilities for thinking, feeling, and being.

Notes

Introduction

1. Gilles Deleuze, *Negotiations: 1972–1990*, trans. M. Joughin (New York: Columbia University Press, 1995), p. 146.
2. A noteworthy exception is Bruce Baugh, "Deleuze and Empiricism," *The Journal of the British Society for Phenomenology* 24, no. 1 (January 1993): 15–31. This is a slightly revised version of his earlier "Transcendental Empiricism: Deleuze's Response to Hegel," *Man and World* 25, no. 2 (March 1992): 133–48.

Chapter 1

1. The history of the problem of representation is undoubtedly equal to the history of philosophy itself. Deleuze is concerned primarily, though not exclusively, with the representationalist theories of Plato, Descartes, Kant, and Hegel.
2. For more on this issue in relation to Kant, see Gilles Deleuze, *Kant's Critical Philosophy*.
3. This point is made by Todd May in "Difference and Unity in Gilles Deleuze," in *Gilles Deleuze and the Theater of Philosophy*, ed. C. V. Boundas and D. Olkowski (New York and London: Routledge, 1994), esp. pp. 34–38. I discuss the "constructivist" aspect of Deleuze's philosophy in the following chapter.

4. Concerning the question of his perspective on morality, Nietzsche writes that it is necessary "to *learn to think differently*—in order at last, perhaps very late on, to attain even more: *to feel differently.*" *Daybreak: Thoughts on the Prejudices of Morality*, trans. R. J. Hollingdale, intro. M. Tanner (Cambridge: Cambridge University Press, 1982), p. 103.

5. Deleuze uses the capitalized term "Ideas" but in a sense other than that given in Plato or Kant, as should become clear over the course of this chapter.

6. Michael Hardt presents a fine reading of Deleuze's work in terms of "practical philosophy" in his *Gilles Deleuze: An Apprenticeship in Philosophy* (Minneapolis: University of Minnesota Press, 1993); see esp. chapters 2 and 3.

7. See Aristotle's *Metaphysics* Book VII, 1032a15–1034a10, in *The Basic Works of Aristotle*, ed. R. McKeon (New York: Random House, 1941). For Aristotle, of course, substance is required for individuation. Compare Plato (*Parmenides* and *Phaedo*) and Aquinas (*Summa Theologica*) concerning this issue.

8. Cf. Michel Foucault, *The Order of Things: An Archaeology of the Human Sciences*, trans. A. M. Sheridan (New York: Vintage Books, 1970), p. 17: "Up to the end of the sixteenth century, resemblance played a constructive role in the knowledge of Western culture. . . . And representation—whether in the service of pleasure or of knowledge—was posited as a form of repetition."

9. "The sort of thing I mean by 'genus' is that in virtue of which two things are both called the same one thing; and which is not accidentally differentiated whether regarded as matter or otherwise . . . this, then, will be a form of contrariety . . . because contrariety was shown to be complete difference." Aristotle, *Metaphysics* Book X, vii, 1058a 1–15.

10. See Aristotle, *Metaphysics* Book III, iii, 998b 5–10.

11. Aristotle, *Metaphysics* Book III, iii, 998b 20–30. Also: "And since everything that *is* . . . is so described in virtue of some one common concept, and the same is true of the contraries (since they can be referred to the primary contrarieties and differences of Being) . . . the difficulty which we stated at the beginning may be regarded as solved—I mean the problem as to how there can be one science of several things which are different in genus." Book XI, iii, 1061b 10–15.

12. Compare this to Deleuze's *Expressionism in Philosophy: Spinoza*, pp. 92–95 and pp. 217–26, as well as *Spinoza: Practical Philosophy*, pp. 26–29 and pp. 97–104.

13. Hegel writes that "every determination, every concrete thing, every Notion, is essentially a unity of distinguished and distinguishable moments, which . . . pass over into contradictory moments. . . . Now the thing, the subject, the Notion, is just this negative unity itself; it is inherently self-contradictory, but it is no less the *contradiction resolved*: it is the *ground* that contains and supports its determinations . . . the absolute is, because the finite is the inherently

self-contradictory opposition, because it is *not.*" *Science of Logic,* trans. A. V. Miller (Oxford: Oxford University Press, 1977), pp. 442–43.

14. According to Leibniz, "the final analysis of the laws of nature leads us to the most sublime principles of order and perfection, which indicate that the universe is the effect of a universal intelligent power." Such principles imply "a necessity of choice whose contrary means imperfection." *Philosophical Papers and Letters,* ed., trans. L. E. Loemker (Dordrecht: D. Reidel, 1970), p. 477, p. 484.

15. See Deleuze's discussion of the Humean problem of habit in *Empiricism and Subjectivity: An Essay on Hume's Theory of Human Nature,* esp. the third chapter.

16. Hume presents a fascinating discussion of how the reproducing and representing function of memory is central to the formation of personal identity by generating relations of resemblance and causation between distinct and separate impressions. *A Treatise of Human Nature,* ed. L. A. Selby-Bigge (Oxford: Oxford University Press, 1978), Book I, Part VI, Section VI.

17. See chapter three of Deleuze's *Bergsonism,* esp. pp. 58–62, for his discussion of Bergson on this matter.

18. On the issues contained in this discussion see Immanuel Kant, *Critique of Pure Reason,* trans. N. K. Smith (New York: St. Martin's Press, 1929), in particular the argument of the Transcendental Deduction. Subsequent references to this work will be cited in the text as *Critique.*

19. This aspect corresponds to the transcendental act of judgment as the condition for the possibility of representational knowledge. See also the Analogies of Experience, A177–A189 and B224–B225.

20. This also applies to the Kantian noumena-phenomena distinction.

21. See Deleuze's comments on this point in *K* 21–24.

22. Deleuze contrasts Nietzsche and Kant on similar issues in order to demonstrate that Kant's "critical" philosophy is, in fact, uncritical of many assumed truths concerning knowledge and morality.

23. In order to save the world of representation Kant attributed to the *a priori* conditions of thought limitations imposed by the harmonious exercise of the faculties, or common sense. Common sense thus forces the assumption of a metaphysical realism, in that the supposed *a priori* conditions of thought are of unsurpassable significance: thought is anticipated by the *a prior* conditions that serve as the ground for the necessity of judgments, which presupposes an internal coherence by which thought "recognizes" itself. As Deleuze argues here, Kant's is a reflexive method that posits an abstracted and generalized aspect of empirical experience as the necessary and sufficient condition of all reality.

24. See the conclusion of Deleuze's *Proust and Signs,* trans. R. Howard (New York: George Braziller, Inc., 1972), esp. pp. 162–65.

25. These are the characteristics Deleuze finds in the work of Foucault. See *Foucault*, trans. S. Hand (Minneapolis: University of Minnesota Press, 1986), pp. 47–69.

26. See the *Critique of Pure Reason*, B80–B82 and B160–B168.

27. For Kant, Ideas are concepts formed from notions (that are themselves pure concepts of the understanding), which transcend even the possibility of experience (*Critique of Pure Reason*, B377). See also *K* 19.

28. Deleuze insists, however, that the negative can appear when actual terms and relations are cut off from their source and from the movement of their actualization. His position on this issue refers to the ethical-practical concerns of transcendental empiricism. That is why, at this point in *Difference and Repetition*, Deleuze opposes Marx to Hegel on the question of the negative, in terms of Marx's insight into *social* actualization and differentiation and in contrast to Hegel's negative determination of abstract concepts.

Chapter 2

1. This has recently been done in two remarkable volumes by Yirmiyahu Yovel, *The Marrano of Reason* and *The Adventures of Immanence*, which together comprise *Spinoza and Other Heretics* (Princeton, N. J.: Princeton University Press, 1989).

2. "Platon, Les Grecs." In *Critique et clinique* (Paris: Editions de Minuit, 1993), p. 171; my translation.

3. *Proust and Signs*, p. 144.

4. Deleuze writes that he conceived of the history of philosophy as a kind of "buggery" or "immaculate conception" in which he imagined himself "taking an author from behind and giving him a child that would be his own offspring, yet monstrous." He explains that it was important that it should be the author's child, "because the author had to actually say all I had him saying. But the child was bound to be monstrous too, because it resulted from all sorts of shifting, slipping, dislocations, and hidden emissions that I really enjoyed." "Letter to a Harsh Critic," in *Negotiations*, p. 6.

5. Gilles Deleuze, "Bergson (1859–1941)." In *Les philosophes célèbres*, ed. M. Merleau-Ponty (Paris: Editions d'Art Lucien Mazenod, 1956), p. 295.

6. The term *élan vital* is left in the French, following the lead of the translators of Deleuze's book, who explain that any English rendering is insufficient.

7. Henri Bergson, *The Creative Mind*, trans. M. L. Andison (New York: Philosophical Library, 1946), p. 103.

8. Henri Bergson, *Mélanges* (Paris: Presses Universitaires de France, 1972), p. 964.

9. Bergson writes that "every summary of my views will distort their general nature and will by doing so expose them to a host of objections, if it does

not set out from in the first place, and constantly return to, what I regard as the core of the doctrine: the intuition of duration" (*Mélanges*, p. 1148).

10. In fact, Deleuze specifies that Bergson's project "is not absolutely new, not even in France, because it defines a general conception of philosophy, and in several respects it is similar to British empiricism, but the methods were profoundly diverse." "Bergson (1859–1941)," p. 299.

11. As we will see in the next chapter, Deleuze proposes a similar interpretation of Hume's empiricism: His empiricism is significant not because it searches for the "origin" of knowledge, but because it criticizes this search as a false problem.

12. It should be noted that Bergson distinguishes duration and time in order to refine his position. Time can be measured, while duration cannot.

13. "La conception de la différence chez Bergson." *Les études bergsoniennes* 4 (1956): 77–112. The quote is from p. 112.

14. Michael Hardt provides a more extensive treatment of Deleuze's Bergsonian critique of Hegel's dialectical method. (See *Gilles Deleuze: An Apprenticeship in Philosophy*, pp. 2–19). I prefer to focus on the positive articulations of Deleuze's work rather than engage in what has become a perhaps overworked and overwrought debate in Continental philosophy over whether or not it is possible to "escape" from Hegel and the dialectic. In addition, the Bergsonian/Deleuzian critique of opposition is aimed at the ontological commitment of the Hegelian dialectic, because to them opposition is a "practical and not ontological" category ("Bergson (1859–1941)," p. 294).

15. Bergson opens his philosophical autobiography on this very point: "What philosophy has lacked most of all is precision. Philosophical systems are not cut to the measure of the reality in which we live; they are too wide for reality. . . . The fact is that a self-contained system is an assemblage of conceptions so abstract, and consequently so vast, that it might contain, aside from the real, all that is possible and even impossible" (*The Creative Mind*, p. 11).

16. The following discussion draws upon Deleuze's commentary on Bergson in *Cinema 1: The Movement-Image*, trans. H. Tomlinson and B. Habberjam (Minneapolis: University of Minnesota Press, 1986).

17. Gilles Deleuze, *Cinema 2: The Time-Image*, trans. H. Tomlinson and R. Galeta (Minneapolis: University of Minnesota Press, 1989), p. 82.

18. Deleuze often speaks of the "magic formula" PLURALISM=MONISM, which prevents a collapse into rigid dualisms and philosophies of transcendence.

19. Hugh Tomlinson, translator of *Nietzsche and Philosophy*, reminds the reader that the French "élément," translated in the text as "element," bears the sense not only of the English "element" but also of "environment" and "grounds for existence" (*N* 199, n. 1). Hence the relevance of closely associating "element" and "condition."

20. Friedrich Nietzsche, *The Will to Power*, trans. W. Kaufmann and R. J. Hollingdale (New York: Vintage Books, 1967), p. 267 (no. 481).

21. I borrow this notion of *a priori* and necessary principles and conditions as "shadows" of a transcendent God from Yirmiyahu Yovel's discussion of Spinoza and Nietzsche in chapter 5 of *The Adventures of Immanence.*

22. Gilles Deleuze, *The Fold: Leibniz and the Baroque,* trans. T. Conley (Minneapolis: University of Minnesota Press, 1993), p. 20.

23. Deleuze refers to Spinoza as the "prince of philosophers" in at least two places, *Expressionism and Philosophy: Spinoza,* p. 11, and *What is Philosophy?,* p. 48. In the latter work, Deleuze also calls Spinoza the "Christ of philosophers" since the thought of pure immanence had been incarnated once, in Spinoza's philosophy (p. 60).

24. All citations from the *Ethics* will be from the version contained in *The Collected Works of Spinoza, Volume I,* ed. and trans. E. Curley (Princeton, N. J.: Princeton University Press, 1985). Subsequent references to this work will be cited in the text as *Ethics.*

25. Descartes writes in the *Principles of Philosophy,* "By *substance* we can understand nothing other than a thing which exists in such a way as to depend on no other thing for its existence" (I, 51). He also writes "each substance has one principal property which constitutes its nature and essence, and to which all its other properties are referred" (I, 53). For Descartes, it is only God which can be truly understood as "needing no other thing in order to exist," while extended and thinking substances are dependent upon God. Nevertheless, Descartes maintains that extended substance and thinking substance can be conceived independently of one another. The problem, as we will see, is that Descartes assigns thinking substance a privileged status. In *The Philosophical Writings of Descartes, Volume I,* trans. J. Cottingham, R. Stoothoff, and D. Murdoch (Cambridge: Cambridge University Press, 1985), p. 210.

26. It is generally agreed that Descartes believed that there are many (numerically) distinct substances sharing the attribute of thought, but there is less agreement about whether he also believed that there are a number of distinct extended substances. Edwin Curley discusses this issue in *Behind the Geometrical Method: A Reading of Spinoza's Ethics* (Princeton, N. J.: Princeton University Press, 1988), pp. 53–59 and p. 142, n. 9.

27. It should be remembered that Spinoza takes the terms substance, God, and Nature to express the same thing: "By God I understand a being absolutely infinite, i.e. , a substance consisting of an infinity of attributes, of which each one expresses an eternal and infinite essence" (*Ethics* IDef6); "That eternal and infinite being we call God, *or* Nature, acts from the same necessity from which he exists" (*Ethics* IVPref). Spinoza's "naturalization" of God is one consequence of his more extensive naturalism. In Chapter 4 I will discuss the possibility of a Deleuzian naturalism that borrows in part from Spinoza.

28. "Except God, no substance can be or be conceived" (*Ethics* IP14).

29. Implied is a critique of essence as "possibility" removed from actual existence. As Deleuze points out, Spinoza rejects the notion that essences are

possibles, since such a notion abstractly divorces that which exists from its real causes. For Spinoza, essences "have a fully actual existence that belongs to them by virtue of their cause" (*EP* 194). Existence accompanies essence on the basis of immanent causality.

30. This is in opposition to Descartes' ontological proof for the existence of God, which admits the eminence of God's divinity and an inequality between forms of being.

31. Antonio Negri also discerns a revolutionary quality in Spinoza's ontology of immanent univocity: "The paradox of this Spinozian category of univocal being is that it is constituted by the totality of reality. Every sign of abstraction is taken away; the category of being is the substance, the substance is unique, it is reality. It is neither above nor below reality, it is all reality. It has the scent and the tension of the world, it divinely possesses both unity and plurality. Absolute being is the surface of the world." *The Savage Anomaly: The Power of Spinoza's Metaphysics and Politics*, trans. M. Hardt (Minneapolis: University of Minnesota Press, 1991), p. 52.

32. This can also be seen in terms of Spinoza's *natura naturans* and *natura naturata*, of a productive substance and cause and its multiple effects "interconnected through a mutual immanence" (*SP* 92).

33. Deleuze clarifies that *conatus* is the "existential function of essence," that is, how essence (degree of power) is affirmed in the existence of a finite mode (*EP* 230).

34. More specifically, decomposition is the other side of composition inasmuch as it is a new combining of relations. For example, the death of a human body does not reduce it to nothingness, but more accurately places its parts into different relationships and compositions within nature; the characteristic composition of such a body is thus transformed.

35. Deleuze provides a brief yet powerful analysis of Spinoza's relationship to Hobbes on the issue of the state of reason and freedom with respect to the state of nature, and how their similar positions are to be contrasted to the "rationalist" moral tradition. This tradition presents human beings as born both reasonable and sociable, possessing unconditional duties determined by a superior authority. Spinoza and Hobbes, however, assign no privilege to reason simply because no one is born reasonable, i.e., one can only *become* reasonable. Furthermore, they regard duties as secondary to each individual's natural right, namely, the power of action that can only be determined and exercised fully by each individual and not by some higher authority. The situation of this "state of nature" thus requires a view of society as the dynamic development and cultivation of reason, freedom, and useful associations on the basis of the actual exercise of power and on experimentation and variation. This position results in a complex naturalistic theory of society. See *EP*, chapter 16. The importance of experimentation in the process of developing ways of living is emphasized in *SP*, especially chapter 6.

36. Nietzsche also claims that "it was suffering and incapacity that created all after-worlds—this and that brief madness of bliss which is experienced only by those who suffer most deeply." *Thus Spoke Zarathustra*, trans. W. Kaufmann (New York: Viking Press, 1966), p. 30. Deleuze's own ethical vision of a naturalist tradition that includes Spinoza, Lucretius, and Hume will be our point of discussion in Chapter 4.

37. Genevieve Lloyd offers a similar comparison of Hegel and Spinoza on these issues, showing that Hegel regarded death as the "liberation" and transcendence of the universal from the "defects" of life. In *Part of Nature: Self-Knowledge in Spinoza's Ethics* (Ithaca and London: Cornell University Press, 1994), pp. 141–47.

38. This point is also rather humorously used to critique the notion that philosophy is merely a grandly played yet ultimately ineffective "conversation" between rival opinions: "This is the Western democratic, popular conception of philosophy as providing pleasant or aggressive dinner conversations at Mr. Rorty's" (*WP* 144). Nicholas Rescher offers a similarly pointed critique of idealized consensus in his *Pluralism: Against the Demand for Consensus* (Oxford: Clarendon Press, 1993). While Rescher's style and idiom are quite different from those of Deleuze and Guattari, he proceeds from a standpoint which can be seen as sympathetic to their own.

39. Deleuze writes little on the role of truth with respect to the concept, possibly for two reasons. First, "truth" must itself be approached on the basis of constructivism and cannot merely be assumed to operate outside of specific contexts, values, and purposes: "A concept always has the truth *that falls to it as a function of the conditions of its creation*" (*WP* 27). Second, restricting philosophy to the search for eternal truth or regarding philosophy as the discovery of absolute knowledge at least potentially inhibits the directions philosophers might move in and also restricts the sources upon which they might draw: "Philosophers do the best they can, but they have too much to do to know whether it is the best, or even to bother with this question. . . . If one concept is 'better' than an earlier one, it is because it makes us aware of new variations and unknown resonances" (*WP* 28). This is not to say that Deleuze denies such a thing as truth (which he does not), but only that any concept of truth is constructed and is therefore not independent of the situational practices by which is contingently determined what is and is not true. As Deleuze would probably say, the tendency of rationalist philosophies to invoke transcendental references in order to justify what is regarded as true is "only a habit" and a particularly bad habit at that, which should be challenged by the creation of new habits.

40. Following his comment that "each plane has its own way of constructing immanence," Deleuze goes on to remark that "every plane of immanence is . . . distributive—it is an 'each'. . . . It is not just the planes that vary but the ways in which they are distributed" (*WP* 50). This is remarkably similar to William James' assertion in *Pragmatism* that "the world we live in exists diffused and

distributed, in the form of an indefinitely numerous lot of *eaches*." In *The Writings of William James*, ed. J. J. McDermott (Chicago: University of Chicago Press, 1977), p. 126. In fact, Deleuze's characterization of the philosophy of immanence as a radical empiricism resonates profoundly with James' own work, which James called radical empiricism. The possibility of interpreting Deleuze's thought in light of James' will be discussed in the following chapter.

41. This might be thought of in terms of Spinoza's parallelism (folding) of body and mind on the basis of the ontological unity of substance.

Chapter 3

1. See chapter 5 of *What is Philosophy?* for an account of the nonreferential nature of concepts.

2. "Intellectuals and Power," in Michel Foucault, *Language, Counter-Memory, Practice*, ed. D. F. Bouchard (Ithaca, New York: Cornell University Press, 1977), p. 208.

3. On the distinction between experience as constitutive and experience as constituted, see *Empiricism and Subjectivity*, pp. 66–72, pp. 92–98, and pp. 107–08. This position would, I believe, lead to an important distinction between Deleuze's empiricism and phenomenology, at least of the Husserlian sort. Husserlian phenomenology reduces the universal and *a priori* features of "lived experience" to necessary features of a transcendental and constitutive ego. Moreover, and this point will become more relevant in my discussion below, Husserl's transcendental phenomenology is ultimately concerned with the discovery of the necessary essences of things, through the eidetic reduction. The issue becomes more complex in the case of Merleau-Ponty's existential phenomenology, which proceeds from a criticism of Husserl's notions of eidetic reduction and transcendental ego.

4. Charlene Haddock Seigfried presents an illuminating discussion of the metaphysical perspective James claimed for his radical empiricism in *William James's Radical Reconstruction of Philosophy* (Albany: SUNY Press, 1990). See especially part five.

5. William James, *Essays in Radical Empiricism* (Cambridge, Mass. and London: Harvard University Press, 1976), pp. 22–23. Subsequent references to this work will be cited in the text as *Essays*.

6. William James, *The Will to Believe and Other Essays in Popular Philosophy* (Cambridge, Mass. and London: Harvard University Press, 1979), p. 6.

7. William James, *The Meaning of Truth* (Cambridge, Mass. and London: Harvard University Press, 1975), p. 6. Subsequent references to this work will be cited in the text as *Meaning*.

8. James does not conclude, however, that such transcendent claims are "meaningless" simply because they do not correspond to some demonstrable

physical objects. It is not possible here to elaborate on James' pragmatic epistemology beyond noting that his radical empiricism is intended to undermine the traditional distinction of thought and thing or consciousness and content as "discontinuous entities" and the belief that knowledge consists in a correspondence of the two (*Essays* 27). My interest, as mentioned above, with both James and Deleuze is in the ontological rather than epistemological issues, even though I realize that this distinction is somewhat fluid.

9. There is, in fact, some confusion in James' writing concerning the predominance of external relations. He consistently criticizes the view, representative of absolute monism, that there are only internal relations. Yet he also states at times that there are "inner relations" (such as between identical "types") although we are able to "arrange them just as freely" as external relations. See *Pragmatism* (Cambridge, Mass. and London: Harvard University Press, 1975), pp. 118–19. It is not clear in any case that by "inner relations" James has in mind the type of internal relations being discussed here. However, the evidence overwhelmingly points toward his belief that the pluralism of radical empiricism must be based on external relations, as James succinctly states in his notes for a course given in 1903–04 on "A Pluralistic Description of the World": "My philosophy and common sense both assume that things whose being is independent, can nevertheless come into relations, which are adventitious & external, not necessarily involved in the being of each thing." *Manuscript Lectures* (Cambridge, Mass. and London: Harvard University Press, 1988), p. 290. Since this type of statement is at the heart of his argument against absolutism, and indeed constitutes a polemic against it on ontological grounds, it shall be the focus of my treatment of James' radical empiricism. The situation will be somewhat different in the case of Deleuze, who clearly states that all relations are external to their terms.

10. A thing's "nature" can be thought, then, in Nietzschean terms, that is, in terms of becoming, relations, appropriations of forces, and perspectives, rather than in Platonic terms of a realm of Being or of eternal essences.

11. William James, *A Pluralistic Universe* (Cambridge, Mass. and London: Harvard University Press, 1977), p. 9. Seigfried usefully discusses James' perspectivism at several points in her book. Again, the similarities on these last points between James and Nietzsche, at least on the Deleuzian reading of Nietzsche which I offered in Chapter 2, is noteworthy.

12. James, *Pragmatism*, p. 126.

13. In his study of James' philosophy, Graham Bird notes that "Pragmatism and radical empiricism are clearly linked with an emphasis on immanence rather than transcendence." *William James* (London and New York: Routledge & Kegan Paul, 1986), p. 147.

14. James, *A Pluralistic Universe*, p. 145. As we will see below, the conjunction "and" is frequently utilized by Deleuze in order to resist the predicative "is" of foundationalist metaphysics.

15. Deleuze had previously edited a collection of Hume's writings with André Cresson entitled *David Hume, sa vie, son oeuvre avec un exposé de sa philosophie* (Paris: Presses Universitaires de France, 1952). He later contributed the entry on Hume for the *Histoire de la philosophie* series edited by François Châtelet (Paris: Hachette, 1972).

16. See "Letter to a Harsh Critic," in *Negotiations*. As Deleuze writes in *Dialogues*, it is "the concrete richness of the sensible" that motivates and sustains empiricism (p. 54).

17. This perspective would support Deleuze's argument, reviewed in Chapter 1, against Kant's attempt to define the necessary conditions for the possibility of all experience, that is, *the* conditions for experience as such inscribed in the transcendental subject.

18. Kant, *Critique of Pure Reason*, p. 606. Deleuze's own empiricism is perhaps better characterized as geographically rather than historically oriented (although it does not exclude historical conditions), since he is concerned ultimately with milieus, planes, fields, contexts, and relationships and not a supposedly linear historical progression from origin to end (i.e., History).

19. Deleuze also comments here that "When James calls himself a pluralist, he does not say, in principle, anything else" (*ES* 99).

20. Deleuze is referring to Hume's statement that "whatever objects are different are distinguishable, and that whatever objects are distinguishable are separable by the thought and the imagination." *A Treatise of Human Nature*, p. 18.

21. Gilles Deleuze and Félix Guattari, *Anti-Oedipus: Capitalism and Schizophrenia*, trans. R. Hurley, M. Seem, and H. Lane (Minneapolis: University of Minnesota Press, 1983), p. 42.

22. James, *The Will to Believe*, p. vii.

23. In an interview conducted in 1980 Deleuze relates that he does not deny the reality of systems, unities, or wholes, but denies only that they are closed and complete rather than open and partial. He notes that what he and Guattari call a "rhizome," which I examine below, is an example of an open and partial system. Such open systems are "based on interactions" that "relate to circumstances rather than essences." See "On *A Thousand Plateaus*," in *Negotiations*, pp. 31–32. This important point is often overlooked by commentators on Deleuze's work.

24. These formulations can be found in Deleuze's discussion of Bergson's notions of relations and change in *Cinema 1: The Movement-Image*, chapter one, third thesis. Deleuze also states: "We know that the relation between two things is not reducible to an attribute of one thing or the other, nor, indeed, to an attribute of the set. On the other hand, *it is still quite possible to relate the relations to a whole if one conceives the whole as a continuum, and not as a given set.*" *Cinema 1: The Movement-Image*, p. 219 n. 6; my emphasis.

25. All of this can be thought of in terms of the Nietzschean form of questioning; not "What is X?" (which seeks to discover a fixed essence) but "Which

one is X?" (which seeks to determine "the continuity of concrete objects taken in their becoming") (*N* 76).

26. James also wrote that "each part of the world is in some ways connected, in some other ways not connected with its other parts, and the ways can be discriminated" (*A Pluralistic Universe*, p. 79).

27. Given the topic of the present chapter, it is worth noting that one of the reasons Deleuze and Guattari characterize their book as a multiplicity of plateaus is because a "book has neither subject nor object; it is made of variously formed matters, and very different dates and speeds. To attribute a book to a subject is to overlook this working of matters, and the exteriority of their relations" (*ATP* 3).

28. André Pierre Colombat briefly discusses the extension of the rhizome beyond its botanical limits and why it is not simply a metaphor in his article "A Thousand Trails to Work with Deleuze," in *SubStance* 20, no. 3 (1991): 10–23. We might consider the rhizome, in all its dimensions, to be an excellent example of the use Deleuze makes of naturalism.

29. It is important to note that by speaking of the nature of the multiplicity, Deleuze and Guattari are referring to the quality that an open system possesses and which changes as the relations of the whole are transformed, and not to the objective essence of a thing and its intrinsic relation to an attribute or property.

30. See Ronald Bogue's discussion of Deleuze and Guattari's "theory of action" in his *Deleuze and Guattari* (London and New York: Routledge, 1989), pp. 136–49.

31. The issue here is, again, to be stated in qualitative and not in quantitative terms. For Deleuze and Guattari, majority refers "not to a greater relative quantity but to the determination of a state or standard in relation to which larger quantities, as well as the smallest, can be said to be minoritarian: white-man, adult-male, etc." (*ATP* 291). This is obviously what is at issue in what is often referred to in terms of the "politics of identity."

32. William James to Mrs. Henry Whitman, 7 June 1899, in *Letters of William James*, ed. H. James (Boston: The Atlantic Monthly Press, 1920), 2: 90. James refers to himself as an anarchist in a letter to William Dean Howells, 16 November 1900 (Howells Papers, Houghton Library, Harvard University). This letter is cited in George Cotkin, *William James: Public Philosopher* (Urbana and Chicago: University of Illinois Press, 1989), p. 174 and p. 210, n. 55. Cotkin discusses James' anarchist sympathies at various points in his book.

33. Gilles Deleuze and Félix Guattari, *Kafka: Toward a Minor Literature*, trans. D. Polan (Minneapolis: University of Minnesota Press, 1986), p. 18.

34. *Kafka*, p. 23.

35. See the critiques of fascism, semiotic law, social and political representationalism, and organicism by Deleuze and Guattari in *Anti-Oedipus*.

36. On the use of "and" and its relation to empiricism, see also *Dialogues*, pp. 56–59. In fact, according to Deleuze "and" is not merely a specific type of

relation or conjunction, it is "a special form of every possible conjunction," that is, it is an affirmative disjunction in the guise of conjunction (*ATP* 526, n. 32).

37. A more complete explanation of Deleuze and Guattari's theory of statements-acts assemblages is found in Dorothea Olkowski, "Semiotics and Gilles Deleuze," in *The Semiotic Web 1990*, ed. T. A. Sebeok and J. Umiker-Sebeok (Bloomington and Indianapolis: Indiana University Press, 1990). In addition, see my "From Relations to Practice in the Empiricism of Gilles Deleuze," *Man and World* 28, no. 3 (June 1995): 283–302, for a discussion of external relations in regard to Deleuze's "logic of sense."

38. Deleuze reinforces this perspective when he writes in *Dialogues* that "it is in concrete social fields, at specific moments, that the comparative movements of deterritorialization, the continuums of intensity and the combinations of flux that they form must be studied" (p. 135).

39. This position is expressed quite well by Foucault, whom Deleuze saw as a fellow empiricist: "I do not think there is anything that is functionally—by its very nature—absolutely liberating. Liberty is a *practice*." See "Space, Knowledge, and Power," in *The Foucault Reader*, ed. P. Rabinow (New York: Pantheon Books, 1984), p. 245. Deleuze's *Foucault* is a magnificent exercise which reads Foucault in light of the type of empiricism Deleuze promotes, and shows how Foucault, too, was a profound theorist and practitioner of relations.

40. *Dialogues*, p. 147. Here Deleuze insists that "quality of life" is to be distinguished from "standard of living," that is, the general quantification of existence at the expense of life's richness, diversity, and complexity.

Chapter 4

1. Michel Foucault, *Politics, Philosophy, Culture*, ed. L. D. Kritzman (New York and London: Routledge, 1988), pp. 119–20.

2. See, however, Lyotard's mostly positive reflections on ecological destruction and ideology in his essay "*Oikos*," in *Political Writings*, trans. B. Readings and K. P. Geiman (Minneapolis: University of Minnesota Press, 1993). Arran E. Gare perceptively notes that although "French poststructuralists have not been centrally concerned with the environment," Deleuze clearly differs in "[r]ejecting the anti-naturalism of other poststructuralists." *Postmodernism and the Environmental Crisis* (London and New York: Routledge, 1995), p. 87, p. 70.

3. General accounts of naturalism can be found in Arthur C. Danto, "Naturalism," *Encyclopedia of Philosophy*, vol. 5 (New York: Macmillan Publishing Co., Inc., 1967); *Naturalism and the Human Spirit*, ed. Y. H. Krikorian (New York: Columbia University Press, 1944); and *American Philosophic Naturalism in the Twentieth Century*, ed. J. Ryder (Amherst, New York: Prometheus Books, 1994).

4. These essays were originally published as "Renverser le platonisme," *Revue de métaphysique et de morale* 71, no. 4 (1966): 426–38, and "Lucrèce et le naturalisme," *Etudes philosophiques* 1 (1961): 19–29. They are included in *The Logic of Sense* as "Plato and the Simulacrum" and "Lucretius and the Simulacrum."

5. Donald W. Livingstone takes a view similar to Deleuze in this respect, and believes that the "concept of convention is, perhaps, the most important in Hume's philosophy." *Hume's Philosophy of Common Life* (Chicago and London: University of Chicago Press, 1984), p. 4 and passim.

6. It is worth noting that Hume does not limit the disposition of sympathy only to humans, but extends the ability to enter into the interests and emotions of others to nonhuman animals, as well. Sympathy is not species specific, and frequently occurs between different species. It is observable, he writes, "thro' the whole animal creation," and "takes place among animals, no less than among men." *A Treatise on Human Nature*, p. 363, p. 398. For an interesting attempt to apply Hume's "biosocial" moral theory to environmental ethics, see J. Baird Callicott, "Animal Liberation and Environmental Ethics: Back Together Again," in *Earth Ethics*, ed. J. P. Sterba (Englewood Cliffs, N. J.: Prentice Hall, 1995): 190–98.

7. Hume writes that the "very first state and situation" of human beings "may justly be esteem'd social." *A Treatise on Human Nature*, p. 493.

8. "Adsorbtion" is when one or more things bond together without eliminating the singularity, uniqueness, or difference of each thing.

9. *Oikos* can mean house, household, family, milieu, vicinity, habitat, or environment.

10. The following discussion is based primarily on *A Thousand Plateaus*, especially Plateau 3, "10,000 B. C.: The Geology of Morals."

11. Michel Serres has made symbioses a central concept of his call for a "natural contract" that is dedicated to the renewal of our relationship with the earth. He argues that humans have maintained a "parasitic" rather than "symbiotic" relationship with the natural world, and that a global ecological revolution requires an awareness of the earth as our "symbiont." See *The Natural Contract*, trans. E. MacArthur and W. Paulson (Ann Arbor: University of Michigan Press, 1995), pp. 35–44.

12. I refer here to the final chapter of *Spinoza: Practical Philosophy*, also published separately as "Ethology: Spinoza and Us," in *Incorporations*, ed. J. Crary and S. Kwinter (New York: Zone Publications, 1992). There are quite a few references to ethology scattered throughout Deleuze's writings and it is unnecessary to refer to them all in this context. However, the reader is urged to consult especially plateaus 10 and 11 of *A Thousand Plateaus*, entitled "1730: Becoming-Intense, Becoming-Animal, Becoming-Imperceptible . . ." and "1837: Of the Refrain."

13. *Negotiations*, p. 100.

14. An example of a similar important statement regarding environmental ethics can be found in Jim Cheney, "Postmodern Environmental Ethics: Ethics as Bioregional Narrative," in *Environmental Ethics* 11 (Summer 1989): 117–34.

15. Nietzsche asks: "When will all these shadows of God cease to darken our minds? When will we complete our de-deification of nature? When may we begin to '*naturalize*' humanity in terms of a pure, newly discovered, newly redeemed nature?" *The Gay Science*, trans. W. Kaufmann (New York: Vintage Books, 1974), pp. 168–69. Significant discussions of Nietzsche's naturalism can be found in Theodore R. Schatzki, "Ancient and Naturalistic Themes in Nietzsche's Ethics," *Nietzsche-Studien* 23 (1994): 146–67; and Lawrence Lampert, *Nietzsche and Modern Times* (New Haven and London: Yale University Press, 1993).

16. Murray Bookchin, *Which Way for the Ecology Movement?* (Edinburgh and San Francisco: AK Press, 1994), p. 17.

17. Murray Bookchin, *Remaking Society: Pathways to a Green Future* (Boston: South End Press, 1990), p. 32, p. 44.

18. These ideas can be found throughout the works cited above, and especially in *Toward an Ecological Society* (Montreal and Buffalo: Black Rose Books, 1980).

19. See Murray Bookchin, *The Ecology of Freedom* (Palo Alto: Cheshire Books, 1982), p. 36, and *The Philosophy of Social Ecology: Essays on Dialectical Naturalism* (Montreal and Buffalo: Black Rose Books, 1990), p. 182.

20. See, for example, the introductory chapter to *Remaking Society*.

21. Foucault clarifies that critically examining the notion of an inviolate, inherently nonoppressive rationality is not by itself evidence of irrationalism: "I think that the blackmail that has very often been at work in every critique of reason or every critical inquiry into the history of rationality (either you accept rationality or you fall prey to the irrational) operates as though a rational critique of rationality were impossible." The point made by Foucault is that there are different kinds of rationality that may or may not be useful or beneficial. See "Critical Theory/Intellectual History," in *Politics, Philosophy, Culture*, p. 27.

22. See Murray Bookchin, "Ecologizing the Dialectic," in *Renewing the Earth: the Promise of Social Ecology*, ed. John Clark (London: Green Print, 1990).

23. *Remaking Society*, p. 41, p. 75.

24. *The Philosophy of Social Ecology*, p. 35.

25. Arne Naess, *Ecology, Community, and Lifestyle: Outline of an Ecosophy*, trans. D. Rothenberg (Cambridge: Cambridge University Press, 1989), pp. 27–28, p. 163, pp. 171–76. Subsequent references to this work will be cited in the text as *Lifestyle*.

26. Bill Devall and George Sessions, *Deep Ecology: Living as if Nature Mattered* (Salt Lake City: Peregrine Smith Books, 1985), p. 65.

27. Arne Naess, "The Shallow and the Deep, Long-Range Ecology Movement," *Inquiry* 16 (1973): 95–100. The quote is from p. 96.

28. Félix Guattari, *Les Trois Ecologies* (Paris: Editions Galilée, 1990). All translations from this text are my own. Subsequent references to this work will be cited in the text as *Ecologies*.

Bibliography

Allison, Henry E. *Benedict de Spinoza: An Introduction.* Revised edition. New Haven: Yale University Press, 1987.
Aristotle. *The Basic Works of Aristotle.* Edited by R. McKeon. New York: Random House, 1941.
Baugh, Bruce. "Deleuze and Empiricism." *Journal of the British Society for Phenomenology* 24 (January 1993): 15–31.
———. "Transcendental Empiricism: Deleuze's Response to Hegel." *Man and World* 25 (March 1992): 133–48.
Bergson, Henri. *The Creative Mind: An Introduction to Metaphysics.* Translated by M. Andison. New York: Citadel Press, 1946.
———. *Duration and Simultaneity.* Translated by L. Jacobson. Indianapolis: Bobbs-Merrill, 1965.
———. *Matter and Memory.* Translated by W. S. Palmer and N. M. Paul. New York: Zone Books, 1988.
———. *Mélanges.* Paris: Presses Universitaires de France, 1972.
———. *The Two Sources of Morality and Religion.* Translated by R. A. Audra and C. Brereton. Notre Dame: University of Notre Dame Press, 1935.
Bird, Graham. *William James.* London: Routledge & Kegan Paul, 1986.
Bogue, Ronald. *Deleuze and Guattari.* London and New York: Routledge, 1989.
Bookchin, Murray. *The Ecology of Freedom.* Palo Alto: Chesire Books, 1980.
———. *The Philosophy of Social Ecology: Essays on Dialectical Naturalism.* Montreal and Buffalo: Black Rose Books, 1990.
———. *Remaking Society: Pathways to a Green Future.* Boston: South End Press, 1990.

———. *Toward an Ecological Society*. Montreal: Black Rose Books, 1980.
———. *Which Way for the Ecology Movement?*. Edinburgh and San Francisco: AK Press, 1994.
Boundas, Constantin and Dorothea Olkowski, eds. *Gilles Deleuze and the Theater of Philosophy*. New York and London: Routledge, 1994.
Callicott, J. Baird. "Animal Liberation and Environmental Ethics: Back Together Again." In *Earth Ethics*. Edited by J. P. Sterba. Englewood Cliffs, NJ: Prentice Hall, 1995.
Cheney, Jim. "Postmodern Environmental Ethics: Ethics as Bioregional Narrative." *Environmental Ethics* 11, no. 2 (Summer 1989): 117–34.
Clark, John, ed. *Renewing the Earth: The Promise of Social Ecology*. London: Green Print, 1990.
Colombat, André Pierre. "A Thousand Trails to Work with Deleuze." *SubStance* 20, no. 3 (1991): 10–23.
Cotkin, George. *William James: Public Philosopher*. Urbana and Chicago: University of Illinois Press, 1989.
Curley, Edwin. *Behind the Geometrical Method: A Reading of Spinoza's Ethics*. Princeton: Princeton University Press, 1988.
Deleuze, Gilles. "A Philosophical Concept. . . ." In *Who Comes After the Subject?*. Edited by E. Cadava, P. Connor and J-L Nancy. New York and London: Routledge, 1991.
———. "Bergson (1859–1941)." In *Les philosophes célèbres*. Edited by M. Merleau-Ponty. Paris: Editions d'Art Lucien Mazenod, 1956.
———. *Bergsonism*. Translated by H. Tomlinson and B. Habberjam. New York: Zone Books, 1988.
———. *Cinema I: The Movement-Image*. Translated by H. Tomlinson and B. Habberjam. Minneapolis: University of Minnesota Press, 1986.
———. *Cinema II: The Time-Image*. Translated by H. Tomlinson and R. Galeta. Minneapolis: University of Minnesota Press, 1989.
———. "La conception de la différence chez Bergson." *Les études bergsoniennes* 4 (1956): 77–112.
———. *Critique et clinique*. Paris: Les Editions de Minuit, 1993.
———. *Difference and Repetition*. Translated by P. Patton. New York: Columbia University Press, 1994.
———. *Empiricism and Subjectivity: An Essay on Hume's Theory of Human Nature*. Translated by C. Boundas. New York: Columbia University Press, 1991.
———. *Expressionism in Philosophy: Spinoza*. Translated by M. Joughin. New York: Zone Books, 1990.
———. *The Fold: Leibniz and the Baroque*. Translated by T. Conley. Minneapolis: University of Minnesota Press, 1993.
———. *Foucault*. Translated by S. Hand. Minneapolis: University of Minnesota Press, 1988.

———. *Kant's Critical Philosophy: The Doctrine of the Faculties.* Translated by H. Tomlinson and B. Habberjam. Minneapolis: University of Minnesota Press, 1984.
———. *The Logic of Sense.* Translated by M. Lester with C. Stivale, edited by C. Boundas. New York: Columbia University Press, 1990.
———. "Mediators." In *Incorporations.* Translated by M. Joughin. New York: Zone Books, 1992.
———. *Negotiations: 1972–1990.* Translated by M. Joughin. New York: Columbia University Press, 1995.
———. *Nietzsche and Philosophy.* Translated by H. Tomlinson. New York: Columbia University Press, 1983.
———. "Nomad Thought." In *The New Nietzsche: Contemporary Styles of Interpretation.* Translated and edited by D. B. Allison. Cambridge, Mass.: MIT Press, 1977.
———. *Périclès et Verdi: La philosophie de François Châtelet.* Paris: Minuit, 1988.
———. *Proust and Signs.* Translated by R. Howard. New York: George Braziller, Inc., 1972.
———. *Spinoza: Practical Philosophy.* Translated by R. Hurley. San Francisco: City Lights Books, 1988.
Deleuze, Gilles and Félix Guattari. *Anti-Oedipus.* Vol. 1 of *Capitalism and Schizophrenia.* Translated by R. Hurley, M. Seem, and H. Lane. Minneapolis: University of Minnesota Press, 1983.
———. *A Thousand Plateaus.* Vol. 2 of *Capitalism and Schizophrenia.* Translated by B. Massumi. Minneapolis: University of Minnesota Press, 1987.
———. *Kafka.* Translated by D. Polan. Minneapolis: University of Minnesota Press, 1986.
———. *What is Philosophy?.* Translated H. Tomlinson and G. Burchell. New York: Columbia University Press, 1994.
Deleuze, Gilles and Claire Parnet. *Dialogues.* Translated by H. Tomlinson and B. Habberjam. New York: Columbia University Press, 1987.
Descartes, René. *The Philosophical Writings of Descartes.* Vol. 1. Translated by J. Cottingham, R. Stoothoff, and D. Murdoch. Cambridge: Cambridge University Press, 1985.
Devall, Bill and Sessions, George. *Deep Ecology: Living as if Nature Mattered.* Salt Lake City: Peregrine Smith Books, 1985.
Forbes, Duncan. *Hume's Philosophical Politics.* Cambridge: Cambridge University Press, 1975.
Foucault, Michel. *The Foucault Reader.* Edited by P. Rabinow. New York: Pantheon Books, 1984.
———. *Language, Counter-Memory, Practice.* Translated by D. Bouchard with S. Simon. Edited by D. Bouchard. New York: Cornell University Press, 1977.

———. *The Order of Things: An Archeology of the Human Sciences*. Translated by A. M. Sheridan. New York: Vintage Books, 1973.

———. *Politics, Philosophy, Culture*. Edited by L. D. Kritzman. New York and London: Routledge, 1988.

Gare, Aaran E. *Postmodernism and the Environmental Crisis*. London and New York: Routledge, 1995.

Guattari, Félix. *Les Trois Ecologies*. Paris: Editions Galilée, 1990.

Hardt, Michael. *Gilles Deleuze: An Apprenticeship in Philosophy*. Minneapolis: University of Minnesota Press, 1993.

Hegel, G. W. F. *Phenomenology of Spirit*. Translated by A. V. Miller. Oxford: Oxford University Press, 1977.

———. *Science of Logic*. Translated by A. V. Miller. Atlantic Highlands, N. J.: Humanities Press, 1969.

Hume, David. *A Treatise of Human Nature*. Second edition. Edited by L. A. Selby-Bigge. Oxford: Oxford University Press, 1978.

———. *Essays: Moral, Political and Literary*. Revised edition. Edited by E. F. Miller. Indianapolis: Liberty Fund, Inc., 1985.

James, William. *The Letters of William James*. Edited by H. James. Boston: The Atlantic Monthly Press, 1920.

———. *The Works of William James*. Edited by F. H. Burkhardt, F. Bowers, and I. K. Skrupskelis. Cambridge, Mass. and London: Harvard University Press, 1975–1988.

———. *The Writings of William James*. Edited by J. J. McDermott. Chicago: University of Chicago Press, 1977.

Kant, Immanuel. *Critique of Pure Reason*. Translated by N. K. Smith. New York: St. Martin's Press, 1929.

Krikorian, Yervant H., ed. *Naturalism and the Human Spirit*. New York: Columbia University Press, 1944.

Lampert, Lawrence. *Nietzsche and Modern Times*. New Haven and London: Yale University Press, 1993.

Leibniz, Gottfried Wilhelm. *Philosophical Papers and Letters*. Translated by L. E. Loemker. Dordrecht: D. Reidel, 1970.

Livingstone, Donald W. *Hume's Philosophy of Common Life*. Chicago: University of Chicago Press, 1984.

Lloyd, Genevieve. *Part of Nature: Self-Knowledge in Spinoza's Ethics*. Ithaca and London: Cornell University Press, 1994.

Lyotard, Jean-François. *Political Writings*. Translated by B. Readings and K. P. Geiman. Minneapolis: University of Minnesota Press, 1993.

May, Todd. G. "Difference and Unity in Gilles Deleuze." In *Gilles Deleuze and the Theater of Philosophy*. Edited by C. V. Boundas and D. Olkowksi. New York and London: Routledge, 1994.

Bibliography

Naess, Arne. *Ecology, Community, and Lifestyle: Outline of an Ecosophy.* Translated by D. Rothenberg. Cambridge: Cambridge University Press, 1989.

———. "The Shallow and the Deep, Long-Range Ecology Movement." *Inquiry* 16 (1973): 95–100.

Negri, Antonio. *The Savage Anomaly: The Power of Spinoza's Metaphysics and Politics.* Translated by M. Hardt. Minneapolis: University of Minnesota Press, 1991.

Nietzsche, Friedrich. *Beyond Good and Evil.* Translated by W. Kaufmann. New York: Vintage Books, 1966.

———. *Daybreak: Thoughts on the Prejudices of Morality.* Translated by R. J. Hollingdale, introduced by M. Tanner. Cambridge: Cambridge University Press, 1982.

———. *The Gay Science.* Translated by W. Kaufmann. New York: Vintage Books, 1974.

———. *Human, All Too Human.* Translated by R. J. Hollingdale. Cambridge: Cambridge University Press, 1986.

———. *On the Genealogy of Morals.* Translated by W. Kaufmann and R. J. Hollingdale. New York: Vintage Books, 1967.

———. *Thus Spoke Zarathustra.* Translated by W. Kaufmann. New York: Viking Press, 1966.

———. *The Will to Power.* Translated by W. Kaufmann and R. J. Hollingdale, edited by W. Kaufmann. New York: Vintage Books, 1967.

Olkowski, Dorothea. "Semiotics and Gilles Deleuze." In *The Semiotic Web.* Edited by T. A. Sebeok and J. Umiker-Sebeok. Bloomington and Indianapolis: Indiana University Press, 1990.

Rescher, Nicholas. *Pluralism: Against the Demand for Consensus.* Oxford: Clarendon Press, 1993.

Ryder, John, ed. *American Philosophical Naturalism in the Twentieth Century.* Amherst, New York: Prometheus Books, 1994.

Schacht, Richard. *Nietzsche.* London and New York: Routledge, 1983.

Schatzki, Theodore R. "Ancient and Naturalistic Themes in Nietzsche's Ethics." *Nietzsche-Studien*, 23 (1994): 146–67.

Seigfried, Charlene Haddock. *William James' Radical Reconstruction of Philosophy.* Albany: SUNY Press, 1990.

Serres, Michel. *The Natural Contract.* Translated by E. MacArthur and W. Paulson. Ann Arbor: University of Michigan Press, 1995.

Smith, Norman Kemp. *The Philosophy of David Hume.* London: Macmillan, 1941.

Spinoza, Benedictus de. *The Collected Works of Spinoza.* Vol. 1. Translated and edited by E. Curley. Princeton: Princeton University Press, 1985.

Sterba, James P. *Earth Ethics: Environmental Ethics, Animal Rights, and Practical Applications.* Englewood Cliffs, N. J.: Prentice Hall, 1995.

Yovel, Yirmiyahu. *The Adventures of Immanence*. Vol. 2 of *Spinoza and Other Heretics*. Princeton: Princeton University Press, 1989.
———. *The Marrano of Reason*. Vol. 1 of *Spinoza and Other Heretics*. Princeton: Princeton University Press, 1989.

Index

Absolute, 28, 45, 57–59, 69, 81, 82, 88, 89, 90, 91, 92, 95, 99, 101, 107, 115, 136 n. 13
Affirmation, 15, 55, 56, 62, 68, 104, 107, 109–10, 115, 118, 132
Aristotle, 12–13, 105, 136 n. 9–11
Assemblage, 95–96, 97–98, 100, 118, 119, 123

Baugh, Bruce, 135 n. 2
Becoming, 7, 22, 23, 30, 45, 51, 54, 55, 71, 76, 78, 79, 90, 93, 95, 96, 97, 98, 102, 115–17, 118, 120–21, 131–32
Being, 7, 12–14, 45, 46, 54–55, 57–60, 61, 62–63, 74, 79, 80, 107, 115
Being of the sensible, 16–17, 27–28, 110
Bergson, Henri, 19, 39–47, 82, 93, 138 n. 9, 139 n. 15; difference, 40–43; duration, 42–47; problems, 38–40
Bogue, Ronald, 146 n. 30
Bookchin, Murray, 125–26

Cheney, Jim, 149 n. 14
Common sense, 13, 26–27, 29, 137 n. 23
Composites, 38, 41–43, 45, 46, 50, 75, 89–93, 101, 108–12, 115, 118, 119, 141 n. 34
Concepts, 69–78, 79
Conceptual personae, 71, 76–77
Consensus, 70, 124, 140 n. 38
Constructivism, 6, 70–72, 74, 77, 80, 94, 101, 115, 129
Creation, 6, 22–23, 28, 55, 69, 70, 71, 76, 88, 90, 97, 104, 110, 112, 116, 121, 122, 123, 125, 128, 130

Deleuze, Gilles, *Bergsonism*, 37–48; *Dialogues*, 1, 16, 69; *Difference and Repetition*, 5–35, 41, 47, 54, 73; *Empiricism and Subjectivity*, 86–93, 112–14; *Expressionism in Philosophy: Spinoza*, 56–69, 110–12; *The Fold*, 54; *Logic of Sense*, 106–10; *Nietzsche and Philosophy*, 6, 48–56; *Spinoza:*

Practical Philosophy, 56–69, 110–12, 118; *Thousand Plateaus*, 94–102, 114–18; *What is Philosophy?*, 69–78, 102, 114–15
Descartes, René, 37, 59–60, 63, 73, 110, 111, 140 n. 25–26, 141 n. 30
Deterritorialization, 95–96, 114–15
Dialectic, 10, 40, 45, 93, 106, 126, 139 n. 14
Difference, 1–2, 5–17, 24–26, 40, 41, 46, 47, 48, 50, 54, 70, 72, 75, 77, 81, 88–89, 106–07, 115, 118, 121, 122, 127–28, 132; of degree, 40–44; in kind, 40–44; and repetition, 8–10, 25–26; and representation, 12–17, 24–26; and unity, 39, 44–46
Diversity, 6, 20, 21, 29, 33, 39, 48, 51, 54, 55, 63, 68, 69, 70, 78, 86, 87, 90, 102, 107, 110, 115, 122, 131
Dualisms, 31, 49, 99, 103, 111, 120, 124
Duration, 19, 42–48, 139 n. 12

Earth, 75, 114–15
Emanation, 57–58, 59, 106, 110
Empiricism, 1–2, 48, 70, 74, 78, 79–94, 101–02, 133
Essence, 48–51, 56–57, 83–84, 91, 94–95, 103–04, 120–21, 140 n. 29, 141 n. 33, 144 n. 10
Eternal return, 22–24, 54–56
Ethics, 7, 54–56, 63, 65–68, 80, 101, 111, 114, 119–23, 131; environmental, 104, 120–23, 125–31
Ethology, 104, 117–19, 148 n. 12
Evaluation, 48, 52–54, 55, 91, 92, 101, 121–23, 131
Evolution, 96, 116

Experience, 6, 16–17, 20, 29–31, 37, 39, 41–43, 45, 47, 49, 50, 52, 55, 71, 78, 81, 85–86, 100–02, 107, 122, 143 n. 3
Experimentation, 32, 68, 73, 77, 80, 98, 101, 122–23, 131, 141 n. 35
Expression, 11, 56–67, 96, 98, 99, 108, 110–11

Faculties, 26–30
Forces, 9, 16, 17, 24, 30, 49–52, 54, 55, 65, 110, 121
Foucault, Michel, 80, 103, 136 n. 8, 143 n. 2, 147 n. 39, 149 n. 21
Fragmentary wholes, 71–72, 89

Gare, Arran E., 147 n. 4
Guattari, Félix, 5, 69–78, 80, 89, 94–100, 114; and ecology, 128–131

Habits, 9, 18–20, 84, 90, 98, 137 n. 15
Habitats, 115, 116, 118, 119, 124, 129
Hardt, Michael, 136 n. 6, 139 n. 14
Hegel, G. W. F., 14–15, 45, 136 n. 13, 138 n. 28, 138 n. 37, 139 n. 14, 142 n. 37
History, 7, 22, 23–24, 30–31, 74, 77, 84, 104
Hobbes, Thomas, 141 n. 35
Hume, David, 85–87, 112–14, 137 n. 16, 139 n. 11, 148 n. 6–8

I, fractured, 22, 32
Ideas, 7, 11, 16, 25–26, 28, 32–35, 136 n. 5
Immanence, 30, 31, 35, 36–78, 79, 81, 90, 93, 100, 102, 104, 109–11, 144 n. 13
Intensity, 5, 24, 31, 32, 63, 64, 120

Index

James, William, 80, 81–86, 93, 98, 105, 142 n. 40, 144 n9, 146 n. 26, 146 n. 32

Kant, Immanuel, 20–22, 30–33, 37, 41, 47, 50, 70, 72, 73, 74, 78, 86, 120, 137 n. 18–19, 137 n. 22–23, 138 n. 27, 145 n. 17
Knowledge, 5–6, 20–21, 29, 30, 32–33, 39, 52, 53, 91, 94, 121

Language, 98–100
Leibniz, G. W., 14–15, 137 n. 14
Livingstone, Donald W., 148 n. 5
Lloyd, Genevieve, 142 n. 37
Lyotard, Jean-François, 104, 147 n. 2
Lucretius, 107–10

Majoritarian, 97–100, 146 n. 31
Marx, Karl, 38, 138 n. 28
May, Todd, 135 n. 3
Memory, 9, 10, 18, 19, 26, 32, 41, 44, 46–47, 50, 137 n. 16
Micropolitics, 97–98, 123–25, 129–31
Milieu, 115–19, 122, 124
Minoritarian, 97–100, 146 n. 31
Morality, 55, 66–67, 113–14, 120
Multiplicity, 1, 6, 7, 33, 34, 37–78, 89, 94–96, 118–19, 146 n. 29

Naess, Arne, 126–28
Naturalism, 102, 103–31
Nature, 62, 68, 104, 107–08, 110–11, 115–19, 124–26
Negative, 8, 15–17, 35, 110, 111, 112, 120, 138 n. 28
Negri, Antonio, 141 n. 31
Nietzsche, Friedrich, 13, 20, 48–56, 109, 114, 125; and empiricism, 48, 50; eternal return, 54–56; evaluation, 48, 52–54; forces, 54–55; interpretation, 48, 52–54; perspectivism, 52–54, and pluralism, 48, 50–52; will to power, 50–52

Olkowski, Dorothea, 147 n. 37
Open systems, 11, 24–25, 34, 91, 92, 95, 97, 107, 111, 115, 117, 145 n. 23, 146 n. 29

Past, 19, 20, 22, 23, 46–47, 54
Philosophy, 69–79, 133–34
Plane of immanence, 71, 72–77, 115–17
Plato, 16, 25–26, 28, 37, 38, 50, 51, 56–57, 74, 105–07
Plotinus, 57–58
Pluralism, 1–2, 15, 17, 38, 46, 47, 48, 50, 51, 80–83, 89, 90, 93, 132
Political ecology, 104, 123–26, 128–31
Politics, 97, 104–05, 113–14, 123–26, 128–31
Problems, 16–17, 32–35, 39–40, 42, 71, 77, 79, 81, 82, 133–34

Questions, 24, 40, 51, 52, 54, 56

Recognition, 9, 10, 26–27, 28, 29
Relations, 63–64, 67, 81–97, 100–02, 115–16, 118, 146 n. 36; external, 83–84, 87–89, 90, 97, 144 n. 9; internal, 84, 87–89, 91, 97, 144 n. 9
Repetition, 8–12, 17–35, 39, 50, 54, 102; and change, 17, 23–25; and difference, 7–35; and representation, 17–25
Representation, 1, 5–35, 37, 71, 79–80, 94, 99–100, 106–07, 130, 137 n. 23; and difference, 12–17, 23–25; and repetition, 8–12, 17–25, and thought, 5–7, 17–35

Rescher, Nicholas, 142 n. 30
Reterritorialization, 95–96, 114–15
Rhizome, 94–102, 146 n. 28

Seigfried, Charlene Haddock, 143 n. 4, 144 n. 11
Sensibility, theory of, 16–17, 22, 26–28, 29, 31, 32, 35, 49
Serres, Michel, 148 n. 11
Signs, 11, 17, 52
Simulacra, 11, 17, 25–26, 106–07
Sociability, 112–13, 119
Spinoza, Baruch, 13, 37, 56–69, 93, 105, 110–12, 140 n. 29, 141 n. 35, 143 n. 41; and affirmation, 67–68; bodies, 64–65; expression, 56–67, God, 60–63, 140 n. 22; Nature, 62–63, 110–12
Subject, 16, 18, 20–22, 30, 31, 32, 33, 46, 50, 51, 52, 54, 73, 74, 81, 110, 126, 128–31
Symbiosis, 116–17, 119, 121, 123, 126, 128, 134, 138 n. 11

Territorialization, 95–96, 114–15
Thought, 2, 5–7, 17–35, 60, 69, 72–76, 78, 81, 90, 109, 114, 121, 128
Time, 18, 20–22, 42–48, 54–55, 84, 109, 139 n. 12; and fractured I, 22, 32
Transcendence, 37–78, 79, 105, 109, 120
Transcendental empiricism, 5–35, 138 n. 28
Transcendental illusions, 75, 79
Truth, 53–54, 69, 70, 73, 126, 142 n. 39

Unity, 38, 39, 43–48, 54, 57, 61, 62, 63, 68, 71, 72, 75, 89, 93, 97–99, 101, 107, 109, 115, 123

Universality, 8, 9, 10, 14, 20, 26, 27, 30, 31, 33, 37, 45, 51, 53, 67, 70, 74, 75, 78, 81, 99, 100, 120, 122, 123
Univocity, 14, 61–63, 110–11

Values, 6, 27, 37, 49, 51, 52, 53, 68, 69, 84, 114, 120–23, 130–31
Virtual, 42, 44, 46, 47, 48

Whole, 14, 15, 19, 45, 47, 64, 72, 91, 127–28

Yovel, Yirmiyahu, 138 n. 1, 140 n. 21

Studies in European Thought

This series of monographs, translations, and critical editions covers comparative and interdisciplinary topics of significance from the early eighteenth century to the present. Volumes, both published and projected, include a collection of essays on German drama, a study of the Künstlerroman, and a study on the aesthetics of the double talent of Kubin and Herzmanovsky-Orlando.

For additional information about this series or for the submission of manuscripts, please contact:

Peter Lang Publishing
Acquisitions Dept.
516 N. Charles St., 2nd Floor
Baltimore, MD 21201

B 2430 .D454 H39 1998
Hayden, Patrick, 1965-
Multiplicity and becoming